CHANIC

(AT DUCATO

TALBOT EXPRESS, PEUGEOT J5 1.8 and 2.0 ltr. PETROL ENGINES

COVERING:

BY PETER RUSSEK

ORDER NO.: 846

Published by:
Peter Russek Publications Ltd.
3rd Floor, Block C,
Commercial Square,
High Wycombe, Bucks. HP 11 2RH,
England
Email: russek@globalnet.co.uk
ww.russek-manuals.co.uk

ISBN NO. 1 - 898780 - 84-6

WITH FAULT FINDING SECTION AT END OF MANUAL

PREFACE

Small though this Workshop Manual is in size, it lacks no detail in covering the whole of the servicing and repair of the Citroen C25, Fiat Ducato, Peugeot J5 and Talbot Express vans with 1.8 litre and 2.0 litre petrol engines with 69, 78 and 85 BHP. The various vans are closely related, but there will be obvious differences between the individual manufacturers, which will however, not influence any of the repair work. The following engines are covered:

1.8 litre = 169 (XM7-engine)
2.0 litre = 170 B (XN1 engine)
2.0 litre = 170 C (XN1-TA engine)

A five-speed transmission is bolted to the rear of the engine.

Brief, easy-to-follow instructions are given, free from all necessary complication and repetition, yet containing all the required technical detail and information, and many diagrams and illustrations.

Compiled and illustrated by experts, this manual provides a concise source of helpful information, all of which has been cross-checked for accuracy to the manufacturer's official service and repair procedures. Where special tools are required, these are identified in the text if absolutely necessary and we do not hesitate to advise you if we feel that the operation cannot be properly undertaken without the use of such tools. Whenever possible, alternative tools or make- shift tools are mentioned to carry out specific operations. If alternative methods are given, these have been tested in practice and have been found satisfactory for the job described.

The readers own judgement must ultimately decide just what work he will feel able to undertake, but there is no doubt, that with this manual to assist him, there will be many more occasions where the delay, inconvenience and the cost of having the car off the road can be avoided or minimised.

The manual is called "Pocket Mechanic" and produced in a handy glove-pocket size with the aim that it should be kept in the vehicle whilst you are travelling. Many garage mechanics themselves use these publications in their work and if you have the manual with you in the car you will have an invaluable source of reference which will quickly repay its modest initial cost.

A fault finding (trouble shooting) section is included at the end of the manual and all items listed are taken from actual experience, together with the necessary remedies to correct faults and malfunctioning of certain parts.

0. INTRODUCTION

Our "Pocket Mechanics" are based on easy-to-follow step-by- step instructions and advice which enables you to carry out many jobs yourself. Moreover, you now have the means to avoid these frustrating delays and inconveniences which so often result from not knowing the right approach to carry out repairs which are often of a comperatively simple nature.

Whilst special tools are required to carry out certain operations we show you in this manual the essential design and construction of such equipment whenever possible to enable you, in many cases, to improvise or use alternative tools. Experience shows that it is advantageous to use only genuine parts since these give you the assurance of a first class job — **Always buy your spare parts from an officially appointed dealer.**

0.0. General Information

The Van Models covered in this publication, are fitted with the engines specified on the previous page. Section 1.0 gives a list of all engines covered.

1 Type indentification plate
2 Chassis number
3 Engine number, 2.5 litre
4 Engine number, 1.9 litre
5 Engine number, petrol engine
6 Transmission number
7 Model year
8 Paint number

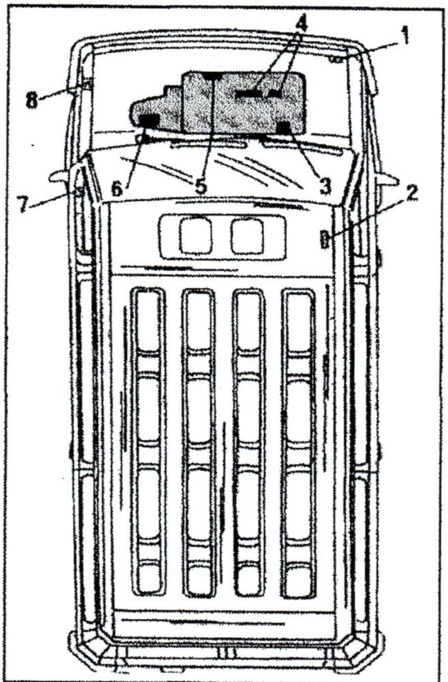

Fig. 0.1. — The location of the various indentification plates and numbers.

0.1. Identification

The type identification plate (1) is located at the R.H. front corner and contains the chassis number, the gross vehicle weight, the gross vehicle weight with trailer and the max. permissible weight on the front and rear axles. The chassis number can also be found at position (2). As can be seen from the illustration there is a a difference in the location of the engine number. Pos. (5) is valid for the engines covered in this manual.

The model year of the vehicle at position (7) is important when spare parts are required. The model year together with the chassis number must always be quoted when new parts are required.

The engine type and engine serial numbers are stamped into plates, attached to the engine, as can be seen from Fig. 0.1. Engine type and serial number are given in the identification plate.

Other numbers can be found in the transmission (6) and relate to the paint code (8).

0.2. General Characteristics

0.2.0. DIMENSIONS (typical for C25)

Wheelbase:	
Short wheelbase:	2923 mm (116.73 in.)
Intermediate wheelbase:	3200 mm (127.14 in.)
Long wheelbase:	3650 mm (145.0 in.)
Front track:	1682 mm (66.83 in.)
Rear track:	1965 mm (78.07 in.)
Overall Length (given for C25):	4765 or 5495 mm (189.3 or 218.3 in.)
Overall Height:	Between 2100 and 2470 mm (83.43 and 98.13 in.)
Overall width:	1965 mm (78.07 in.)
Ground clearance (depending on tyres):	170 to 210 mm (6.75 - 8.35 in.)

0.2.1. FILLING CAPACITIES

Fuel tank:	70 litres
Cooling system :	9.0 litre (16 Imp. pts approx.)
Engine:	
Without oil filter:	3.5 litres (6.25 Imp. pts.)
With oil filter:	4.0 litres (7.0 Imp. pts.)
Between "Max." and "Min." marks on oil dipstick:	1.0 litre (2.0 Imp. pts. approx.)
Transmission:	
With two-wheel drive	1.6 litres (1.25 litre to July 1989)
With four-wheel drive:	2.5 litres

0.3. General Servicing Notes

The servicing and repair instructions in this Workshop Manual are laid out in an easy-to-follow step-by-step fashion and no difficulty should be encountered if the text and diagrams are followed carefully and methodically. The intention has been to include all possible technial data that may be required and, in order this this can be done without adding unnecessary bulk and expense, we do not repeat each time the simple and obvious steps necessary to conform to good engineering practice. It may, however, be useful to many of our readers to summarise a few of the more important procedures which should be adopted at all times, and to briefly draw your attention to some points of general interest.

Always use the torque settings given in the various main sections of the manual. These are grouped together in separate sub-sections for convenient reference.

Bolts and nuts should be assembled in a clean and very lightly oiled condition and faces and threads should always be inspected to make sure that they are free from damage, burrs or scoring. DO NOT degrease bolts or nuts.

All joint washers, gaskets, tabs and lock washers, split pins and "O" rings must be replaced on assembly. Oil seals will, in the majority of cases, also need to be replaced, if the shaft and seal have been separated. Always lubricate the lip of the seal before assembly and take care that the seal lip is facing the correct direction.

References to the left-hand and right-hand sides are always to be taken as if the observer is at the rear of the van, facing forwards, unless otherwise stated.

Always make sure that the vehicle is adequately supported, and on firm ground, before commencing any work on the underside of the car. A small jack or a make shift prop can be highly dangerous and proper axle stands are an essential requirement for your own safety. ***Remember that the vehicle is high and is more likely to topple over.***

Always use genuine manufacturer's spares and replacements for the best results.

Since the manufacturer uses metric units when building the cars it is recommended that these are used for all precise units. Inch conversions are given in most cases but these are not necessarily precise conversions, being rounded off for the unimportant values.

Removal and installation instructions, in this Workshop Manual, cover the steps to take away or put back the unit or part in question. Other instructions, usually headed "Servicing", will cover the dismantling and repair of the unit once it has been stripped from the vehicle. It is pointed out that the major instructions cover a complete overhaul of all parts but, obviously, this will not always be necessary and should not be carried out needlessly.

There are a number of variations in unit parts on the range of vehicles covered in this Workshop Manual. We strongly recommend that you take care to identify the precise model, and the year of manufacture, before obtaining any spares or replacement parts.

The front wheel drive of the vehicles covered have a number of features which provide much easier servicing and adjustment than will be found on many conventional vehicles. It is recommended that the reader should familiarise himself with these features. With the aid of the instructions given in this Workshop Manual we feel that there is little in the way of overhaul and servicing that cannot be undertaken with confidence.

The following abbreviations are sometimes used in the text and should be noted:

Std.: To indicate sizes and limits of components as supplied by the manufacturer. Also to indicate the production tolerances of new unused parts.

O/S Parts supplied as Oversize or Undersize, or recommended limits for such parts, to enable them to be used with worn or re-machined mating parts. O/S indicates a part that is larger than Std. size. U/S may indicate a bore

Fig. 0.3. — View of the vehicle from underneath. The arrows show where a mobile jack, a scissor jack or chassis stands can be placed. Note that chassis stands should have flat support pads (not "V"-shaped).

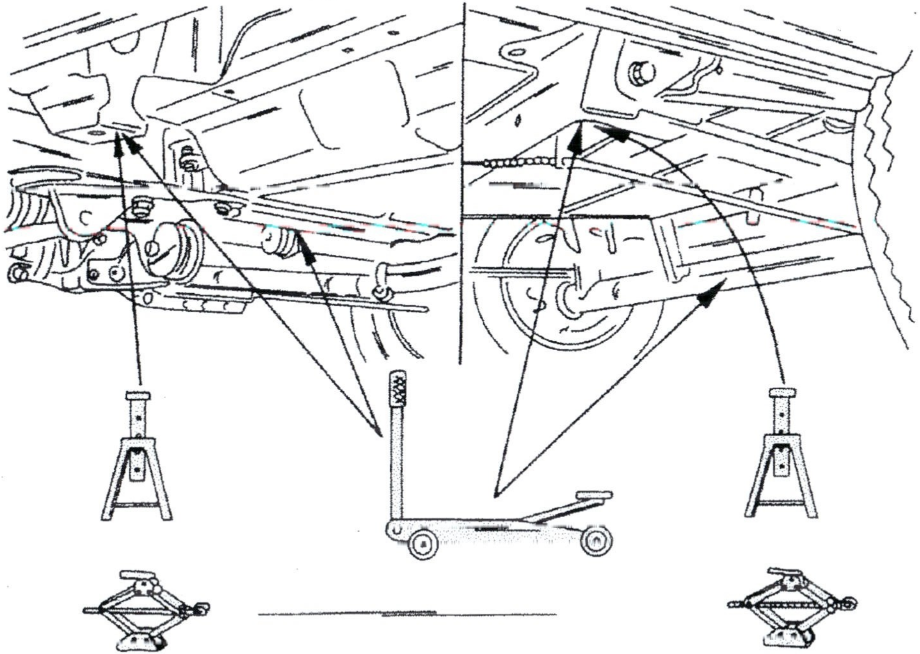

U/S of a bushing or female part that is smaller than Std.

Max.: Where given against a clearance or dimension indicates the maximum allowable. If in excess of the value given it is recommended that the appropriate part is fitted.

TIR: Indicates the Total Indicator Reading as shown by a dial indicator (dial gauge).

TDC: Top Dead Centre (No. 1 piston on firing stroke).

MP: Multi-Purpose grease.

0.4. Jacking-up of the Vehicle

Due to the construction of the vehicle, a jack and/or chassis stands should only be placed under the vehicle as follows:

For smaller jobs the vehicle jack can be used in accordance with the instructions in the Operators Manual and then place a chassis stand underneath the side of the body. Take care not to damage the paint work.

To jack up the front end of the vehicle, apply the handbrake and if available, chock the rear wheels with wedges (a brick will do in emergency). To jack up the rear end of the vehicle, engage the reverse or 1st gear. Avoid to lift-up one side of the vehicle higher than necesary to remove a wheel.

Always use secure chassis stands when working underneath the vehicle. The pads of the chassis stands should be flat, i.e. the normally used stands with "V"-shaped pads should be avoided. Always make sure that the ground where you place the jack, is not too soft. It cannot be emphasised enough. Accidents must be avoided by all means.

Ramps are perhaps the best solution to carry out operations underneath the vehicle, but again we must stress the height of the vehicle.

It has happened: Never jack up the vehicle inside your garage without checking the height of the ceiling. Before you know, the van roof will touch the ceiling and could be damaged.

1. ENGINES

1.0. Main Features

Fitted Engine Type:

1.8 litre: 169 (XM7-T)
2.0 litre: .... 170 B (XN1)
2.0 litre: .... 170 C (XN1-TA)

Note: The first letters/numbers refer to the engine family. The following information will only refer to the engine type. It should be remembered that not all engines are fitted to vehicles marketed in the U.K.

Engine Capacity::

169 engine: .... 1796 c.c.

1. Engines

170 engines:	1971 c.c.
Number of cylinders:	4
Cylinder arrangement:	In-line
Firing order:	1—3—4—2 (No. 1, flywheel side)
Valve arrangemen:	Overhead valves, two rocker shafts
Camshaft:	In side of cylinder block
Cylinder block:	Cast-iron, "wet" cylinder liners
Timing drive:	With timing chain
Pistons:	Aluminium-alloy with three piston rings

Cylinder Bore:

1.8 litre:	84.0 mm (3.3373 in.)
2.0 litre:	88.0 mm (3.4962 in.)

Piston Stroke:

1.8/2.0 litre:	81.0 mm (3.218 in.)

Compression Ratio:

1.8 litre:	7.5 : 1
2.0 litre, 78 BHP:	8.0 : 1
2.0 litre, 85 BHP:	8.8 : 1

Max. Power (DIN):

1.8 litre:	69 BHP (50 kW) at 4800 rpm
2.0 litre (170 B):	78 BHP (56.5 kW) at 5000 rpm
2.0 litre (170 C):	85 BHP (62.5 kW) at 4750 rpm

Max. Torque (approx.):

1.8 litre engine:	13.4 kgm (96.5 ft.lb.) at 2300 rpm
2.0 litre engine (170 B):	15.0 kgm (108 ft.lb.) at 2500 rpm
2.0 litre (170 C) engine:	16.0 kgm (115.2 ft.lb.) at 2500 rpm

Oil Pressure:

At 800 rpm:	2.7 ± 0.8 bar
At 2000 rpm:	3.3 ± 0.7 bar
At 4000 rpm:	3.8 ± 0.7 bar

Valve Timing	**169B/170B**	**170 C**
Inlet valve opens:	6° ATDC	2° ATDC
Inlet valve closes:	33° ABDC	35° ABDC
Exhaust valve opens:	21° BBDC	34° BBDC
Exhaust valve closes:	6° ATDC	4° 30' ATDC

Above opening and closing angles are given with a theoretical valve clearance of 0.7 mm

BTDC	= Before top dead centre
ATDC	= After top dead centre
BBDC	= Before bottom dead centre
ATDC	= After top dead centre

Valve clearances:

Inlet valves:	0.10 mm
Exhaust valves:	0.25 mm

Note: Throughout the engine section the engine will either be referred to as "169" or "170". Differences within the "170" engine groups will be referred to with the actual engine type, i.e. "170 B" or "170 C", enabling you to identify the modifications that have taken place on the latter of the two engines.

1.1. Engine — Removal and Installation

The engine and transmission is removed from the car as a complete unit, i.e. a substantial lifting device must be available to lift the assembly from the vehicle. The workshop uses a special lifting bracket of the shape shown in Fig. 1.1 which is "hooked" into the lifting brackets at the top of the cylinder head. Where no lifting brackets are fitted to the cylinder head, you will have to improvise again and make-up some brackets. Pay special attention to the construction of any lifting brackets used. Accidents must be avoided under all circumstances when engine and transmission are lifted out of the vehicle. Some operations are not explained in detail in the following instructions, as there will be difefrences within the various manufacturers. To remove the engine and transmission, proceed as follows, but note that the instructions are given in general for all models, but additional operations may have to be carried out as applicable, as it is not possible to refer to all models.

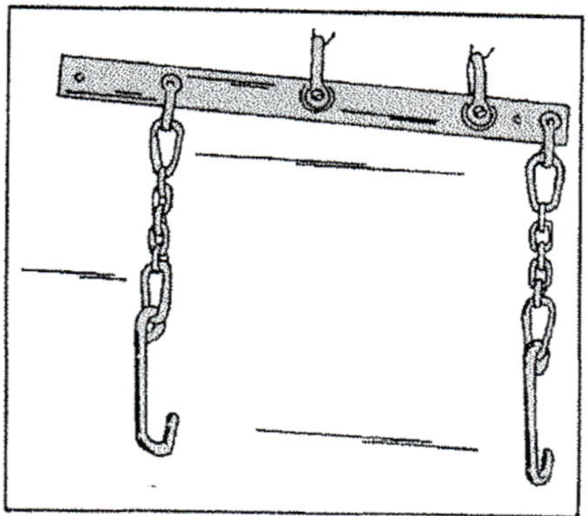

Fig. 1.1. — Lifting bracket for the removal and installation of engine and transmission.

There are a few basic instructions which must be followed in all cases:

- The front of the vehicle is jacked-up with the wheels hanging doww. A jack should not be placed underneath the suspension arms, as they will have to be disconnected.
- There is no need to drain the engine and/or transmission oil.
- There is no need to separate the track rod ball joints or the suspension ball joints. To separate the connection is is preferable to unscrew the swivel joint from the steering knuckle.
- There are differences in the removal and installation of the L.H. and R.H. drive shaft. A chisel is required to remove the R.H. shaft (see description later on).
- The R.H. drive shaft has a central support bearing, bolted to the cylinder block.
- The cooling system must always filled with the recommended anti-freeze solution.

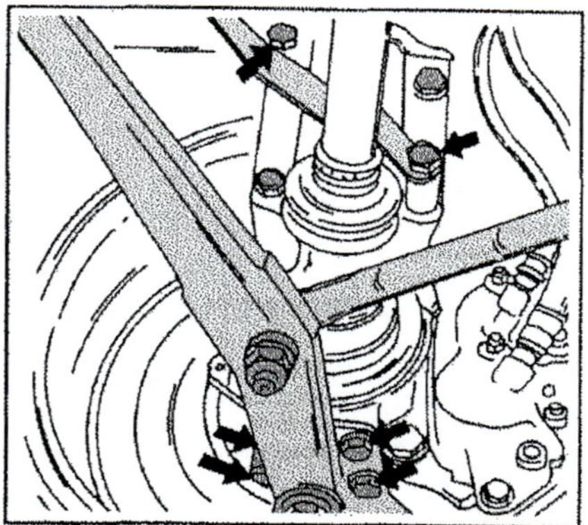

Fig. 1.2. — Suspension ball joint and steering lever must be disconnected from the steering knuckle.

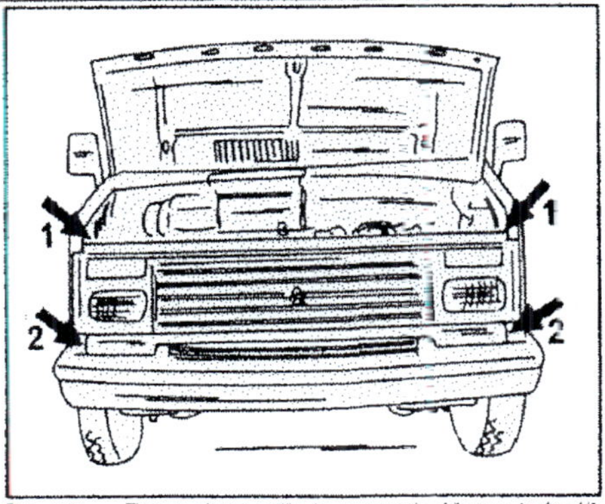

Fig. 1.3. — The radiator grille is secured with two bolts (1) and two nuts (2).

- The hub grease cap can easily be damaged during removal. Take special care when removal takes place.
- The brake master cylinder must be removed. Remove the four nuts securing the master cylinder to the brake servo unit. In the inside of the vehicle remove the four nuts securing the brake servo support and extract the whole assembly. Tie the master cylinder to the bulkhead where it cannot be in the way.

  Remove the engine and transmission as follows:

- Remove the spare wheel.
- Slacken the wheel nuts of the front wheels and jack up the front of the vehicle. The wheels must be hanging free. Remove both wheels.
- Disconnect the negative and the positive cable of the battery. The battery can be also be removed.
- Remove the radiator grille to gain better access to some of the engine parts (optional). Fig. 1.3 shows where the grille is attached.
- Drain the cooling system. Anti-freeze can be collected if it appears to be in good condition. A drain tap is fitted to the bottom of the radiator; a plug must be unscrewed from the cylinder block.

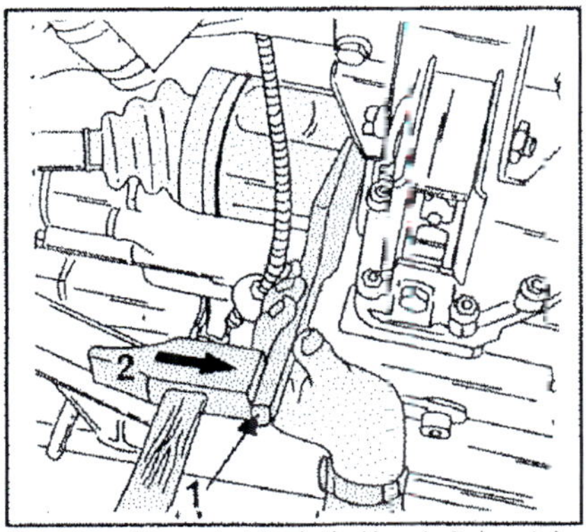

Fig. 1.4. — Removal of the L.H. drive shaft. Insert the chisel in the direction of the arrow (1) and then hit it with a hammer in direction (2). The shaft will come out of the gearbox connection.

The following operations are carried out from below the vehicle:

- Remove the bolts shown in Fig. 1.2 to free the suspension ball joint from the steering knuckle (lower arrows) and the steering lever (upper arrows).

On the L.H. side of the vehicle:

- Insert a chisel in the manner shown in Fig. 1.4 between the CV joint housing and one of the bolt heads of the final drive housing. Check that the chisel is in the correct position and hit the end of the chisel with a hammer, as shown by arrow (1) in the illustration. Then hit the side of the chisel (arrow 2), until the shaft is freed from the gearbox.

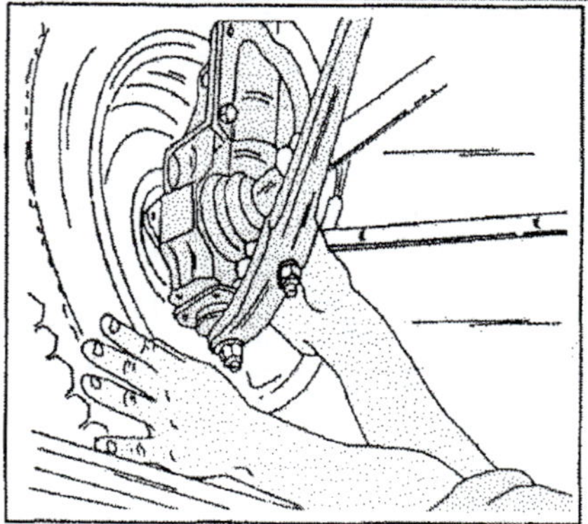

Fig. 1.5. — Pull the suspension arm downwards, at the same time pushing the wheel towards the outside until the drive shaft can be fully withdrawn from the gearbox.

- Grip the suspension arm as shown in Fig. 1.5 and pull it towards the bottom, away from the suspension ball joint. With the other hand push the wheel towards the outside. The drive shaft will now be fully freed from the inside of the transmission and can be "deposited" on the suspension arm.

On the R.H. side of the vehicle:

- Remove the suspension arm ball joint and the steering lever as described for the L.H. side.
- Use a circlip pliers, as shown in Fig. 1.6, squeeze together the circlip and push the shaft in the direction of the arrow. Slacken the nuts (2) in the illustration and unscrew the bolts (1) by half a turn to release the bearing outer track.
- Remove the three bolts securing the bearing block to the cylinder block.
- Push the suspension arm downwards to separate the suspension ball joint from the suspension arm.
- The suspension arm is now gripped as shown in Fig. 1.7 and push the steering knuckle together with the wheel towards the outside. This will free the inner tri-axe joint from the shaft. Take off the aluminium bearing assembly. and "deposit" the drive shaft onto the lower suspension arm.

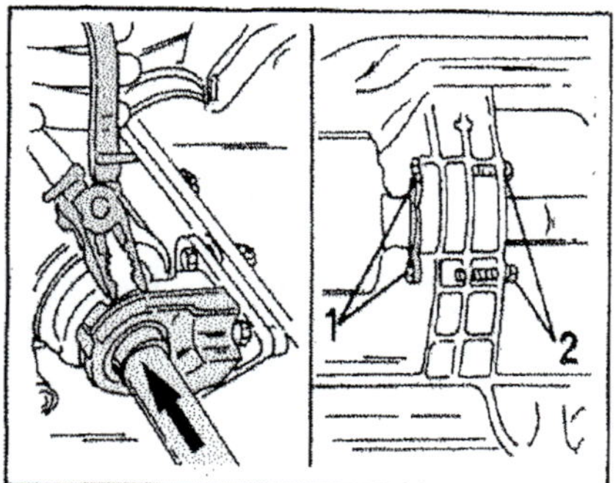

Fig. 1.6. — Removal of the R.H. drive shaft. First remove the circlip on the L.H. side and push the shaft in the direction of the arrow. Then slacken the bolts (1) and the nuts (2) as described in the text.

The following operations are carried out on the transmission:

- Disconnect the clutch operating cable on the clutch cable bracket by unscrewing the two nuts until the cable is long enough to unhook the cable from the clutch release lever.
- Follow the speedometer drove cable and unscrew the nut connecting the cable to the transmission.
- Above the clutch cable remove the nut securing the rear power unit mounting and drive out the bolt.

The following operations are carried out at the rear of the cylinder block:

- Evenly unscrew the two nuts securing the exhaust pipe to the exhaust manifold and remove the two springs and spacers. The connectio must be tightened in a certain manner during installation. Retain the springs, as they will be needed. Immediately below the exhaust pipe, disconnect a hose from the rear water pipe. Details of the parts mentioned above can be seen in Fig. 1.8 (behind the oil sump).

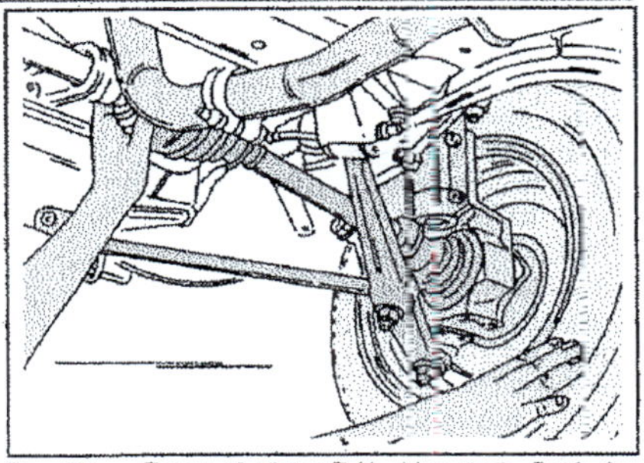

Fig. 1.7. — Removal of the R.H. drive shaft. Push the wheel towards the outside, until the tri-axe joint can be removed from the support bearing.

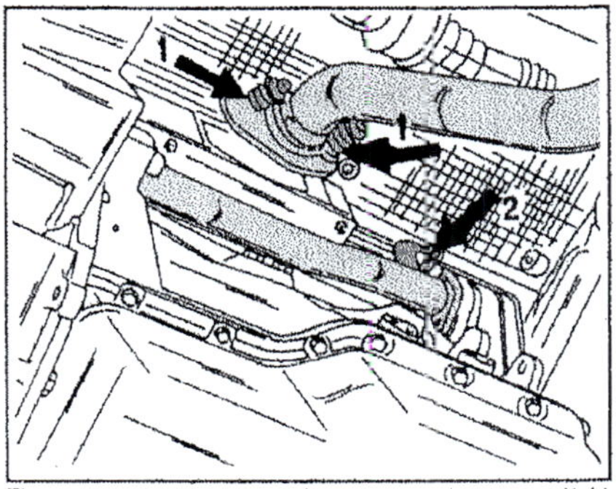

Fig. 1.8. — Attachment of the exhaust pipe-to-manifold connection (1) and the water hose-to-water pipe connection (2).

- **The following operations are carried out under the bonnet:**
- Disconnect the bonnet prop from the R.H side of the bonnet, carefully open the bonnet towards the rear and with a piece of string tie the bonnet to the R.H. rear view mirror.
- Remove the spare wheel, the spare wheel carrier bracket and the air intake.

Remove the complete front panel as follows:

- Disconnect the wires and the connector plugs from the following electrical consumers: headlamps and direction indicators, the electric cooling fan, the temperature switch on the radiator, the ignition coil.
- Remove the two lower fastenings from the electric fan unit and free the wiring clips. Fig. 1.9 shows where some of the connections are located.
- Disconnect the upper and lower radiator hoses at the engine end, the de-aerating hose at the de-aeration chamber end (expansion tank end), the bonnet latch. The latter is secured by two screws.
- Remove two bolts at the upper end and two bolts at the lower end of the front panel and remove the complete assembly together with the radiator, the cooling fan and the headlamps towards the front. The two radiator hoses must be disconnected from the engine connections at the same time. A helper should be around to facilitate the operation.
- Remove the lower pin from the gearchange control.
- Remove the heater inlet and outlet hoses and the brake servo vacuum hose.

- Disconnect the following units: The earth cable from the gearbox, the cable from the reversing light switch, the cable from the temperature switch and from the thermistor switch on the cylinder head.
- The following cables can be disconnected by referring to Fig. 1.10 (shown by the arrows): The starter motor cables, the alternator cables, the cables from the oil pressure switch and the cables from the fuel cut-off valve. Also disconnect the fuel hose from the fuel pump.

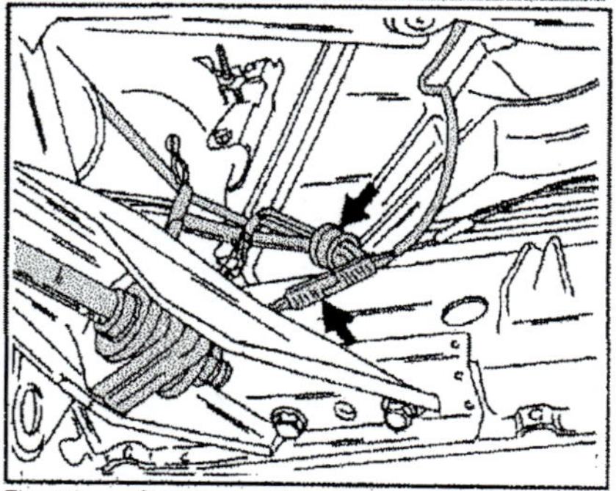

Fig. 1.9. — Cables must be disconnected at the positions shown by the arrows.

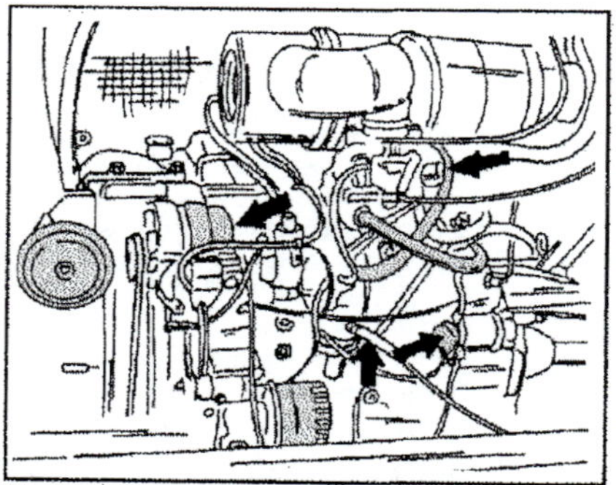

Fig. 1.10. — View of the engine compartment. Cables must be disconnected at the points shown by the arrows.

Remove the engine and transmission as follows:

- The lifting brackets already mentioned earlier on must now be bolted to the engine. First remove the two front securing bolts from the engine mounting (one bolt at a time), fit the lifting bracket and retighten the bolts. To prevent damage to the horn, slacken its attachment and push it as far as possible into the direction of the arrow (L.H. bottom, Fig. 1.11).
- On the L.H. side remove the clutch housing upper securing bolt, fit the lifting bracket and refit and tighten the bolt. Make sure that both lifting brackets are fitted securely in position.
- Remove the upper nut from the mounting rubber pad.
- Attach the lifting device shown in Fig. 1.1 or a similar arrangement to the two lifting brackets, using suitable chains and suspend the complete assembly onto a lifting tackle or hand crane. Lift the assembly until the engine/transmission mountings are under tension.
- Remove the four upper bolts from the intermediate mounting at the transmission end.
- Check once more that all connections, cables, pipes, etc. have been separated and lift the power unit slowly out of the engine compartment, continuously checking that none of the engine auxiliary parts or cable connections can get caught in the engine or transmission. Lower the complete assembly onto the floor after it is free from the engine compartment.

- Remove the transmission from the engine if required. The starter motor must be removed. Take care not to distort the clutch drive shaft when the transmission is lifted off.

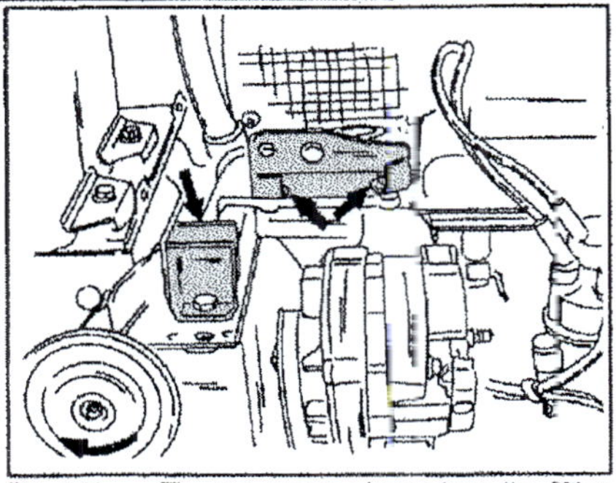

Fig. 1.11. — The two arrows show where the lifting brackets are attached. The horn is moved towards the outside to prevent damage.

Installation

The installation is a reversal of the removal procedure. The following points must be noted in general:

- All self-locking nuts, lock washers, etc. and all parts which are no longer in good condition must be replaced.
- Prepare the engine compartment for a trouble-free lowering of the engine and transmission.
- All disconnected cables, pipes, hoses, etc. must be moved out of the way. Use sticky tape and attach them to the outer panels, if necessary.
- Thoroughly clean all connections. Check for rust, if applicable.
- When fitting the L.H. drive shaft make sure that the circlip in the end of the shaft engages in the inside of the side gear in the differential. Check by moving the drive shaft to and fro.
- The exhaust manifold to exhaust pipe connection must be made as follows:

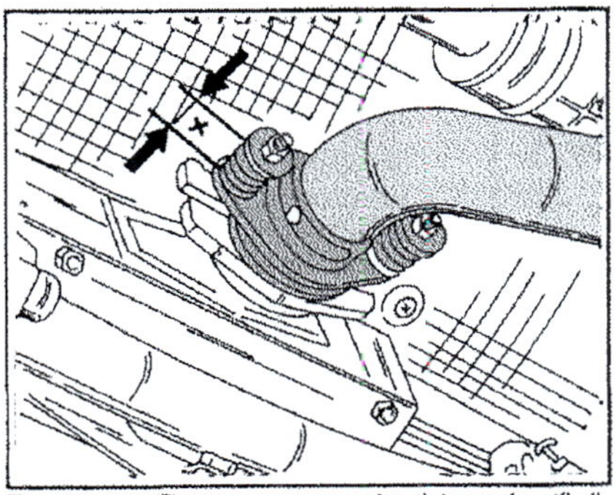

Fig. 1.12. — The two nuts must be tightened until dimension "X" is 22 mm on both sides of the pipe.

- Coat the sealing cones with a heat-resistant grease, such as "Gripcott A-F", as used by Citroën workshops. Place the springs and washers in position, fit the two nuts and tighten the nuts evenly until the dimension "X" in Fig. 1.12 is 22 mm. This will assure a gas-tight connection.
- Adjust the clutch pedal free travel. This is obtained by adjusting the clutch pedal height. A helper is required to observe the position of the pedals as the two nuts are adjusted. After joining the clutch operating cable with the clutch release lever, adjust the two nuts, shown by the arrows in Fig. 1.13, until clutch and brake pedals are at the same height. Lock the two nuts against each other after the adjustment has been obtained.
- Fill the cooling system with 9 litres of anti-freeze solution. Refer to the "Cooling System" section for the filling procedure.
- Re-connect the various cable connections. Some of them are shown in Fig.

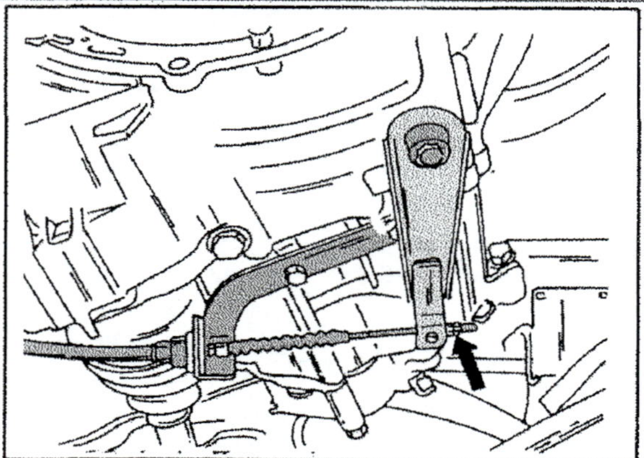

Fig. 1.13. — The clutch pedal height is adjusted by rotating the two nuts at the outer end of the clutch release lever.

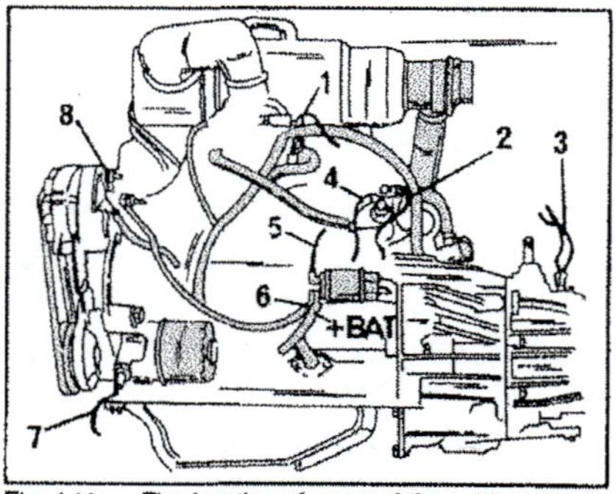

Fig. 1.14. — The location of some of the cable connections on the engine.

1 Idle cut-off valve
2 Temperature sensor
3 Reversing lights
4 Temperature switch
5 Starter motor
6 Alternator
7 Oil pressure switch
8 Alternator

1.14. Some of the cable colours are as follows: Idle cut-off valve (1) = orange, temperature sensor (2) = green/white, reversing light switch (3) = white, cooling temperature switch (4) = white, starter motor (5) = red, alternator (6) = brown or green, depending on ignition system, oil pressure switch (7) = green, alternator (8) = black/violet. Take care not to interchange the cables for the ignition coil.

- When tightening the engine mountings refer to the section at the end of Chapter "Engine".
- Joint the suspension ball joints and the steering knuckles. Refer to section "Front Suspension" for details.
- After starting the engine check the cooling system for leaks, the oil level and the correct operation of the gearchange mechanism.

1.2. Engine — Dismantling

Before commencing dismantling of the engine, all exterior surfaces should be cleaned as far as possible, to remove dirt or grease. Plug the engine openings with clean cloth first to prevent any foreign matter entering the cavities and openings.

1. Engines

Detailed inforation on engine dismantling and assembly is given in the sections dealing with the servicing and overhaul (commencing at 1.3.) and these should be followed for each of the sub-assemblies or units to be dealt with.

Follow the general dismantling instructions given below. The two engine types are described under different headings.

Dismantling must be carried out in an orderly fashion to ensure that parts, such as valves, pistons, bearing caps, shells and so on, are replaced in the same positions as they occupied originally. Mark them clearly, but take care not to scratch or stamp on any rotating or bearing surfaces. A good way to keep the valves in order is by piercing them through an upside-down cardboard box and writing the number against each valve (see Fig. 1.15). Segregate together the springs and retainers with collets for each valve, if possible in small plastic bags for each individual valve.

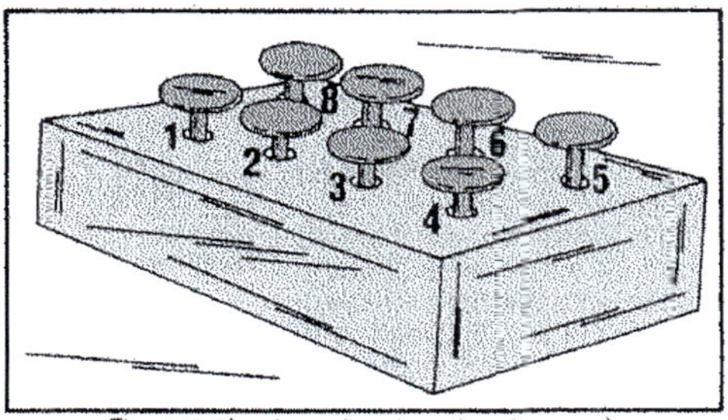

Fig. 1.15. Keeping valves in order of removal.

If a proper engine dismantling stand is not available, it will be useful to make up wooden support blocks to allow access to both the top and bottom faces of the engine. The cylinder head, once removed from the block, should be supported by a metal strap, screwed to the manifold face and secured by two nuts onto the manifold studs.

The following text describes the general dismantling of the engine. Specific instructions for the removal of a certain parts can be found in the following sections.

- On one side of the engine remove the oil filter. A suitable oil filter wrench must be available. Otherwise drive the blade of a screwdriver through the side of the filter and unscrew it. The filter must be replaced in any case.
- Remove all accessible parts from the engine, including cylinder head cover, air intake and exhaust manifold (with carburettor), alternator and drive belt, ignition distributor, fuel pump, one oil pipe, cable harnesses, etc.
- Unscrew the 5 nuts securing the rocker shaft assembly.

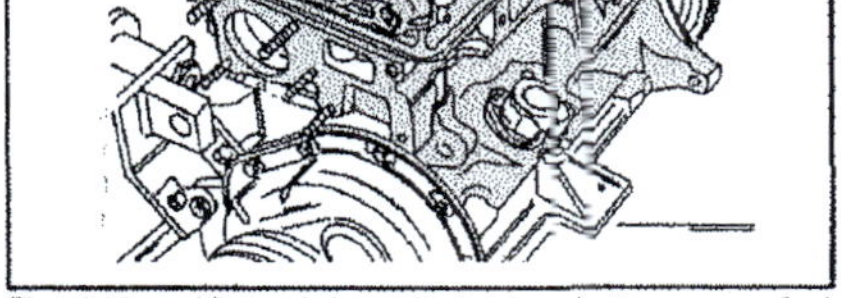
Fig. 1.16. — View of the cylinder head after removal of the cylinder head cover.

Slacken the 10 cylinder head bolts from the outside towards the inside in several stages. Fig. 1.16. shows a view of the engine with the cylinder head cover removed.

- Lift off the rocker shaft assembly and withdraw the push rods in their order of installation. Immediately mark each push rod. We recommend to push them through a piece of cardboard, writing the number against each rod as it is removed (No. 1 on timing side).
- The cylinder head should be lifted off as shown in Fig. 1.17. Insert two iron bars (1) and (2) as shown and lift the head with the bars. This will break the seal between cylinder head and cylinder liners. Immediately secure the cylinder liners in position as shown in Fig. 1.18. Each pair of cylinder liners must be secured with suitable clamps and bolt.

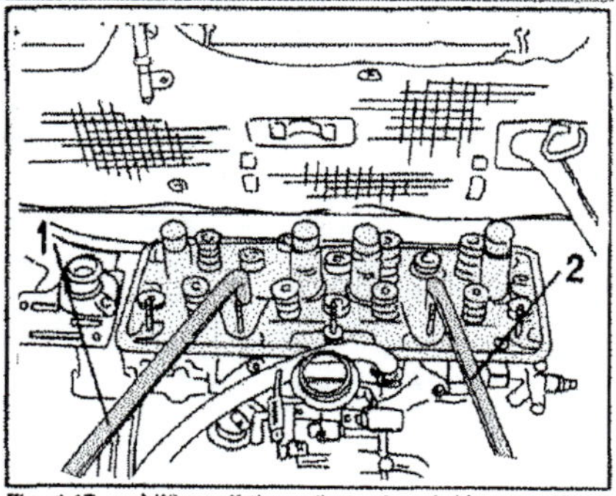

Fig. 1.17. — Lifting off the cylinder head. Use two lifting bars (1 and 2) as shown.

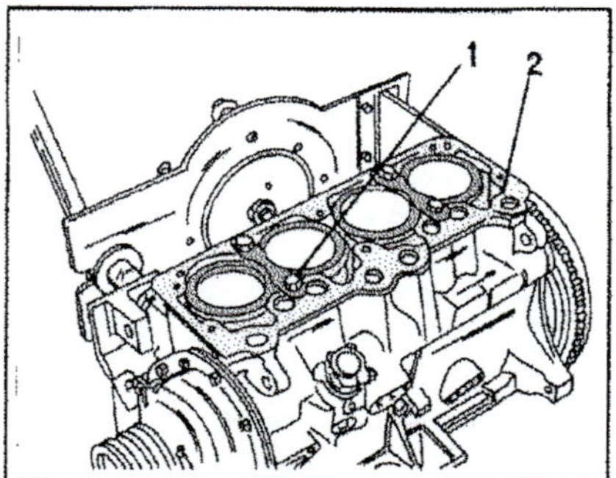

Fig. 1.18. — Cylinder liners can be clamped in position with two clamps (1) as shown. Bolt the clamps to the block (2).

- Remove the valve tappets from the cylinder block bores. Either use a magnet or insert a pointed piece of wood into the tappets to remove them. Store the tappets in their fitted order.
- Unscrew the distributor support housing. Below the housing you will find the distributor drive shaft which can also be removed.
- Unscrew the oil sump with the engine in the upright position. This will allow the oil to remain in the sump, preventing the contamination of the crankshaft assembly with old oil. It is assumed that the oil is already drained. Otherwise do it now.
- Invert the cylinder block and remove the oil pump from the bottom of the crankcase.
- Insert a wooden block between one of the crankshaft throws and the wall of the cylinder block to block the crankshaft against rotation and unscrew the clutch securing bolts evenly in a diagonal manner. Use a centre punch and mark the flywheel and the clutch at a point opposite each other. If clutch and/or flywheel are not to be replaced, refit the parts in the original position. Remove the clutch driven plate from the flywheel.
- With the crankshaft still locked against rotation unscrew the flywheel bolts. There is no need to mark the fitted position of the flywheel, as it can only be fitted in one position. Remove the flywheel with a mallet, if necessary.

- From the front end of the engine remove the crankshaft pulley nut. A tight pulley can be removed with two tyre levers, inserted at opposite points underneath the pulley. Unscrew the timing cover.
- Next is the removal of the chain tensioner. Two types were used during production and must be removed accordingly:

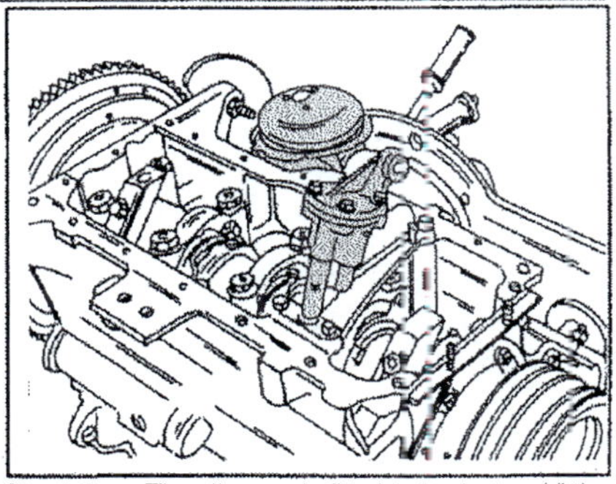

Fig. 1.19. — The oil pump is fitted to the bottom of the crankcase.

Sedis Chain Tensioner

- Insert a screwdriver as shown in Fig. 1.20 into the chain tensioner bore and press against the chain tensioner pad to release it from the chain. Lock the chain tensioner by turning the screwdriver in the direction of the arrow. The ratchet inside the tensioner will lock the pad in position.

Renold Chain Tensioner

- This type of chain tensioner has no locking mechanism. It must therefore locked mechanically, before it is removed. You require a piece of wire to lock the tensioner as shown in Fig. 1.21. Make sure the end is twisted securely.

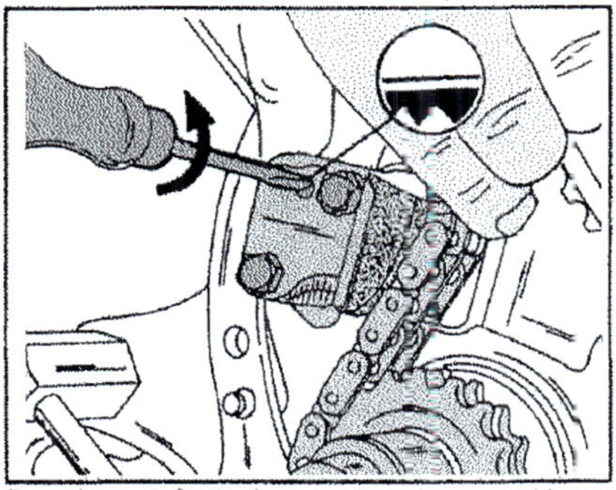

Fig. 1.20. — A Sedis chain tensioner is operated by an internal mechanism which must be locked in position before it can be removed.

All Chain Tensioners

- Undo the two securing screws and remove the chain tensioner. Treat the chain tensioner with care to ensure it can not unlock. Below the chain tensioner there is a filter which can now be withdrawn.
- In the given order remove the camshaft timing sprocket, the timing chain, the crankshaft timing sprocket and the camshaft. Before removing the chain check for timing marks. If none are visible mark the chain and the corresponding sprockets accordingly. The camshaft is held in position by a keeper plate and three bolts.
- Remove the timing cover back plate.
- The removal of the connecting rod and pistons is next. If no markings can be seen on connecting rods and big end bearing caps, use a centre punch and mark each rod and cap with the cylinder number (No. 1 = 1 punch mark, No. 2 = two marks and so on). One after the other remove the big end bearing cap nuts and remove the caps with the bearing shells. The crankshaft must be rotated to gain easy access to two of the bearing caps in turn.

Note: Big end bearing bearing caps and bearing shells must be kept together if they are to be refitted.

- The crankcase will now look as shown in Fig. 1.22. The main bearing caps can be marked in the manner described below. Starting from the flywheel end (cap No. 1), the following paint marks can be seen:

Cap No. 1	No marks
Cap No. 2	Red
Cap No. 3	Green
Cap No. 4	White
Cap No. 5	Blue

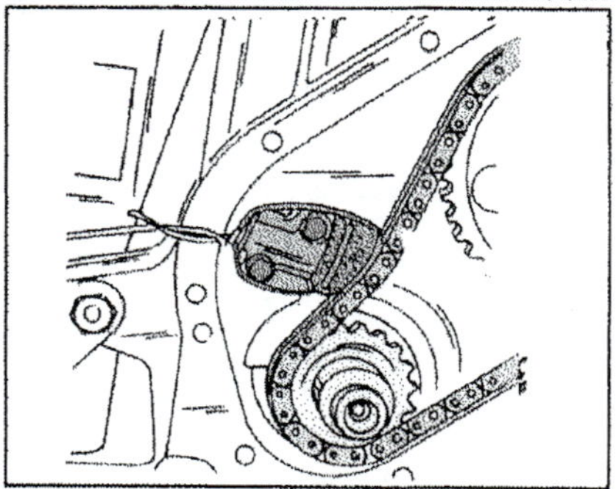

Fig. 1.21. — A Renold chain tensioner must be tied together with a piece of wire before it can be removed from the cylinder block.

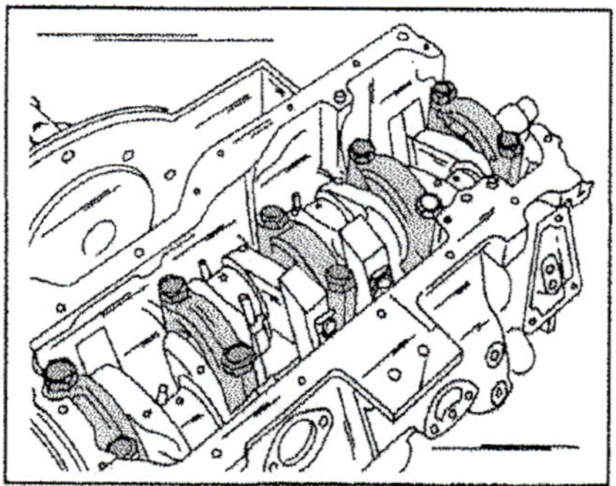

Fig. 1.22. — The crankshaft main bearing caps must be checked for identification marks before they are removed.

In addition to the paint marks given above, you may also find reference marks in bearing caps 4 and 5 and bearing caps 2 and 3. *If no marks are visible, mark each bearing cap either with paint or a centre punch with the respective bearing cap number.*

- Unscrew the main bearing cap bolts from the outside towards the inside in several stages until the bolts and bearing caps can be removed. Keep each bearing cap together with its bearing shell.
- Carefully lift out the crabnkshaft and remove the remaining bearing shells from the crankcase bores. Mark the bearing shells in accordance with their position in the cylinder block and keep the together with the bearing shell and the bearing cap
- Remove the cylinder liner clamps and withdraw the cylinder liners together with the piston/connection rod assemblies. Mark each cylinder liner with the cylinder number, if they are to be refitted. A sticking cylinder liner will have to be removed with a piece of wood and a hammer. Place the cylinder block on one side to do this. Remove the pistons and con rods out of the cylinder liner bores. Mark the piston crowns with the cylinder number.
- Dismantle the pistons and connecting rods as described later on. We recommend to attach the big end bearing caps and bearing shells to the connecting rods (the correct ones) until you dismantle the assemblies. The pistons and connecting rod assemblies can then be stored as shown in Fig. 1.23 on a clean sheet of paper or cloth.

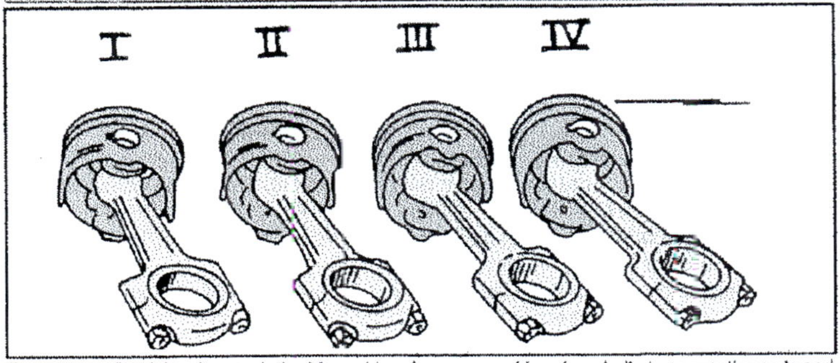

Fig. 1.23. — Provisionally attach the big end bearing caps and bearing shells to connecting rods and pistons and lay them out in the manner shown.

- The cylinder head can be dismantled as described in Section 1.4.
- If work is to be carried out on the crankshaft remove the counter weights. These are attached as shown in Fig. 1.24. Plugs are fitted to the crankshaft throws and can be removed with an Allen key of suitable size to clean the oil galleries. In the end of the crankshaft (flywheel side) you will find a pilot bearing for the clutch shaft. A puller is required to withdraw the bearins.

Fig. 1.24. — The crankshaft counter weights are secured to the crankshaft as shown. **Mark each counter weight for installation position before removal.**

1.3. Engine — Assembly

The following general instructions are applicable to all engines. When assembling the engine, follow the general proceedings outlined in this section and refer to the later sections, commencing at 1.4. for any detailed information that is necessary. In the following description it is assumed that all sub-assemblies have been overhauled or replaced, as necessary.

Carefully clean the cylinder block, paying particular attention to the crevaces which are easily overlooked.

Lubricate each rotating or moving part BEFORE it is assembled. Lubricating it after the assembly has little purpose, as the oil cannot reach the gliding surfaces at all times. Oil seals should be replaced as a matter of course. The same goes for the lock washers and lock plates. Check that all oilways are thoroughly clean.

Refer to the technical data to check important dimensions before parts are re-used. In doubt it is always better to replace a part.

Assemble the engine in the following general order, referring to particular sections as indicated for individual details:

- Check the protrusion of the cylinder liners before assembly of the engine. The liners are fitted with paper gaskets or steel shims at their bottom ends, which govern the fitted position of the liners. In most cases you will find that the instalation height is correct, should however, be checked. Note that either paper gaskets or steel shims are used, depending on the year of production. Proceed as follows during the measurement:
- Insert the cylinder liners without gaskets into the cylinder block. Make sure that the marks in liner and cylinder block bore are opposite each other. Push each liner fully home.
- Measure the protrusion of each liner as shown in Fig. 1.25, using the gauge shown. First place the stylus at points A to D against the cylinder block face and write down each dimension. Then place the stylus against the edge of the liner at positions A to D in Fig. 1.26, again writing down the dimension. Compare the value obtained for each point The difference between the first and the second measurement must not exceed 0.07 mm. If this is the case, there may be some foreign matter between the liner and the liner seating. Remove thje liner and check.

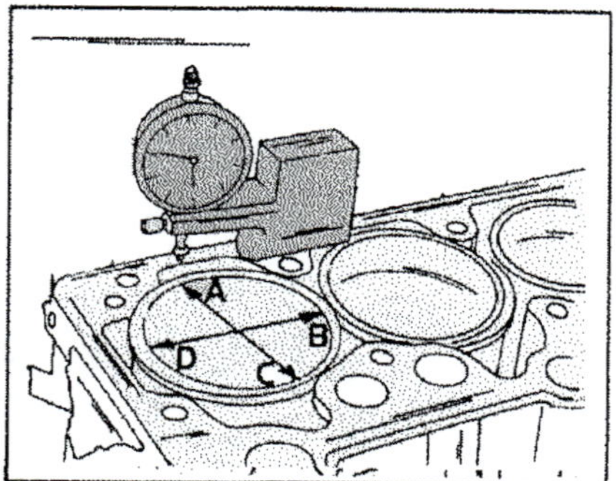

Fig. 1.25. — Place the dial gauge with a suitable block onto the cylinder block face. The stylus is placed in turn over points A to D.

Before proceeding with the operation note the following:

- The cylinder liners must protrude by 0.07 to 0.14 mm above the cylinder block face in the case of engines produced to April 1989, with the liner seal fitted. Always try to obtain the 0.14 mm value. On engines produced after the date given above, the protrusion has been reduced to 0.03 - 0.10 mm. Again the higher value should be considered.
- Liner seals are made of different material, depending on the year of production of the engine. Up to July 1985 they were made of paper and white, synthetic fibre material. From July 1985 steel shims with aluminium coating are used.

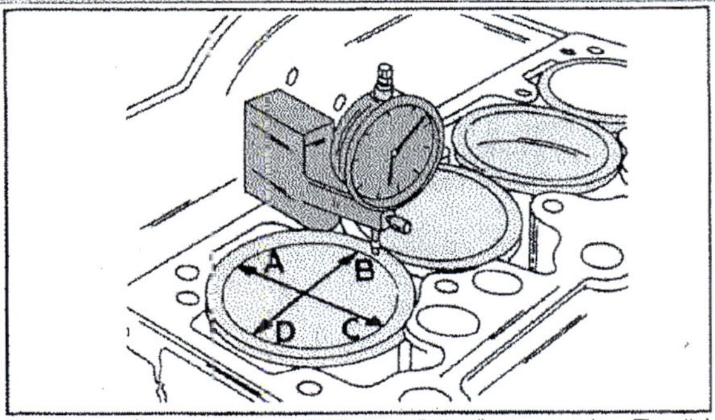

Fig. 1.26. — Second stage to check the cylinder liner protrusion. The dial gauge stylus is now placed over the shoulder of each liner, at points A to D.

All seals/shims have tags on the outside, which are, however, also different on the old and the new version. The table below lists the allocation of the liner seals for the engines in question:

Paper Gaskets to July 1985

Highest point of liner without seal	*No. of tags*	*Thickness*
+0.039 to 0.045 mm	1	0.07 mm
+0.019 to 0.038 mm	2	0.085 mm
—0.006 to + 0.018 mm	3	0.105 mm
—0.095 to 0.007 mm	4	0.130 mm

Steel Shims from July 1985

Highest point of liner without seal	*No. of tags*	*Thickness*
+0.039 to 0.045 mm	1	0.10 mm
+0.019 to — 0.006 mm	2	0.12 mm
—0.095 to 0.007 mm	3	0.15 mm

Note: Only one seal is placed underneath each cylinder liner. Mesure each liner on both sides of the cylinder block.

If the correct protrusion cannot be obtained, remove the liner and check the joining surface of the liner/seal for foreign matter.

- Remove the cylinder liner and fit the liner seals in accordance with Fig. 1.27, but note the following points: The seal has a tag (1), which is inserted into a locating groove in the liner. A second tag (tab) is used to identify the thickness of the liner seal and must be arranged so that it is in line with the flat (3) at the upper end of the liner. If all cylinder liners are removed at once, make sure they are identified where they come from.

The engine can now be assembled in the following manner. It is assumed that all parts have been checked and/or replaced as necessary:

- Screw the plugs into the crankshaft. As the original plugs were peened in position, it is possible that the threads are no longer in perfect condition. Damaged threads can be re-cut with a M25 x 1.5 thread cutter, but not deeper than 10 mm (0.4 in.). Use new plugs and tighten them to 5.5 kgm (40 ft.lb.).

- After the plugs have been tightened, use a pointed centre punch and peen the plug in the inside to the crankshaft. As you may notice, the plug will be rather deep in its bore and must be peened as shbown in Fig. 1.28. Make sure that the plug is well secured.

Note: *Crankshafts without closing plugs are also used. These crankshaft also have a different arrangement of the main bearing shells and will be referred to later on.*

- Refit the crankshaft counter weights in accordance with the identification and fit and tighten the bolts to 6.8 kgm (41 ft.lb.). Lock plates are used underneath the bolt heads and must be locked after installation of the weight(s). Make sure that the bolts are well locked to prevent the weights from coming off. The best way to secure the lock plates is shown in Fig. 1.29.

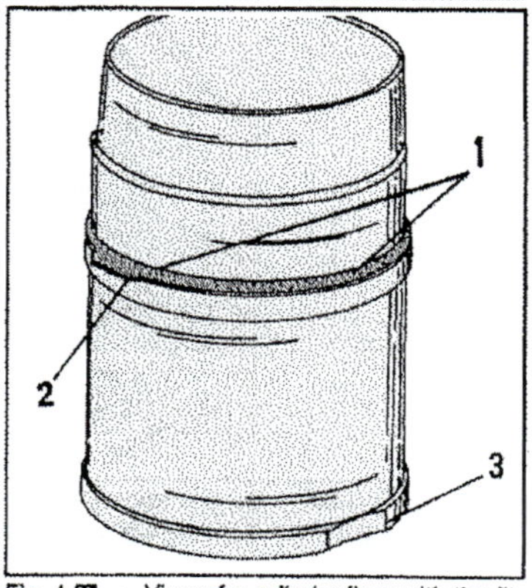

Fig. 1.27. — View of a cylinder liner with the fitted seal. Refer to text.

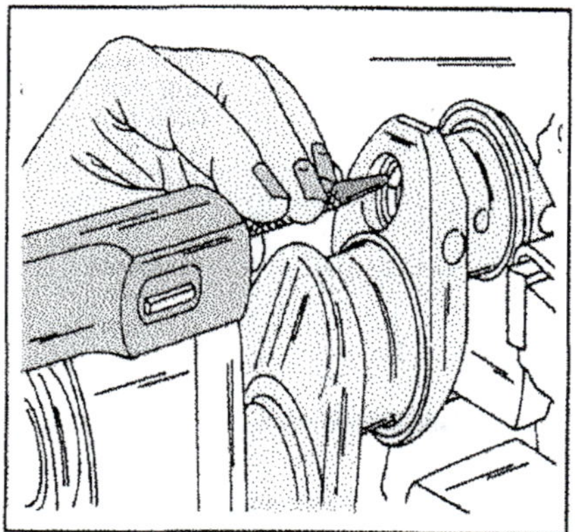
Fig. 1.28. — Oil gallery plugs are peened in position in the manner shown after they have been tightened to the specified torque.

- If removed, fit a new bush for the clutch shaft (chamfer towards the outside). Fit a new oil seal and lubricate the bush and the seal with engine oil.

The crankshaft bearing shells are now fitted to the crankcase in accordance with the type of crankshaft fitted. Refer to Fig. 1.30 on the next page to avoid mistakes:

Crankshafts with Pluigs

- Insert the bearing shells **with oil grooves** into bearing bores I, III und V, the bearing shells **without oil grooves** into the bearing bores II and IV.

Crankshafts without Plugs

- The bearing shells **with oil grooves** are fitted into the cylinder block bores, the bearing shells **without oil grooves** are fitted into the main bearing caps.
- Generously lubricate the main bearing shells with engine oil and insert the crankshaft into the bearing bores. Rotate the shaft a few times to settle the bearings.
- Fit the two half thrust washers for the crankshaft end float on the flywheel side

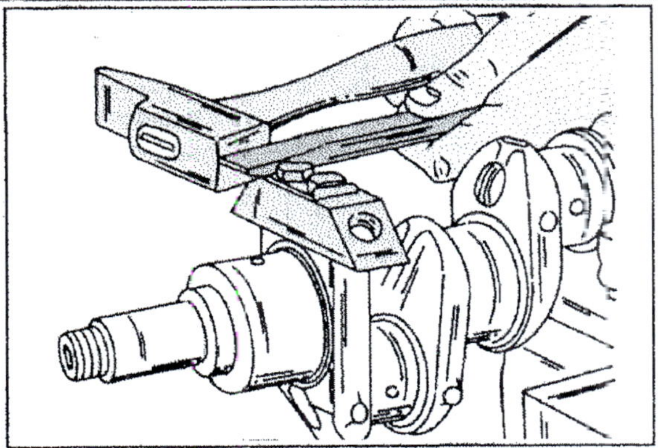

Fig. 1.29. The locking plates for the crankshaft counter weights are locked with a chisel and a hammer as shown.

- Insert the bearing shells into the main bearing caps (noting the identification marks), lubricate the shells with engine oil and fit the caps in position (again in accordance with their markings).
- Fit the rear bearing cap without the side seals but with the half thrust washer for the crankshaft end float. The oil lubricating grooves of the thrust washer must be facing towards the crankshaft side. Make sure to oil the thrust washer face.
- Insert and tighten the main bearing cap bolts. Tighten from the inside towards the outside in several stages to a final torque reading of 7.5 kgm (54 ft.lb.).

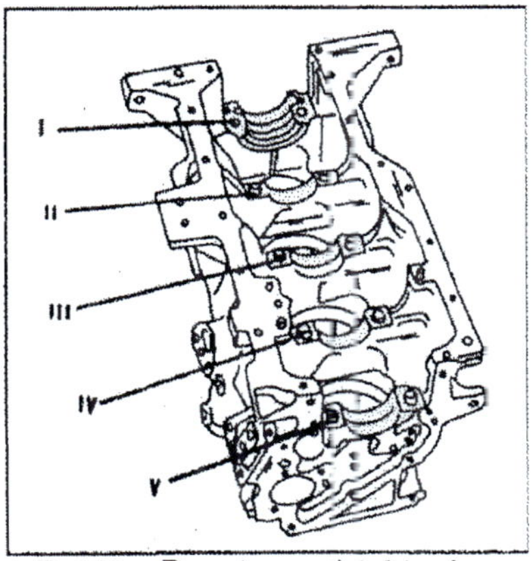

Fig. 1.30. — The various crankshaft bearings.

- The end float of the crankshaft must now be checked. Arrange a dial gauge with a suitable holder as shown in Fig. 1.31, placing the stylus against the counter weight face.
- Use a screwdriver and push the crankshaft all the way to one side. Set the dial gauge to "Zero" and push the shaft into the opposite direction. The indication on the dial gauge is the end float and should be between 0.08 and 0.20 mm (0.003 and 0.008 in.). If the end float is greater than the maximum value, two oversize half thrust washers must be fitted. Both washers must have the same thickness and are available in thicknesses of 2.30, 2.35, 2.40 and 2.45 mm are available. If the end float is smaller than 0.8 mm you can assume that "something" has not been fitted properly during the installation of the crankshaft and the whole assembly must be investigated.

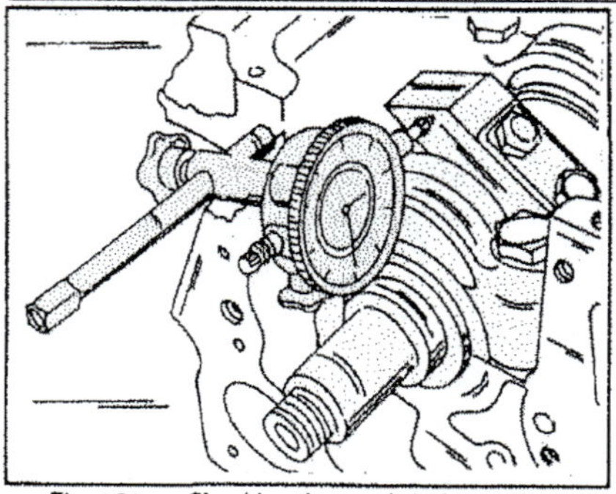

Fig. 1.31. — Checking the crankshaft end float.

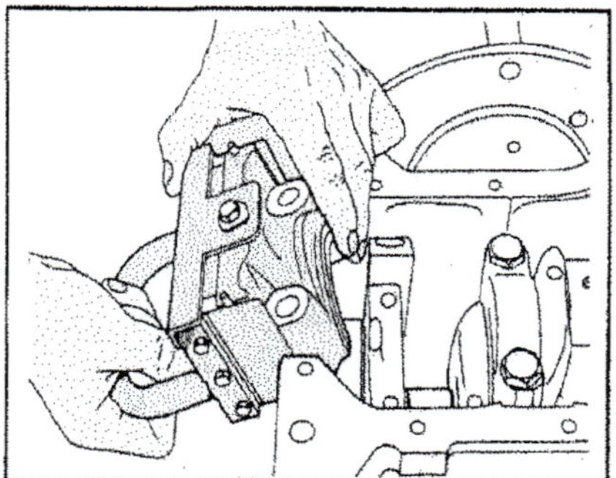

Fig. 1.32. — Fitting the rear main bearing cap with the special tool to fit the side seals. The two side shims must be inserted on the L.H. and R.H. sides.

The rear main bearing cap and the two side seals are now fitted as follows. The workshop uses a special tool to fit the seals to prevent their damage.

- Insert new rubber seals into the bearing cap and fit the tool shown in Fig. 1.32 to the cap. Insert the assembly into the cylinder block, taking care that the two side shims are pushing against the seals. Lubricate the shims and fit the whole assembly into the block. As the special tool shown is most probably not available, you can use thin sheet metal and insert them between the cylinder block and the side seals. Knock the bearing cap in position and remove the special tool (or the sheet metal pieces).
- Re-tighten the two bearing cap bolts evenly across to a torque of 7.5 kgm (54 ft.lb.).
- The side seals will protrude above the crankcase sealing face and must be cut-off. 2.0 mm of the seals must, however, remain. To obtain the exact length, use a piece of sheet metal of this thickness and drill a hole of the diameter of the seals into it. Place the sheet metal in position as shown in Fig. 1.33 and cut off the emerging ends. Both seals must be treated in this manner. ***The flat metal piece must have a thickness of exactly 2.0 mm.***
- Thoroughly clean the flywheel face on the crankshaft and the flywheel itself and fit the flywheel to the crankshaft (only one position possible). Coat the flywheel bolts with "Loctite" and tighten them evenly to 6.75 kgm (49 ft.lb.). The crankshaft must be blocked against rotation in suitable manner.
- Insert the clutch driven plate into the flywheel and fit the clutch (refer to the relevant section). If the original parts are refitted, align the marks made during dismantling before tightening the clutch securing bolts. The bolts are tightened evenly to 1.5 kgm (11 ft.lb.).
- Fit the marked cylinder liners with the seals or steel shims into their marked bores. The identifications tabs must be arranged on opposite sides of the cylinder block, i.e. on one side for the fist cylinder and on the opposite side for the second cylinder.
- The protrusion of the cylinder liners should now be measured with the

seal/shim fitted. This requires that the liners are pushed into the cylinder block under pressure. The workshop uses a special applianance as shown in Fig. 1.34. The same operation can, however, be carried out under a large drilling machine. Important is that the liners are pushed fully down. The maximum protrusion to April 1989 must not exceed 0.14 mm, after this date it must not exceed 0.10 mm. Also measure the difference between two adjacent liners. Proceed in a similar manner as described earlier on, but place the dial gauge stylus onto the shoulders of two adjacent liners. If the difference is more than 0.04 mm, replace the seal/shim of the liner with the higher protrusion.

- After all liners have been measured in the manner described, secure them in position with the clamps.
- Assemble the pistons and connecting rods and fit the pistons into the cylinder liners as described later on.
- Insert the big end bearing shells in accordance with the markings into the con rods (if the original shells are used). The tabs on the shells must enter the locating recesses in the connecting rods. Fit the bearing caps to the connecting rods and tighten the bolts to 4.0 kgm (30 ft.lb.). Refer to "Pistons and Connecting Rods" for details of fitting direction, piston rings, etc.

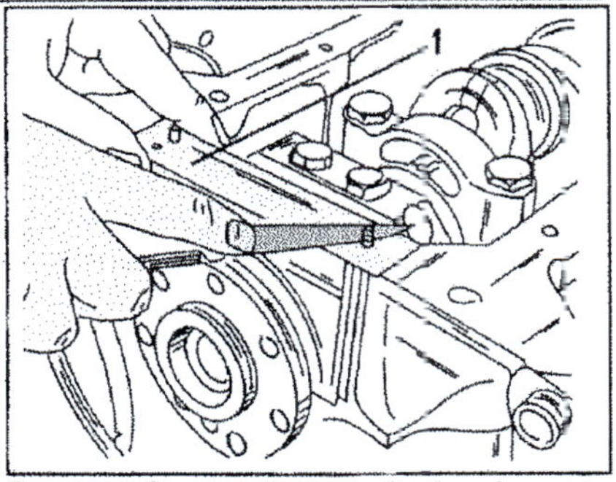

Fig. 1.33 — The protruding ends of both seals must be cut-off with a sharp knife. The sheet metal piece (1) is placed in position as shown.

Fig. 1.34. — Special tools to push the cylinder liners in position, compressing the seals/shims. The exact protrusion can only be established with the liners under pressure.

- Lubricate the camshaft journals with engine oil and insert the shaft into the cylinder block. Insert the keeper plate into the groove of the camshaft, align the plate with the threaded bores of the cylinder block and insert and tighten the two bolts to 1.7 kgm (12.5 ft.lb.).
- Place a new paper gasket over the cylinder block and attach the intermediate plate to the block (1.0 kgm/7.5 ft.lb.).
- Slide the double timing sprocket over the end of the crankshaft with the Woodruff key entering the groove. The timing mark must be positioned on the outside.
- Rotate the crankshaft and the camshaft until the timing marks in the two

sprockets are opposite each other. Compare the aligment with Fig. 1.35.

- Place the timing chain over the crankshaft timing sprocket and insert the sprocket on the other side into the timing chain. Check that the timing marks are aligned as shown in Fig. 1.36 and bolt the camshaft sprocket to the camshaft. Timing chains without marks must be fitted in accordance with the marks made during dismantling.
- Place a new lockplate over the camshaft sprocket and fit the three bolts. Tighten the bolts to 2.3 kgm (17 ft.lb.).

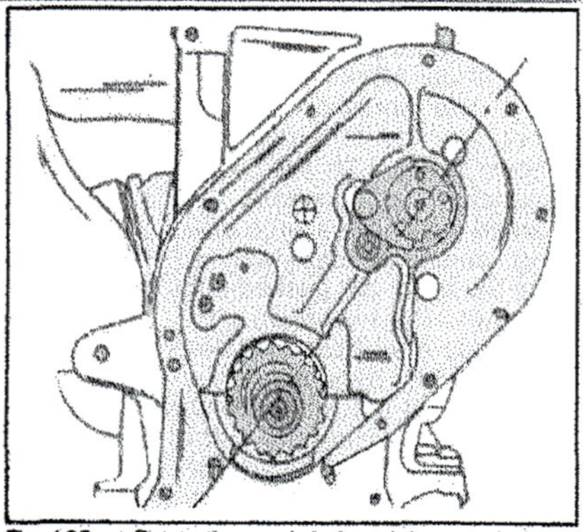

Fig. 1.35. — Rotate the crankshaft and the camshaft until the two timing marks are aligned as shown.

The lock plate tabs must be bent over the sides of the three bolts.

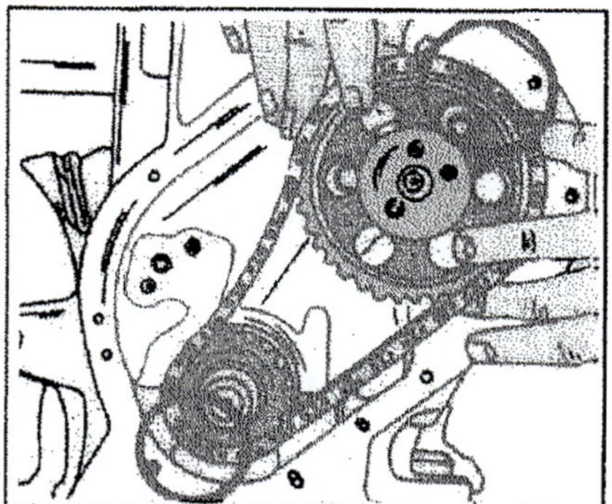

Fig. 1.36. — When fitting the timing chain make sure that the timing chain marks and the timing sprocket marks are aligned as shown.

Dismantling and Assembling the Chain Tensioner

As already mentioned, one of two chain tensioner types can be fitted. The following description assumes that the chain tensioner has been dismantled. If the overhaul of the engine is extensive, it is always necessary to dismantle the tensioner, as this will make sure that the glide shoe can move easily and that the oil bores are free of obstructions. After dismantling, the tensioner must be assembled and pretensioned to ensure its correct operation after installation. The work required is described separately for the two chain tensioner types.

Sedis Chain Tensioner

This is the chain tensioner shown in Fig. 1.37. Dismantle this type of tensioner as follows:

- Place the ratchet into the position shown in box (1) and withdraw the glide shoe and the spring as an assembly. Lock the tensioner by turning the ratchet into the position shown in box (2).
- After cleaning the tensioner parts, assembly in reverse order, finally locking the tensioner in accordance with box (2). A screwdriver is inserted into the hole shown by the arrow to turn the ratchet inside the tensioner body.

Renold Chain Tensioner

- Insert a 3 mm Allen key as shown in Fig. 1.38 into the internal hexagonal bore and rotate the key until the tensioner is locked. In this position fit the glide pad into the tensioner body.
- A new tensioner is supplied together with a plastic washer which is inserted between the tensioner body and the glide shoe as shown in Fig. 1.39, which is removed after the tensioner has been refitted. If the old tensioner is used, you need a piece of wire of 2 mm in diameter at the position shown in the illustration. This will prevent the tensioner from accidently unlocking itself.

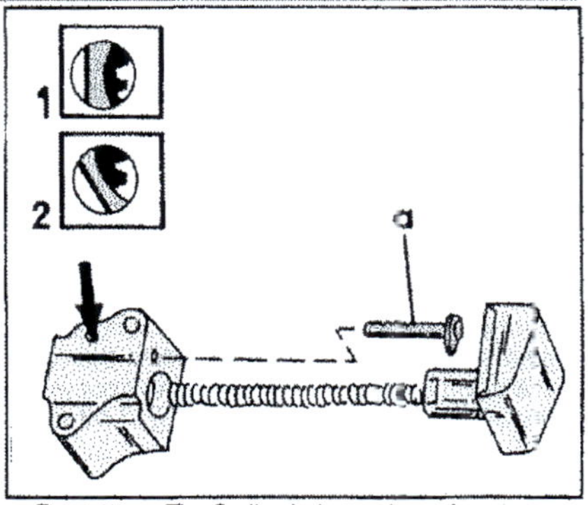

Fig. 1.37. — The Sedis chain tensioner (see text).

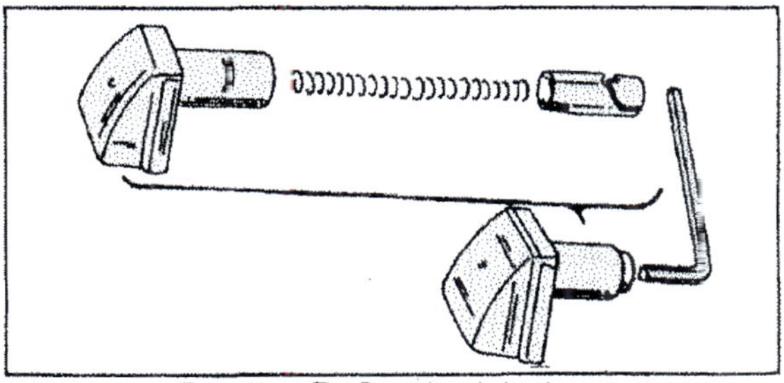

Fig. 1.38. — The Renold chain tensioner.

- Insert the filter into the cylinder block opening and fit the tensioner to the cylinder block. Tighten the bolts (0.6 kgm).
- The chain tensioner must now be pre-tensioned before the glide shoe is released onto the timing chain.

Sedis Chain Tensioner

- Insert a screwdriver into the hole shown in Fig. 1.20 and turn the ratchet inside the tensioner body towards the right, *not to the left, as shown in the illustration.* The location of the hole is also shown in Fig. 1.37 by the arrow

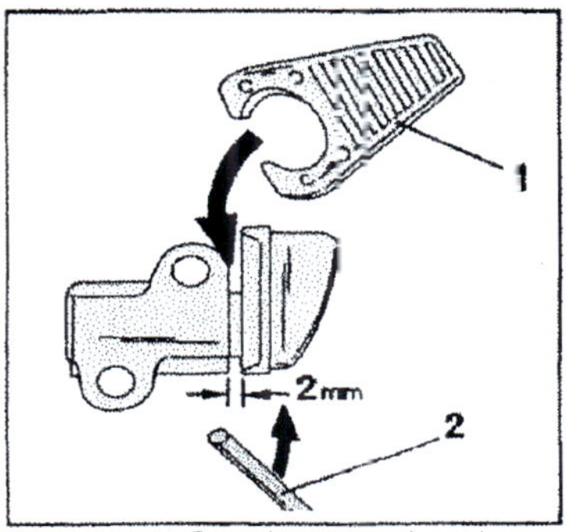

Fig. 1.39. — A Renold chain tensioner is supplied with the plastic lock washer (1) and must be inserted as shown. A steel wire (2) must be inserted when the original tensioner is assembled. Remove the washer/wire after installation of the tensioner.

Renold Chain Tensioner

- Refer to Fig. 1.39 and remove the lock washer (1) or the wire (2) and push the chain from the inside towards the outside in order to push the glide shoe/plunger into the tensioner body. After releasing the timing chain the tensioner will be in the operating position.

Note: Never pre-tension the chain tensioner by moving the glide shoe/plunger to and fro. This warning is valid for both types.

- Refit the timing cover with a new gasket. The cover must be centred to fit the front oil seal. A piece of tube is used to drive the oil seal in position. Insert the oil seal into the timing cover, place the tube over the oil seal and use the large crankshaft pulley nut to draw the seal in position. Insert and tighten the cover screws to 1.3 kgm (9.5 ft.lb.). Fig. 1.40 shows the operation.
- Knock the Woodruff key into the crankshaft and slide the pulley over the key and onto the crankshaft. Block the crankshaft against rotation and tighten the pulley nut to 17.0 kgm (122.5 ft.lb.). A piece of hardwood can be jammed between crankshaft and crankcase to jam the crankshaft.

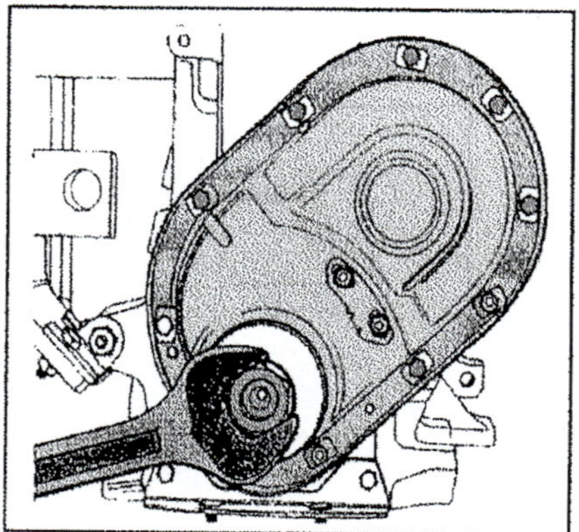

Fig. 1.40. — Fitting the front oil seal.

If the timing plate has been removed it will have to be re-adjusted to establish the top dead centre:

- Rotate the crankshaft until the pistons of No. 1 and No. 4 cylinder are at top dead centre.

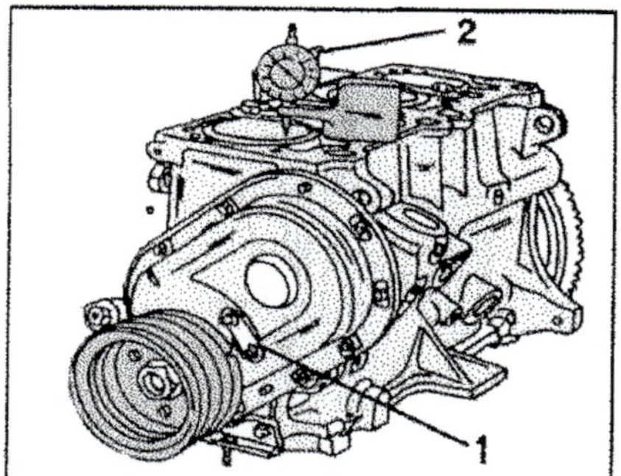

Fig. 1.41. — To fit the timing plate (1) in the correct position, use a dial gauge (2) to set the No. 1 piston to top dead centre. The zero on the timing plate must be in line with the notch in the crankshaft pulley.

The valves of No. 4 cylinder must be "rocking", i.e. one valve must be opening and the other one closing. The exact TDC point should, however, be set with a dial gauge, applied as shown in Fig. 1.41. Rotate the crankshaft until the dial gauge needle shows that TDC is obtained.

- Fit the timing plate and rotate it until the "Zero" in the plate is opposite the timing mark on the pulley. Tighten the two nuts. One of the nuts and the plate should be marked with paint for future use of the timing plate.

- Fit the oil pump and distributor shaft. The piston of No. 1 cylinder must be at top dead centre. Insert the shaft so that the slot in the shaft end is parallel with the engine centre line. The slot is off-centre and the shaft must be fitted with the smaller segment facing towards the cylinder block. Push the shaft fully in position. The shaft will turn as it engages with the drive gear or the camshaft and the slot should be orientated from the bottom left to the top right, with the wider segment of the driver towards the rear of the engine. Fit the distributor support/clamp and tighten.
- Fit the oil pump. First check that the dowel pin is in position in the cylinder block. Fit a new "O" seal and fit the pump to the crankcase. Turn the shaft to engage the drive. Tighten the screws to 1.0 kgm (7.2 ft.lb.)
- Fit the oil sump with a new gasket. Tighten the screws to 1.0 kgm (7.2 ft.lb.).
- Generously lubricate the valve tappets with engine oil and insert them into their original bores, if the old ones are used. New tappets can be inserted in any bore.
- Remove the cylinder liner clamps. Once more check that the flats on the end flanges of liners No. 1 and No. 2 and No. 3 and No. 4 are parallel with each other.

The next operation is the installation of the cylinder head. The tightening method has been altered since introduction of these engines, i.e. you will have to know when the engine was manufactured. It is also imperative to obtain the correct cylinder head gasket.

- Insert two locating pins into two corners of the cylinder block (into the side opposite the distributor). Cut the ends of two old cylinder head bolts and cut a slot for the application of a screwdriver into the end. Any bolt/stud of suitable diameter and thread will do.
- Place the cylinder head gasket over the block. Gaskets are marked (for example DESSUS, top) and the writing must be visible after the gasket has been fitted.
- Place the cylinder head in position, tapping it down with a mallet.
- Insert the push rods into the tappets in accordance with the cylinder number and valve number. Lubricate the rod ends with engine oil.
- Fit the rocker shaft assembly. The cylinder head will now have the appearance shown in Fig. 1.42.

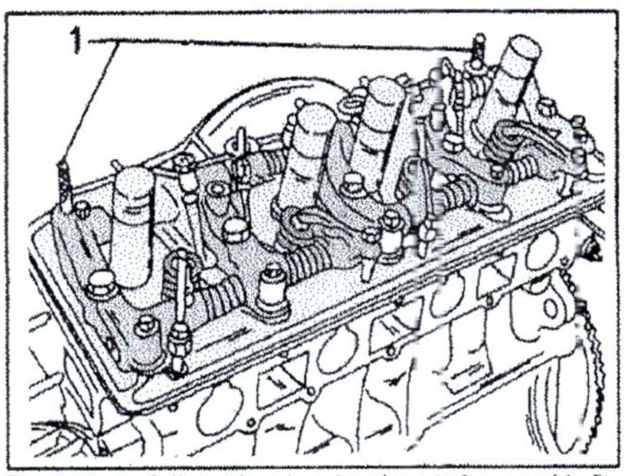

Fig. 1.42. — Cylinder head and rocker shaft assembly fitted to the engine. The two locating pins are fitted to positions (1).

- Coat the cylinder head bolts with engine oil and screw them in position. Two versions can be encountered: Bolts with 12 mm diameter are fitted with washers, bolts with 11 mm diameter with a shoulder underneath the bolt head require no washers.

The cylinder head bolts are now tightened in the sequence shown in Fig. 1.43.

1. Engines, Assembly

The introduction of the modified engine has not taken place at the same time on all vehicles (manufacturers). The engine types listed below are given as a general guide line and you will have to make sure which engine is fitted to your vehicle:

Engine 169 B (XM7-)): .... To end of 1986
Engine 170 B (XN1-T): .... To end of 1986
Engine 169 B (XM7-T): .... To April 1989
Engine 170 B (XN1-TA): .... To April 1989
Engine 169 B (XM7-T): .... From April 1989
Engine 170 B (XN1-TA): .... From April 1989

Different cylinder head wrenches are also required, again depending on the year of manufacture. Engines produced after April 1989 require a "Torx 55" in conjunction with a graduated disc. The following differences must therefore be observed:

- In the case of all engines tighten the bolts to 5.0 kgm (36 ft.lb.).
- Tighten the rocker shaft pedestal bolts to 1.5 kgm (11 ft.lb.).

ATTENTION: Follow the instructions step by step. We have taken great care to describe each engine carefully to make sure you cannot encounter any problems.

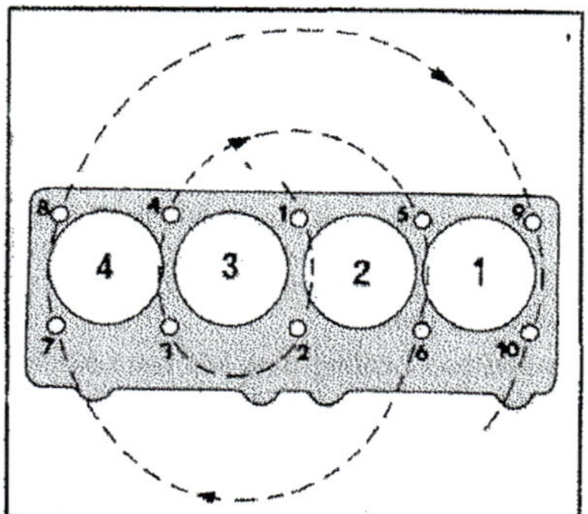

Fig. 1.43. — The tightening sequence for the cylinder head bolts. Valid for all engines.

To End of Model Year 1986:

- Slacken all bolts in the reverse order to the one shown in Fig. 1.43 and re-tighten them in the order 1 to 10 to 2.0 kgm (14.5 ft.lb.).
- Place the socket without torque wrench over bolt No. 1, make a note of the position of the bolt, as shown in Fig. 1.44 and tighten the bolt exactly by one quarter of a turn. This is the socket travel indicated in the illustration by 90°. The easiest way to do this, is to apply the socket and tommy bar parallel to the cylinder head and then tighten the bolt until the tommy bar is parallel to the small end of the head.
- Tighten the remaining cylinder head bolts in the same manner, following the tightening sequence.

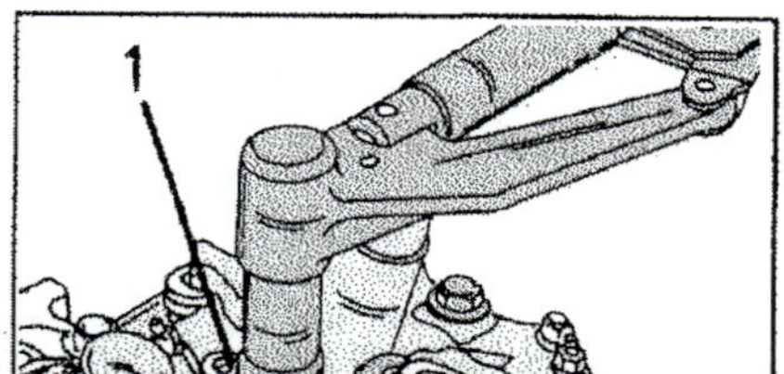

Fig. 1.44. — Angle-tightening of the cylinder head bolts when the angle is 90°. The socket (1) must be marked as shown.

Attention: If you think you may have omitted one of the bolts, restart the tightening of the head from the beginning. *The cylinder head bolts must* *be re-tightened after a certain mileage as described below.*

From Model Year 1986

- Slacken all cylinder head bolts in the reverse order to the one shown in Fig. 1.43 and tighten them in numerical sequence to 2.0 kgm (14.5 ft.lb.).
- Place the socket with a tommy bar over the bolt No. 1 and mark the bolt head as shown in Fig. 1.45. Tighten the bolt by half a turn. This is shown in the illustration by the 180°. Arrange the tommy bar parallel with the long side of the cylinder head and tighten the bolt until it is once more parallel, but on the other side of the head. This will give you the 180°.

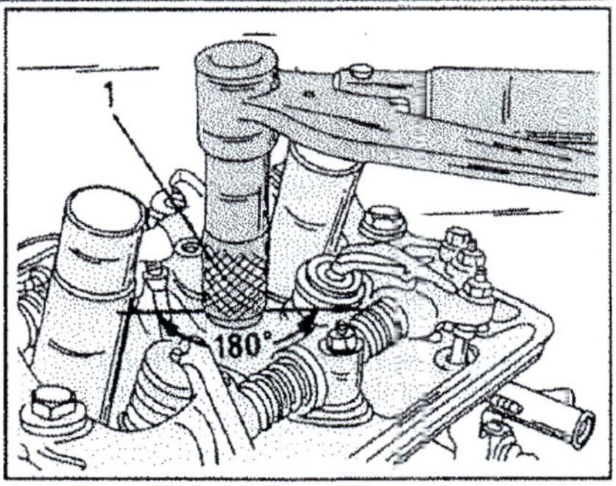

Fig. 1.45. — Angle-tightening the cylinder head bolts when the anlge is 180°. The socket (1) must be marked as shown.

- Tighten the remaining cylinder head bolts in the order shown in Fig. 1.43. *Read the not above if you have omitted one of the bolts during the angle-tightening.*

Note: The cylinder head bolts must be re-tightened as described below after the initial torquing, but not after a certain mileage, as is the case on engines to the end of model year 1986.

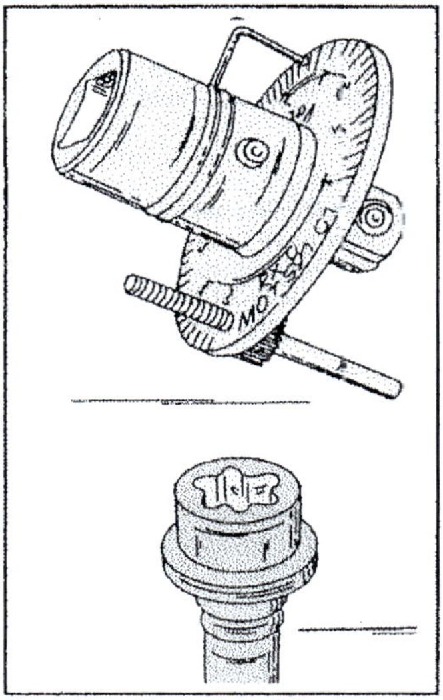

Fig. 1.46. — The graduated disc is used to re-tighten the cylinder head bolts to any of the angles required. Cylinder head bolts for engines after April 1989 have a "Torx" recess.

From April 1989

Cylinder head bolts with a so-called "Torx" head are used on these engines. If the cylinder head bolts have the shape shown in Fig. 1.46, tighten the bolts in the manner described below. You will also need a graduated disc, also shown in Fig. 1.46), but the description below will show you how to carry out the operation without one.

- Insert the bolts and tighten them finger-tight from the inside towards the outside.
- Tighten the bolts in the order shown in Fig. 1.43 to 6.0 kgm (43.5 ft.lb.). Only use a "Torx 55" insert to prevent damage to the bolt heads. "Torx" socket inserts are available in sets containing various sizes, but make sure a "55" is included.
- Slacken all bolts in reverse order and re-tighten them to 2.0 kgm (14.5 ft.lb.) in

the tightening sequence.

- The bolts must now be re-tightened to a certain angle which is 300°. If the disc shown in Fig. 1.46 is used, there will be no problem, i.e. you place the disc between the socket and the tommy bar and with the pointer on "Zero", tighten the bolt until the pointer reaches "300". If the disc is not at hand, you will have to set out that three quarters of a turn will give you 270°. The remaining 30° are one third of a quarter of a turn. To sum up, tighten the bolts by 3/4 of a turn and then the remaining 30°. A little confusing perhaps, but is has been tried.

There is no need to re-tighten the cylinder head bolts of these engines.

Re-tightening of Cylinder Head Bolts

As in the case of the original tightening procedure there are also differences between the various engines when the cylinder head bolts are re-tightened.

To end of Model Year 1986

After the vehicle has been driven with the new cylinder head gasket approx. 1300 miles, slacken each bolt in the order shown in Fig. 1.43 (never more than one bolt at a time) and re-tighten it immediately to 2.0 kgm (14.5 ft.lb.).

- Re-tighten each bolt in the order shown in Fig. 1.43 by a quarter of a turn, as described for this engine.
- The valve tappet clearance must be adjusted after the bolts have been re-tightened.

From Model Year 1986 (to April 1989)

The cylinder head bolts of these engines require no re-tightening after a certain mileage has been covered. After the cylinder head bolts have been tightened as described for these engines, tighten them a further 35°. The graduated disc shown in Fig. 1.46 is, of course, a great help. To obtain this angle without the disc, divide half a turn by 6 and tighten the bolts by one segment and a little more. The engine can either be cold or warm (not hot).

- The valve clearances must be checked with the engine cold and again after a mileage of approx. 1200 miles has been covered.

From April 1989

We will mention it. There is no need to re-tighten the bolts. The valve clearances must be adjusted with the engine cold.

1.4. Engine — Servicing and Overhaul

1.4.0. CYLINDER HEAD AND VALVES

1.4.0.0. Technical Data

Cylinder Head:

Material: .... Aluminium
Cylinder head height: .... 92.5 ± 0.15 mm (3.675 ± 0.006 in.)
Min. cylinder head height: .... 92.10 mm (3.659 in.)
Head surface, max. distortion: .... 0.10 mm (0.004 in.)
Identification of cylinder head gasket: .... According to engine type and number

Valve Guides

Outer diameter, size 1: .... 14.02 mm (0.557 in.)

Outer diameter, size 2: .... 14.13 mm (0.561 in.)
Outer diameter, repair size 1: .... 14.29 mm (0.568 in.)
Outer diameter, repair size 2: .... 14.59 mm (0.580 in.)
Inner diameter, Std.: .... 8.02 ± 0.022 mm (0.319 ± 0.0009 in.)
Valve guide length: .... 58.4 ± 0.3 mm (2.320 ± 0.012 in.)

Locating Bores in Cylinder Head:
- Standard size 1: .... 13.965 ± 0.032 mm (0.555 ± 0.001 in.)
- Standard size 2: .... 14.035 ± 0.032 mm (0.558 ± 0.001 in.)
- Repair size 1: .... 14.195 ± 0.032 mm (0.564 ± 0.001 in.)
- Repair size 2: .... 14.495 ± 0.032 mm (0.576 ± 0.001 in.)

Installation Height between lower guide edge and Valve Seat ("x" in Fig. below):
- Inlet valves (A): .... 31.50 mm (1.2515 in.)
- Exhaust valves (B): .... 21.30 mm (0.858 in.)

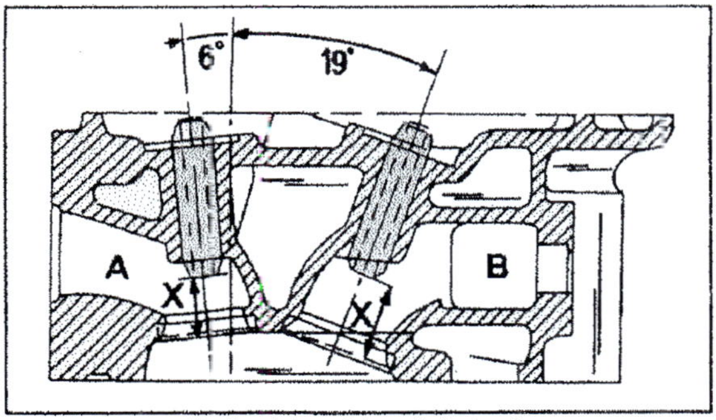

Sectional view of the cylinder head.

Installation Angle of Valve Guides (see Fig. above):
- Inlet valves (A): .... 19°
- Exhaust valves (B): .... 6°

Valves

Valve Head Diameter:
- Inlet valves: .... 42.50 mm (1.689 in.)
- Exhaust valves: .... 35.5 mm (1.4104 in.)

Valve Length:
- Inlet valves: .... 116.25 mm (4.698 in.)
- Exhaust valves: .... 112.00 mm (4.450 in.)

Valve Stem Diameter:
- Inlet valves: .... 8.02 mm (0.319 in.)
- Exhaust valves: .... 8.00 mm (0.318 in.)
- Max. permissible grinding off of valve stem: .... 0.20 mm (0.008 in.)

Min. permissible valve edge thickness: .... 0.50 mm (0.0.02 in.)

Valve Stem Running Clearance:
- Inlet valves: .... 0.02 - 0.042 mm (0.0008 - 0.0017 in.)
- Exhaust valves: .... 0.04 - 0.060 mm (0.0016 - 0.0024 in.)

Valve Clearances:

Inlet valves: .... 0.10 mm (0.004 in.)

Exhaust valves: .... 0.25 mm (0.010 in.)

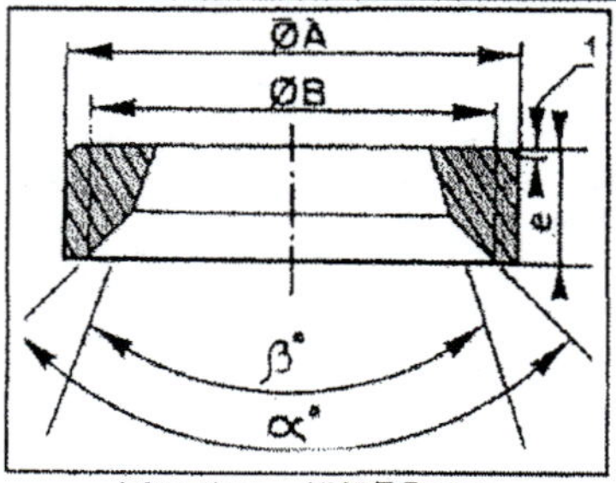

Inlet valves — XM7-T Engine

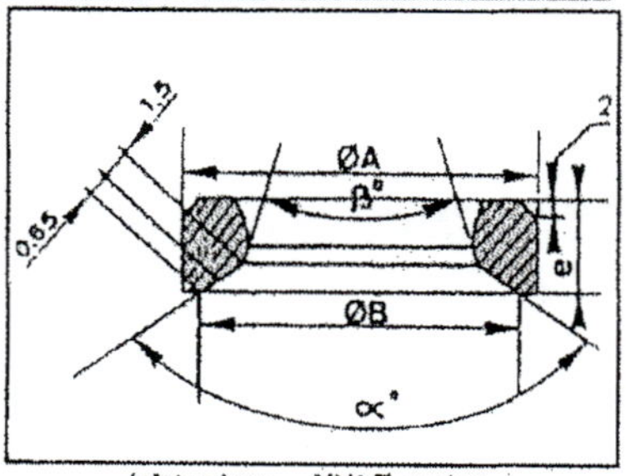

Inlet valves — XN1-T engine.

Valve Seats:

Valve Seat Angles:

Inlet valves: . . . . 120°
Exhaust valves: . . . . 90°

Inlet Valve Seat Diameters — XM7-T Engine (above left and right) — in Millimetres:

Diameter A, Std. size 1: . . . . 43.51 mm
Diameter A, Std. size 2: . . . . 43.71 mm
Diameter A, repair size 1: . . . . 43.81 mm
Diameter A, repair size 2: . . . . 44.01 mm
Diameter B: . . . . 41.00 mm
Dimension "e" — 169 B engine: . . . . 7.33 mm
— 170 engine: . . . . 10.257 mm
Valve angle (alfa): . . . . 120°
Valve angle (beta) — 169 B engine: . . . . 17°
— 170 engine: . . . . 70°

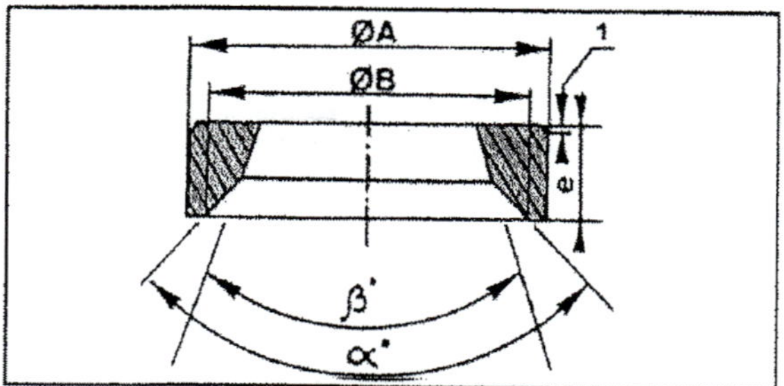

Exhaust valves — All engines

Exhaust Valve Diameters — Cast Iron (see above):

Diameter A, 170B, to 11/83, 169B from 4/85 Std. size 1: . . . . 37.01 mm
Diameter A, 170B, to 11/83, 169B from 4/85, Std. size 2: . . . . 37.21 mm
Diameter A, 170B, to 11/83, 169B from 4/85, repair size 1: . . . . 37.31 mm
Diameter A, 170, to 11/83, 169B from 4/85, repair size 2: . . . . 37.51 mm
Diameter B, all engines: . . . . 35.00 mm
Valve seat angle (alfa): . . . . 90°
Angle (beta): . . . . 15°

Exhaust Valve Diameters — Steel (see Page 36, bottom):

Diameter A, 170B, to 11/83, Std. size 1:	38.01 mm
Diameter A, 170B, to 11/83, Std. size 2:	38.21 mm
Diameter A, 170B, to 11/83, repair size 1:	38.31 mm
Diameter A, 170B from 11/83 and 169 B from 4/85, Std. 1:	37.01 mm
Diameter A, 170B, from 11/83 and 169 B from 4/85, Std. 2:	37.21 mm
Diameter A, 170B, from 11/83 and 169 B from 4/85, repair size 1:	38.31 mm
Diameter B, all engines:	35.00 mm
Dimension "e", all engines:	6.462 mm
Valve seat angle (alfa):	90°
Angle (beta), all engines:	15°

The above dimensions and angles are also valid for the 170 C engine.

Valve Springs

Number of springs:	2 inner springs, two outer springs
Wire diameter:	3.0 mm, inner springs, 4.3 mm, outer springs
Identification colour:	white
Fitting direction:	Not important
Free Lenghts:	
Inner springs:	39.60 mm
Outer springs:	44.00 mm
Direction of Coil Windig:	
Inner springs:	Anti-clockwise
Outer springs:	Clockwise
Length under Load — Inner springs:	
Under load of 8.8 kg:	35.9 mm
Under load of 30.0 kg:	26.80 mm
Length under Load — Outer springs:	
Under load of 17.0 kg:	39.80 mm
Under load of 59.0 kg:	39.70 mm

Camshaft

Number of bearings:	3, pressure lubricated
Camshaft end float:	0.05 - 0.14 mm
Max. run-out of shaft:	0.02 mm
Colour identification of camshaft:	
New shafts:	pink
Repair size:	brown

Timing Drive:

Timing chain:	Double-roller chain, 58 links
Number of teeth on crankshaft sprocket:	19
Number of teeth on camshaft sprocket:	38
Hydraulic chain tensioner:	Renold or Sedis

1.4.0.1. CYLINDER HEAD — REMOVAL AND INSTALLATION

A special socket may be required to undo the cylinder head bolts. The engine will have to be lifted out of its mountings, i.e. a suitable jack will have to be available.

Note: Remember that the cylinder head bolts are tightened in a different manner. Before removal ensure that you know the type of head fitted.

- Disconnect the battery plus cable. Push the cable to one side to make sure it cannot jump back accidently.
- Drain the cooling system.
- Remove the spare wheel.

- Remove the air intake housing and the air cleaner. Disconnect the upper hose from the water pump.
- Disconnect the following hoses between engine (cylinder head) and body: inlet hose to heater, hose for the inlet manifold pre-heating on the exit of the cylinder head, the outlet hose for the pre-heating of the inlet manifold on the manifold side and the vacuum hose for the brake servo unit on the servo side.
- In the following order disconnect the parts from the cylinder head: The cables from the temperature switch for the temperature gauge and from a second temperature switch, the cable from the fuel cut-off valve on the carburettor, the throttle operating cable, the choke cable and the oil hose for the rocker shaft assembly.
- Unscrew the diagnostic box and place it to one side.
- Unscrew the cylinder head cover.
- Remove the spark plug seals and pins from the spark plug tubes, the alternator and the drive belt.
- Jack up the front of the engine to gain access from underneath. First remove the water pump drive belt. The easiest way to remove the belt is to insert a screwdriver as shown in Fig. 1.47 and then turning the crankshaft pulley with a 35 mm socket. The belt will slip off and can be removed.
- Remove the two bolts securing the rear pipe assembly from the water pump, located immediately above the drive shaft.
- Remove the connection between the exhaust manifold and the exhaust pipe, as described during the removal of the engine.
- Support the engine from below (jack with wooden block underneath the oil sump) or lift the engine with a suitable lifting tackle and ropes or chains, without obstructin the access to the cylinder head.
- Remove the engine mounting in Fig. 1.48. First remove the two bolts near the water pump, then the nut (1) in the centre of the engine mount and finally the aluminium carrier bracket (2). Make sure that the engine is well supported before the mounting parts are removed.

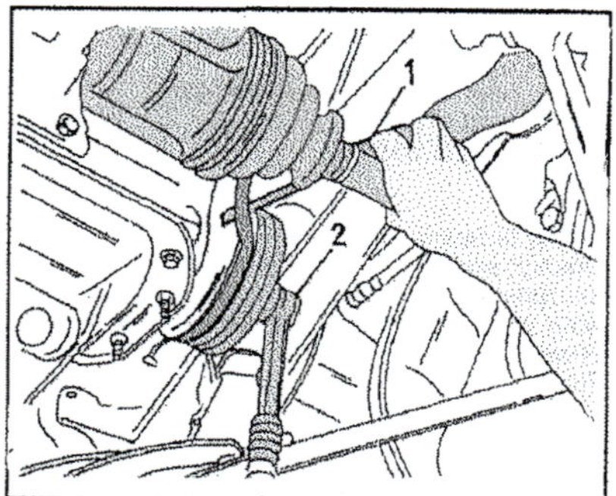

Fig. 1.47. — Removal of the drive belt. Insert a screwdriver (1) below the V-belt and rotate the pulley with a socket (2) until the belt is free.

- Slacken the 10 cylinder head bolts in reverse order shown in 1.43 until they can be removed. Remove the 5 rocker shaft assembly securing nuts and lift off the assembly. The push rods can be withdrawn from the cylindert block.
- The cylinder head can now be removed. Fig. 1.17 shows two iron bars which can be inserted as shown. Lift the ends of the bars until the hed is free. This will break the seal between cylinder head gasket and cylinder liners. Otherwise grip the two manifolds and rock the head to and fro until it is free. Never lift the head upwards, as the liners may stick to the gasket. Make absolutely sure it is free before it is lifted off.

- Remove the cylinder head gasket and secure the cylinder liners with clamps, as shown in Fig. 1.19. Immediately clean the cylinder head and the cylinder block faces and remove the remaining parts of the cylinder head without damaging the surfaces. Emery cloth must not be used to clean off the faces. Take care not to drop any gaskets rests into the cylinder bores. If possible "fill" the bores with rags. The same applies to any other openings or bores in the cylinder block.

The installation of the cylinder head is covered in detail in the section covering the assembly of the engine.

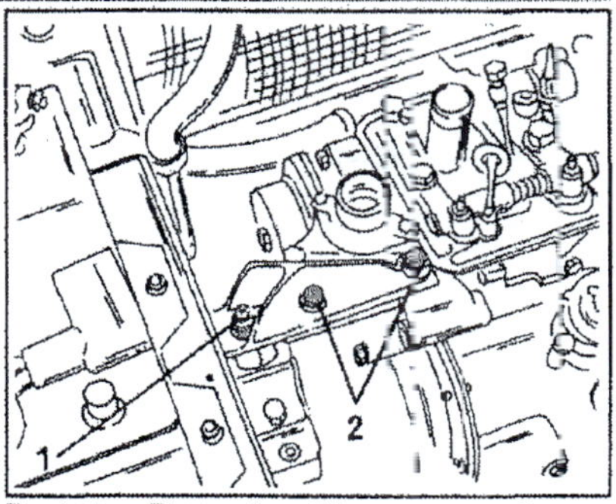

Fig. 1.48. — The location of the engine mountings on the R.H. side of the engine.
1 Engine mounting nut 2 Engine carrier.5

1.4.0.2. Cylinder Head — Dismantling and Overhaul

Remove all external parts from the cylinder head. The valves must now be removed as follows:

- A valve lifter, similar as shown in Fig. 1.49 is the best tool for the removal of the valves. Valve lifters are now available from most tool hire companies and there should be no problem obtaining one. It is also possible to remove the valves by placing a piece of wood into the combustion chamber, to support the valve head, and then to proceed as follows:

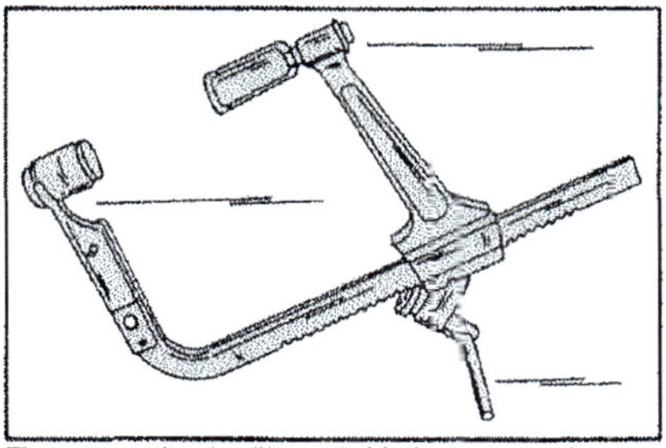

Fig. 1.49. — A valve lifter suitable for these engines.

- Use a piece of tube, the same diameter as the valve spring cap and place the tube over the valve spring. With a hammer give a short and sharp blow onto the tube. The valve springs will be compressed and the valve cotter halves remain inside the tube.
- Take the parts off the valve and withdraw the valve from the other side. Mark the valves. This is best done by piercing them through the bottom of an upside-down cardboard box and writing the valve number next to each valve. No. 1 valve is the one nearest to the timing end of the engine.

Valves: Check the valve faces for wear or grooving. If the wear is only slight, regrind the valves to their appropriate angle in a valve grinding machine. All inlet valves and all exhaust valves of all engines have the same angle. Important is the valve head edge. This is the dimension shown in Fig. 1.50 between the arrows and must not be less than 0.50 mm (0.0.02 in.)

Check the valve stem diameters and in this connection the inside diameters of the valve guides. Professional tools required are a micrometer and an internal precision gauge. Fig. 1.51 shows how the valve stems and the valve guide bores are measured and where the measurements should take place. If there is a deviation from the nominal values, it may be necessary to replace the valve guides (see below). Also check the end of the valve stems. There should be no visible wear in this area. Valve ends can be re-ground to a maximum value.

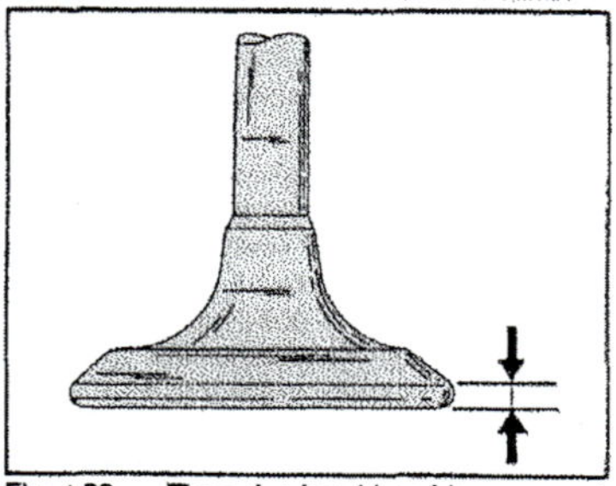

Fig. 1.50. — The valve head head is measured between the arrows. Make sure to observe the minimum permissible dimension.

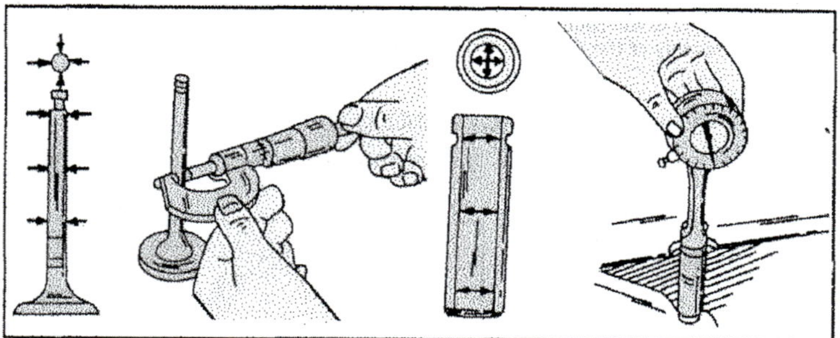

Fig. 1.51. — Measuring the valve stem diameters on the left and the internal diameters of the valve guides on the right.

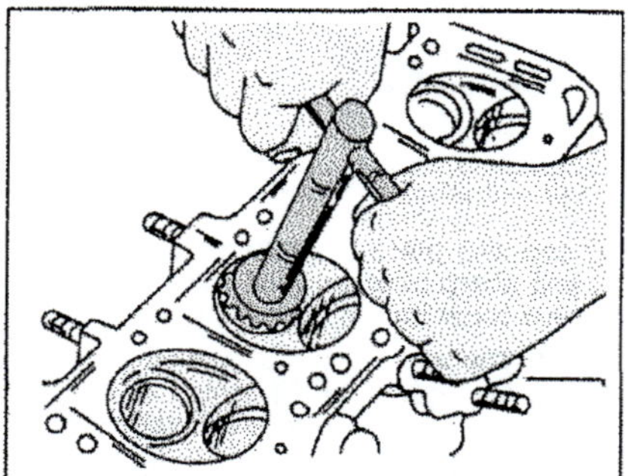

Fig. 1.52. — Re-cutting a valve seat. Rotate the cutter with even pressure.

Valve Seats: Valve seats may be re-cut to their original angle with the appropriate cutters, but note that a 45° cutter (exhaust valves) and a 60° cutter (inlet valves) are required. If this operation is carried out properly, there should be no need to grind-in the valves. Fig. 1.52 shows how such a cutter is employed. Use correction cutters to bring the valve seating area into the centre of the valve seat. Refer to the views of the valve seats on page 36 and the technical data for specific dimensions. Both the valve seat angles (90 or 120°) and the correction angles are given. Note that the valve seat diameters have changed since introduction of the engines. Make sure you check under the engine in question.

Valves should be ground into re-cut valve seats. To this, coat the valve seat with fine lapping compound and use a suction tool. Move the valve backwards and forwards, as demonstrated in Fig. 1.53. Ever so often lift the suction tool, move it forward by ¼ of a turn and continue grinding. Work the seat until an uninterrupted ring is visible around the face of the valve. After grinding-in, clean the cylinder head, and even more important the inside of the valve guide bores thoroughly. Any lapping paste inside the cylinder head will accelerate the wear of the new parts.

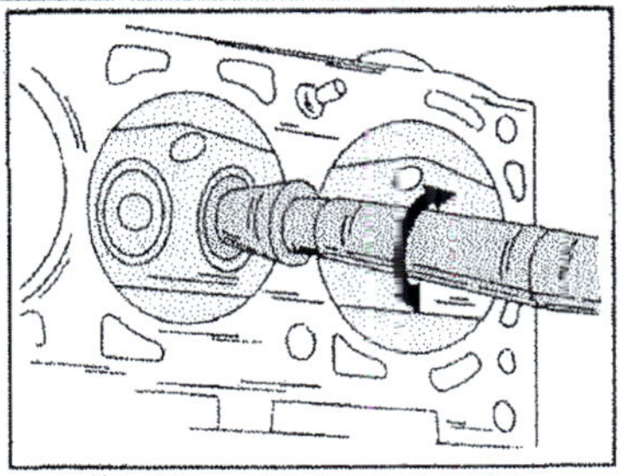

Fig. 1.53. — Grinding-in of a valve.

Use a pencil and mark across the valve seat closely spaced. Drop the valve into the respective valve guide and turn the valve by 90°, using the suction tool, applying slight pressure to the tool. Remove the valve and check if the pencil marks have been removed from the entire circumference. The gap created will indicate the width of the valve seat and can be measured with a ruler or caliper. Otherwise repeat the grinding-in until this is the case.

Valve Springs: If the engine has a high mileage, always replace the valve springs as a set. To check a valve spring, place the old spring and a new spring end to end over a long bolt (with washer under bolt head) and fit a nut (again with a washer). Tighten the nut until the springs are under tension and measure the length of the two springs. If the old spring is shorter by more than 10%, replace the complete spring set. Check the free length of the valve springs (Fig. 1.54) and compare the values with the dimensions given in Section 1.4.0.0.

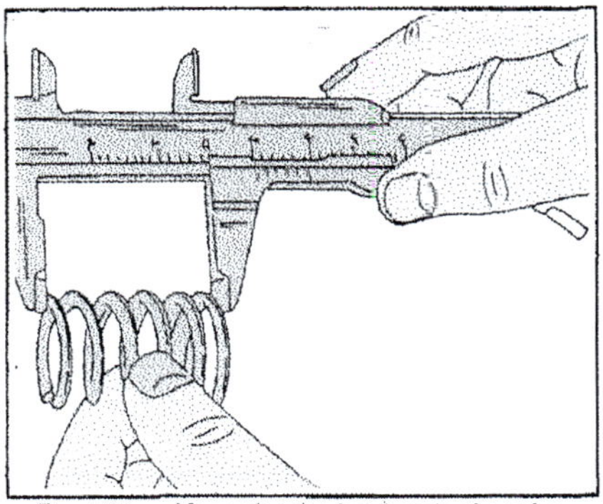

Fig. 1.54. — Measuring the free length of a valve.

Valve Guides: Measure the inside diameter of the guides, as shown on the R.H. side in Fig. 1.51. As an inside micrometer is necessary for this operation, which is not always available, you can insert the valve into its guide and withdraw it until the valve head is approx. level with the cylinder head face. Rock the valve to and fro and check for play. Although no exact values are available, it can be assumed that the play should not exceed 1.0 - 1.2 mm (0.04 - 0.047 in.).

Valve guides are available with oversize outside diameter (see Section 1.4.0.0.) and the locating bores in the cylinder head must be bored out to take the new guides. This may be a job for the workshop. Drive out the guide with a suitable mandrel. The cylinder head should be heated in boiling water to facilitate the operation. Measure the protruding end of the guide (write it down) before driving the old guide out and drive in the new guide to obtain the same dimension.

New valve guides always require the fitting of new valves and the valve seats must be re-cut and the valves ground into the seats.

If you fit the guides yourself, lubricate them with engine oil and press or drive them into the cylinder head until dimension "X" in Fig. 1.55 has the required value. From the illustration you will also see the inclination of the guides, i.e. the cylinder head must be supported on one side to have the respective guide in vertical position. Valve guides must be reamed after installation to the diameter given in Section 1.4.0.0. The guides of all engines have the same inner diameter. Use an adjustable reamer. The correct running clearance is automatically obtained when the guides have the correct internal diameter.

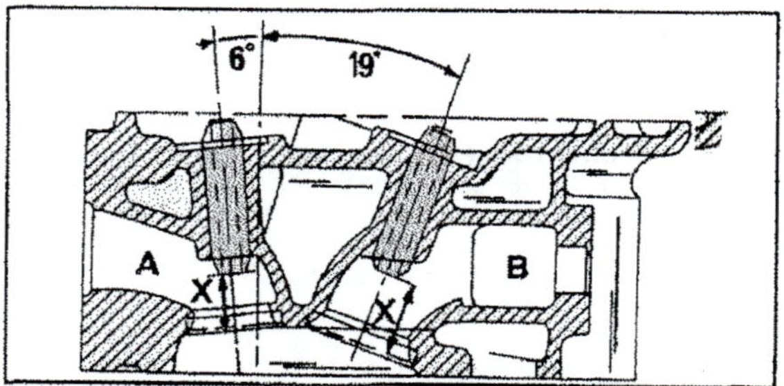

Fig. 1.55. — Sectional view of the cylinder head with the location of the exhaust valve guides (A) und the inlet valve guides (B). Dimension "X" shows the installation depth. Inlet valve guides = 31.5 mm, exhaust valve guides 21.3 mm.

Attention: The valve seats must be re-cut after fitting new valve guides. Valve guides and valves should always replaced as a set.

Cylinder Head: Thoroughly clean the cylinder head surface and measure the surface for distortion. To do this, place a fine-edge steel ruler across the cylinder head face as shown in Fig. 1.56 and measure the gap between ruler and head with feeler gauges. If a feeler gauge of more than specified in Section 1.4.0.0. can be inserted, replace the cylinder head. The head can be re-ground as long as the min. height is retained (92.10 mm).

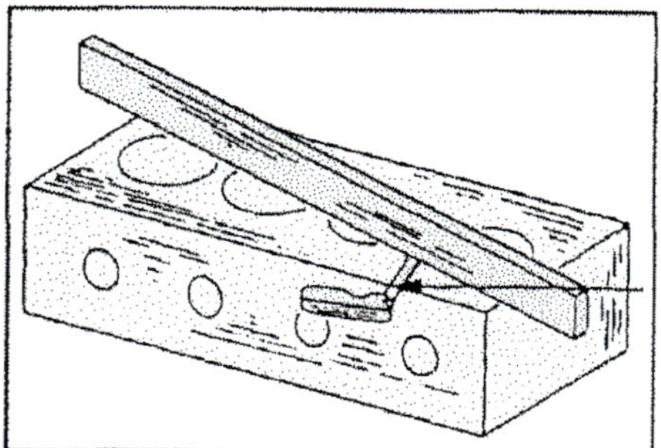

Fig. 1.56. — Checking a cylinder head gasket face for distortion. Check in diaginal and longitudinal direction and across the gasket face.

Camshaft: All engines use the same camshaft. The camshaft is secured to the cylinder block by means of a keeper plate, inserted into a groove in the shaft and secured by two screws.

To remove the camshaft, remove the Woodruff key with a side cutter and unscrew the plate. Carefully withdraw the shaft wityhout hitting with the cams against the bearing shells.

Place the camshaft with the two outer bearing journals into "V" blocks, as shown in Fig. 1.57 or clamp the shaft into a lathe and apply a dial gauge to the centre. Slowly rotate the camshaft and read off the indication of the dial gauge. If the run-out of the shaft is more than 0.01 mm, replace the shaft, as it is bent.

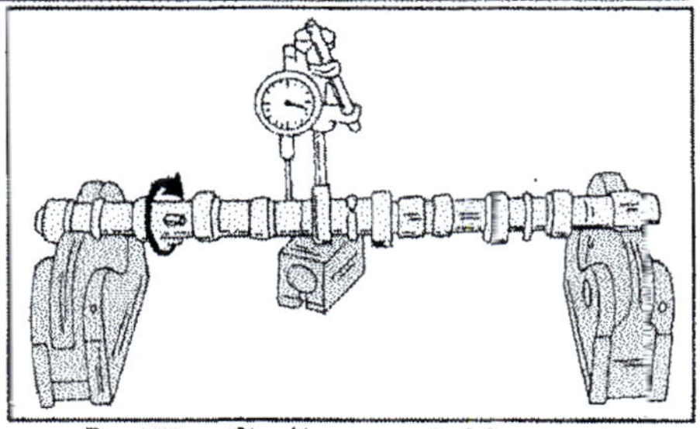

Fig. 1.57. — Checking a camshaft for run-out.

Check the bearing journals for visible wear. Obvious wear requires the replacement of the camshaft. Note that replacement camshafts have a different identification colour.

Check all cams for obvious wear, usually shown by shiny faces.

To measure the end float of the camshaft, fit it into the cylinder block and attach a dial gauge to the cylinder block, with the stylus resting against the end of the shaft. Move the shaft to and fro and read the dial gauge. If the reading is more than 0.14 mm, replace the keeper plate. In severe cases the thrust face of the camshaft could be worn, i.e. replace the camshaft.

1.4.0.3. Cylinder Head — Assembly

If the cylinder had has been replaced, transfer exhaust manifold, spark plugs, thermo switches, etc. from the old to the new head. Make sure all parts are clean. All sliding and rotating parts should be lubricated with oil.

- Insert the well oiled valves into the respective valve guides. If the original valves are used, fit them to the same valve guides; if the valves have been ground-in, make sure that the valve is fitted to the valve seat in which it has been ground-in.
- Assemble the valves. First place the valve spring seat over the cylinder head and push the valve stem seals over the valve stems and valve guides. Fit the valve springs and the upper valve spring cup to the valve spring and compress the spring with a valve spring compressor. When the valve stem end protrudes from the valve spring cup, insert the two valve cotter halves with a pair of pointed pliers. Slowly release the valve spring compressor, checking continuously that the cotter halves are kept in position.

  With a plastic mallet, tap against the end of all valve stems. If the valve cotter halves have not engaged properly, they will jump out. A piece of rag should be replaced over the valve stem ends — just in case.
- The remaining assembly is carried out in reverse order to the removal procedure. Adjust the valve clearance as described in Section 1.4.0.5.
- The fitting and adjustment of the drive belts for the water pump and alternator are described in Section "Cooling System".

1.4.0.4. Cylinder Head — Installation

The installation of the cylinder head has already been described during the assembly of the engine. The following points must be noted when the head is fitted with the engine in the vehicle:

- The nut securing the engine mount (1 in Fig. 1.58) must be tightened to 5.5 kgm (40 ft.lb.), the bolts (2) near the water pump to 5.0 kgm (36 ft.lb.).
- Tighten the exhaust pipe-to-exhaust manifold connection until the dimension "X" in Fig. 1.12 is 22.0 mm.
- Fill the cooling system with anti-freeze.
- Remember that the cylinder head bolts must be re-tightened after a certain mileage. Refer to 31 to 34 for details.

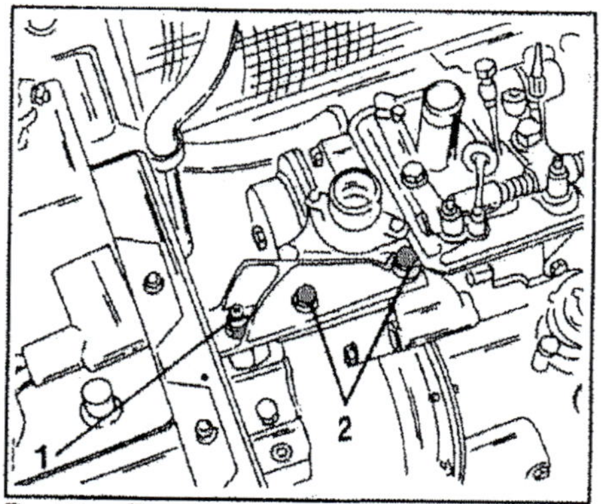

Fig. 1.58. — The engine mounting at the front of the engine.
1 Nut = 5.5 kgm 2 Bolts = 5.0 kgm

The following instructions should also be noted:

- When fitting the cylinder head cover use new seals and packings for the spark plug tubes. A new rubber gasket must be bonded to the cover. Attach the cylinder head cover with the two screws. Fit new rubber tubes. Fig. 1.59 shows how the cylinder head cover is lowered in position.

Fig. 1.59. — Fitting the cylinder head (rocker) cover.

- On the flywheel side fit the oil lubrication pipe for the rocker shaft between the cylinder head and the cylinder block connections. New seals are used on the banjo bolts.
- Adjust the initial setting of the dsitributor. First rotate the crankshaft until the notch in the pulley is in line with the pointer on the timing plate, as shown in Fig. 1.60. Check the position of the driver for the distributor shaft. The larger offset of the drive dog must face towards the rear of the engine when the piston of No. 1 cylinder is at top dead centre (firing point). If this is not the case, rotate the crankshaft **one** turn.
- Insert the distributor into the cylinder block. Set the distributor in the centre po-

sition of its elongated clamp slot. The engine will start, enabling you to adjust the ignition with the engine running.

- Fit the water pump to the cylinder head, using new rubber seals. Note the tightening torques: 8 mm nuts = 2.3 kgm, 10 mm nuts = 4.2 kgm, 10 mm bolts = 2.75 kgm.

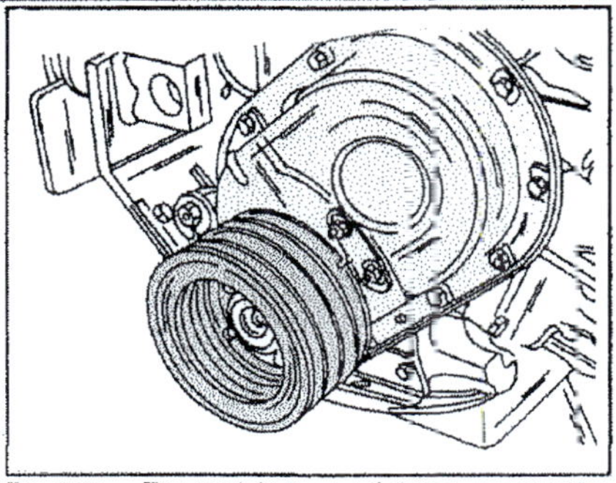

Fig. 1.60. — The notch in the crankshaft pulley must be opposite the pointer on the timing plate before installation of the distributor.

1.4.0.4. Valve Clearance Adjustment

If the adjustment is carried out with the engine fitted, as is the case during a routine check of the valve clearances, remove certain parts to gain access to the valves. These include the cylinder head (rocker) cover, air cleaner, certain hoses, etc. Valve clearances can be adjusted by two different methods, both are described.

- Rotate the engine until the exhaust valve of No. 1 cylinder is full open. In this position adjust the inlet valve of No. 3 cylinder and the exhaust valve of No. 4 cylinder. To rotate the engine either apply a socket to the crankshaft pulley nut (35 mm A/F) or jack up one of the front wheels, engage the highest gear and rotate the wheel until the crankshaft is in the correct position. The spark plugs can be removed to facilitate the rotation of the crankshaft.

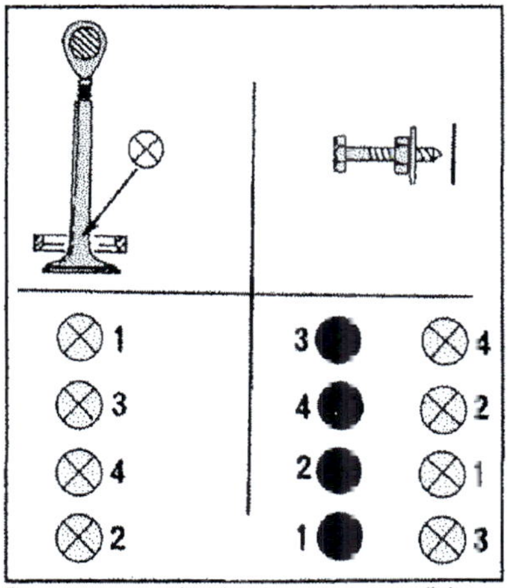

Fig. 1.61. — Adjusting the valve clearances. Exhaust valves are marked with "X" in circle, inlet valves are marked black. With the exhaust valves on the left opened, adjust the valves shown on the right.

- Rotate the engine further until the next exhaust valve is fully open. Adjust the valves in accordance with Fig. 1.61. On the left you see the exhaust valves. The cam must be in the position shown when the valve is fully open. On the right you will see the valves to be adjusted.
- The valves can also be adjusted when one set of valves is fully closed. Following this method, rotate the crankshaft until the valves of No. 1 cylinder are fully closed, i.e. the cams of the two valves must be in the position shown in Fig. 1.62. This can be checked on No. 4 cylinder, where one valve should be opening and the other one closing, i.e. the valves are whats technically known "rocking". If you now move the rocker levers of No. 1 cylinder up and down you

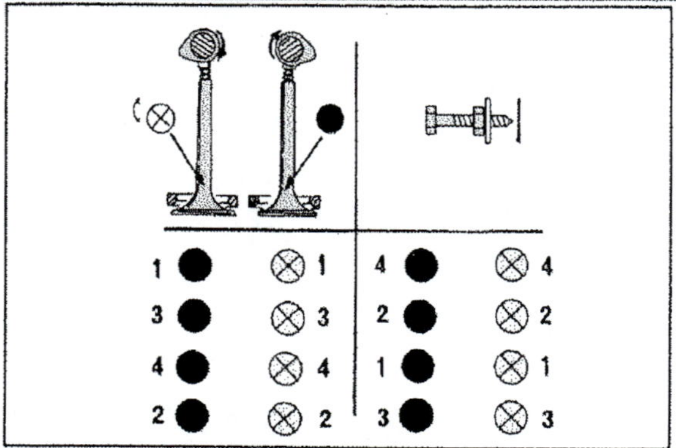

Fig. 1.62. — Adjusting the valve clearances when the valves shown on the L.H. side are fully closed. Adjust both valves of the cylinder shown on the R.H. side. Note the positions of the cams.

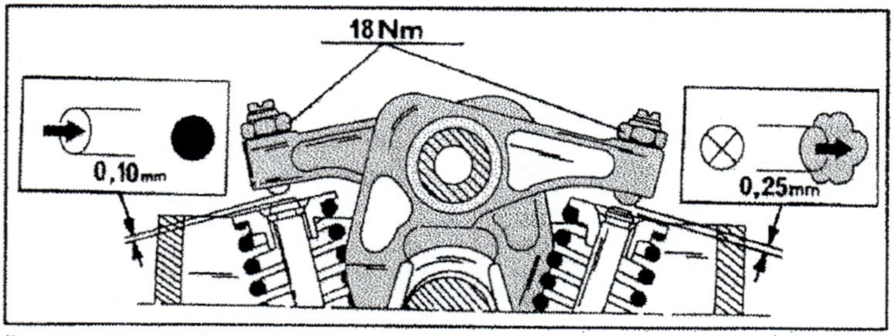

Fig. 1.63. — Insert feeler gauges of the thickness shown between the ends of the valve stems and the rocker arm pads. Tighten the locknuts to 1.8 kgm.

will notice that some play can be felt. After adjusting the valves of No. 4 cylinder, turn the crankshaft by half a turn and adjust the next closed pair of valves. Follow the table below:

Valves closed	*Valves to be adjusted*
Cylinder No. 1	Cylinder No. 4
Cylinder No. 3	Cylinder No. 2
Cylinder No. 4	Cylinder No. 1
Cylinder No. 2	Cylinder No. 3

To adjust the valves insert a feeler gauge of the applicable size between the end of the valve stem and the rocker arm pad as shown in Fig. 1.62. The feeler gauge should have a gliding fit. A good indication of a perfect play is when the feeler gauge can be inserted easily, tries to offer a slight resistance and then "jumps" into the gap.

To adjust the clearance slacken the adjusting screw locknut with a ring spanner and turn the screw with a screwdriver. Re-tighten the nut (Fig. 1.62).

We advise you to re-check the adjustment after all valves have been adjusted in the manner described above.

If the engine is in the vehicle, refit the parts removed. This includes the parts of the cylinder head cover.

1.4.1. PISTONS AND CONNECTING RODS

1.4.1.0. Technical Data

Piston pin fit: .... Floating fit in piston and connecting rod, secured by two snap rings

Piston assembly direction: .... Arrow in piston towards timing side

Piston Rings:
- Number: 3
- Type: .... 1 straight compression ring, 1 taper compression ring 1 oil control ring

Ring Thickness (in mm):
- Upper ring: .... 1.50 mm
- Centre ring: .... 2.00 mm
- Oil scraper ring: .... 3.96 mm

Piston Diameters — 169 B Engine:
- Standard: .... 84.000 mm
- Class A: .... 83.930 - 83.941 mm
- Class B: .... 83.942 - 83.952 mm
- Class C: .... 83.953 - 83.963 mm
- Class D: .... 83.964 - 83.974 mm
- Oversize pistons: .... As per parts catalogue/microfiche

Piston Diameters — 170 Engines:
- Standard: .... 88.000 mm
- Class A: .... 87.925 - 87.936 mm
- Class B: .... 87.937 - 87.947 mm
- Class C: .... 87.948 - 87.958 mm
- Class D: .... 87.959 - 87.969 mm
- Oversize pistons: .... As per parts catalogue/microfiche

Cylinder liner diameter: .... See under "Cylinder Block and Liners"

Piston running clearance: .... 0.06 - 0.08 mm

Raised Piston Crown (2.0 litre only):
- 170 B engine: .... 0.51 mm
- 170 C engine: .... 2.98 mm

Connecting Rods

Material of connecting rods: .... Forged steel

Material of big end bearing shells: .... Steel with bearing metal

Length between centres: .... 132 mm ± 0.07 mm

Big end bearing diameter (without shells): .... 53.555 ± 0.019 mm

Big end bearing journals and bearing shells: .... See under "Crankshaft"

Small End Bush Bore — Standard: .... 24.408 ± 0.068 mm
— Repair size: .... 24.708 ± 0.068 mm

Piston Ring Gaps:
- Upper piston rings: .... 0.20 - 0.50 mm

Centre rings: .... 0.40 - 0.55 mm
Lower rings: .... 0.25 - 0.40 mm

Piston Pins:
Piston Pin Bore in Piston:
Blue mark: .... 23.009 - 23.005 mm
White mark: .... 23.005 - 23.000 mm
Red mark: .... 23.000 - 22.995 mm

Piston Pin Diameter:
Pin colour code blue: .... 23.005 - 23.001 mm
Pin colour code white: .... 23.001 - 22.996 mm
Pin colour code red: .... 22.996 - 22.992 mm

Piston pin length: .... 74.00 mm

1.4.1.1. General

The pistons and connecting rods can be only be replaced when the engine has been removed from the vehicle and the transmission disconnected from the engine. New pistons and cylinder liners are matched to each other and must be kept together. This also applies to original parts, if they are to be refitted. In this case mark the pistons, connecting rods and the liner with the cylinder number.

Each piston is fitted with two compression rings and one oil control ring. The upper compression ring is chromium-plated on its outside, the second piston ring has a taper section and is therefore marked with "Top" to prevent incorrect fitting. The marking must be visible from above.

Although the pistons and connecting rods are not the same in all engines, you will find that the following description is valid for all engine types. New piston/cylinder liner assemblies mus, however, be obtain by quoting the engine number.

1.4.1.2. Dismantling Pistons and Connecting Rods

No special tools are necessary to dismantle the pistons and connecting rods. Securing rings are used to hold the piston pins in position. Proceed as follows to dismantle:

- Use a pair of piston ring pliers and remove the piston rings one after another from the crown end of the piston, as shown in Fig. 1.64. If no piston ring pliers are available, use three thin metal strips and slide the rings over the strips to remove them one by one. One of the strips must be placed underneath the piston ring ends to avoid scratches.
- Remove the securing rings out of the two piston pin bores. Either use a small screwriver or a pair of circlip pliers for this operation.
- Use a stepped mandrel to drive out the piston pin. Hold the piston in

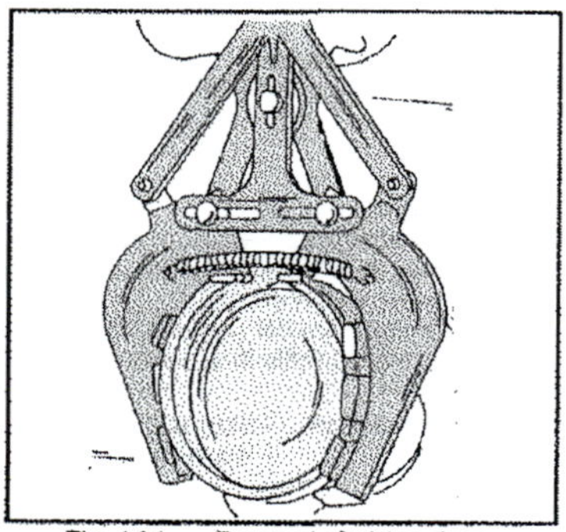

Fig. 1.64. — Removal of piston rings.

one palm of the hand whilst the pin is removed. If the piston pin has a tight fit, heat the piston in warm water.

Note: Pistons and connecting rods should only be separated if pistons or connecting rods must be replaced.

1.4.1.3. Checking Pistons and Connecting Rods

Thoroughly clean and check all parts. Signs of seizure, scratches or wear mean that the respective parts must be replaced.

- One after the other insert each piston ring into the top or bottom of the cylinder bore (from where it was removed) and push the ring squarely into the bore, using an up-side-down piston to do so, as shown in Fig. 1.65, until the ring is inserted by approx. 15 to 20 mm (0.5 - 0.8 in.). Insert a feeler gauge into the gap between the two ring ends and check that the value obtained is not greater than specified in Section 1.4.0.0. Ring gaps cannot be adjusted and new rings must be fitted if the gap of any of the rings is greater.
- Measure the piston diameter with a micrometer. Apply the jaws of the micrometer at right angles to the piston pin bore at the bottom of the piston skirt. The pistons are graded in four tolerance groups. Additionally the piston pins are provided with colour codes. Pistons and piston pins are manufactured in pairs and are marked accordingly. Piston crowns are marked with a letter, a code number for the matching of the assembly and an arrow which points to the timing side of the engine. If the piston crown is covered with carbon you will not be able to see the marking. Careful scraping will, however, the marked details.

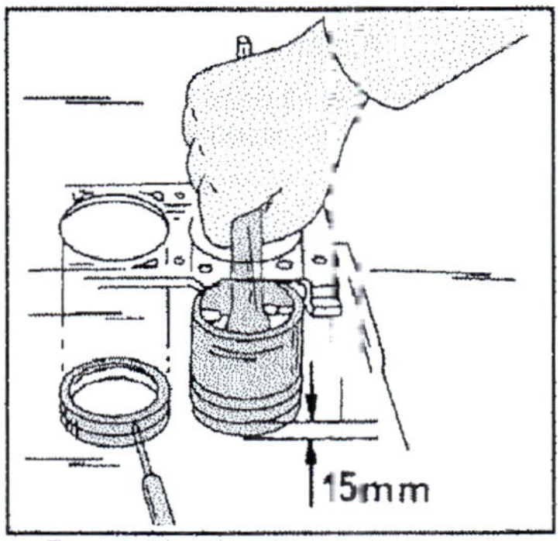

Fig. 1.65. Checking the piston ring gaps

- Pistons of the 2.0 litre XN1-TA engine were modified, i.e. the pistons of an older engine cannot be fitted to the later engine. The same applies visa versa. Fig. 1.66 shows a sectional view of a piston. The dimension between the arrows shows to which engine the piston is fitted.
- To check the piston running clearance measure the cylinder bore diameter with an internal micrometer. Bores are measured in longitudinal and transverse direction and in three different depths of the cylinder bore. The resulting measurements will give the smallest and the largest diameter. Deduct the piston diameter from the bore diameter. The difference is the running clearance which should be as given in Section 1.4.1.0. New pistons/liners must be fitted if a greater difference is established.
- Check piston pins and the bores in the pistons for wear. Piston pins must have a sliding fit in the pistons and connecting rod small ends, with the parts well oiled.
- Excessive wear required the replacement of pistons, pins and liners.

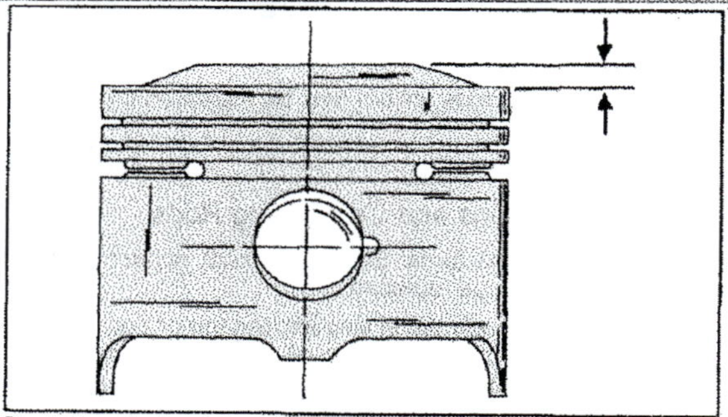

Fig. 1.66. — Sectional view of a piston as fitted to the earlier engine. Pistons for later engines have a different piston crown.

1.4.1.4. Assembling Pistons and Connecting Rods

It is assumed that all parts have been checked as described in the last section and parts have been replaced as necessary. The connecting rods should be checked for twist or distortion. A special jig is available for this operation and we recommend that the con rods are taken to a dealer to have them checked. The big end bearing cap studs in the connecting rods can be replaced individually, if the threads are damaged.

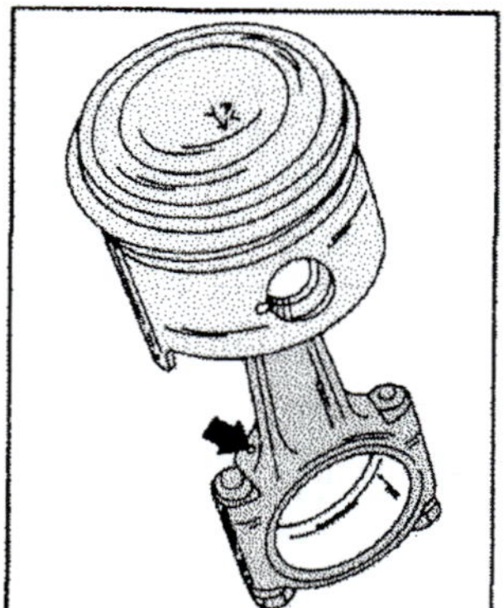

Fig. 1.67. — Correct assembly of pistons and connecting rods. The arrow in the piston crown and the oil splash hole must be on the same side.

- Coat the *piston pin and the piston bore* with engine oil and place the piston over the connecting rod small end. The arrow in the piston crown and the oil splash hole in the connecting rod must be aligned as shown in Fig. 1.67.
- Lubricate the piston pins, piston pin bores and small end bores of the connecting rods and push the piston pin into piston and small end as shown in Fig. 1.68. A tight piston pin can be fitted easier if the piston has been warmed-up in hot water. The pin securing clip must be fitted to one side of the piston. Push the pin in position until it rest against the circlip and the fit the clip on the other side (engage fully).
- Use an oil can and generously splash engine oil onto the piston pin bore area.
- Fit the piston rings one after the other, using a pair of piston ring pliers shown earlier on. Check the fitting direction of each rind before installation. Remember that piston rings are brittle and easisy snap — Take care.
- Coat the piston rings with engine oil and arrange the ring gaps around the circumference of the piston. The ring gaps must, however, be located at specific

intervals. Refer to Fig. 1.69 and turn the oil control ring until the gap is at position "a". Then rotate the two remaining rings until the gaps are spaced 20 to 50 mm from the gap of the oil control ring, one to the left and the other one to the right.

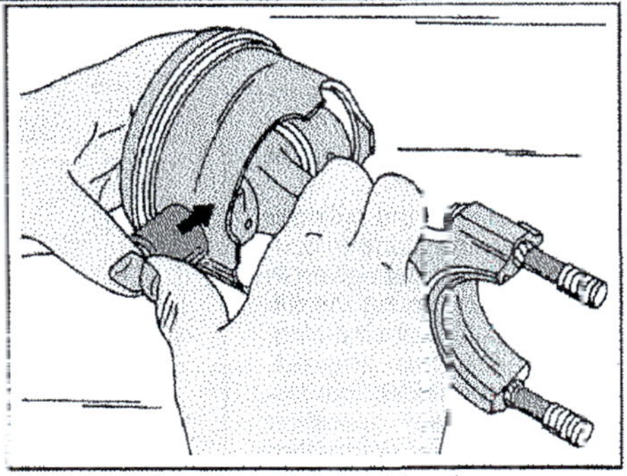

Fig. 1.68. — Fitting a piston pin.

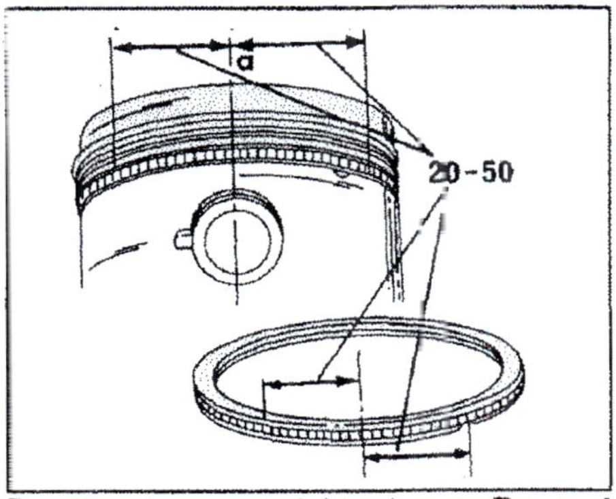

Fig. 1.69. — Arrangement of piston ring gaps. The gap of the oil control ring is positioned at "a". The gaps of the other rings left and right as shown.

- Lubricate the piston with engine oil and insert it into the cylinder liner. Suitable piston ring clamps must be available to push the piston rings into their grooves. With the cylinder liners fitted, place the clamp around the piston as shown in Fig. 1.70 and carefully push the piston/connecting rod assembly downwards, using a hammer handle, until the clamp slips off and the piston rings have entered the bore.
- After fitting all pistons in the manner described check once more that the arrows in the crowns of all pistons face towards the timing side of the engine.
- Fit the big end bearing caps, noting the alignment marks in caps and rods. Tighten the nuts evenly to a final torque setting of 4.0 kgm (30 ft.lb.). After installation check once more that each cap has been fitted to the correct connecting rods and that marks in rods and caps are opposite each other.
- Rotate the crankshaft a few times to check for hard spots. An easy way to rotate a crankshaft is to screw two of the flywheel bolts into the crankshaft flange. Inserting a screwdriver plate between the bolts will allow you to rotate the crankshaft.

1.4.2. CYLINDER BLOCK (Technical Data see Page 53)

The cylinder block consists of the crankcase and the actual block with the cylinder liners. Special attention should be given to the cylinder block at each major overhaul of the engine, irrespective of whether the liners are to be replaced or not. Thoroughly clean all cavities and passages and remove all traces of foreign matter from the joint faces. If any machining or cylinder block face has taken place, it is essential that all swarf is removed before assembly of the engine takes place.

Fig. 1.70. — Fitting a piston with a piston ring clamp.

Measurement of the cylinder liners should be made in conjunction with the data given in Section 1.4.1.0., noting the different diameters of size classes and the two engines. Measuring a cylinder liner bore is not an easy operation and can be rather confusing, mainly as there are intermediate sizes and class sizes. We strongly recommend to have the work carried out by an engine shop which is familiar with these engines.

Cylinder liner bores are measured in both transverse and longitudinal planes and at three positions down the bore. The worst measurement must be taken when deciding the wear of an individual bore.

Measure the gasket face of the cylinder block in similar manner as shown for the cylinder head. If feeler gauge of more than 0.10 mm (0.0004 in.) can be inserted, the block is distorted. Re-machining of the gasket face is permissible, as long as the minimum height of the cylinder head is retained.

1.4.3. CRANKSHAFT AND FLYWHEEL

1.4.3.0. Technical Data

Number of main journals: 5
Material: .... Forged steel

Main Bearings:

Type — Crankshaft WITH plugs: ...... Plain bearing shells with oil holes in bearings I, II and V, without oil holes in bearings II and IV.

Type — Crankshaft WITHOUT plus: ..... Plain bearing shells, with oil holes in cylinder block (all), without oil holes in main bearing caps.

Crankshaft end float: .... 0.08 - 0.20 mm (0.003 - 0.008 in.)
End float regulation: .... Four half thrust washers at flywheel end main bearing
Thrust washer thicknesses:
Std.: .... 2.30 mm
Oversizes: .... 2.35, 2.40, 2.45 and 2.50 mm

Main Bearing Journal Diameter — All Engines (in millimetres):

Nominal diameter — Bearing No. 1 (clutch side) : .... 54.92 mm
— Bearing II: .... 56.165 mm
— Bearing III (centre): .... 57.573 mm
— Bearing IV: .... 58.573 mm
— Bearing V (Timing side): .... 59.416 mm

Repair diameter — Bearing I: 54.62 mm
— Bearing II: 56.865 mm
— Bearing III: 56.889 mm
— Bearing IV: 58.273 mm
— Bearing V: 59.116 mm

Bearing Journal Width:
Bearing No. I: 37.00 mm
Bearing No. II: 30.00 mm
Bearing No. III: 38.00 mm
Bearing No. IV: 30.00 mm
Bearing No. V: 38.00 mm

Main Bearing Shell Widths:
Bearing No. I: 29.35 mm
Bearing No. II: 21.50 mm
Bearing No. III: 29.50 mm
Bearing No. IV: 21.50 mm
Bearing No. V: 29.50 mm
Main Bearing Shell Thickness:
New: 1.885 mm
Repair size: 2.035 mm

Crank Journal Diameter:
Diameter — Std.: 50.00 mm
Repair size: 49.70 mm
Width of journals: 30.05 mm

Big End Bearing Shells:
Thickness: 1.815 mm
Oversize: 1.965 mm

Cylinder Block and Cylinder Liners
Cylinder block height: 285.9 ± 0.15 mm
Height between cylinder head face and liner locating flange: 90.00 mm
Liner material: Centrifugal cast iron
Type: "Wet" cylinder liners
Liner length: 136.20 mm
Lower locating diameter: 93.00 mm

Cylinder Liner Protrusion:
To April 1989: 0.07 - 0.14 mm
From April 1989: 0.03 - 0.10 mm

Seals/Shims for Liner Protrusion Adjustment:
To July 1987, paper: 0.07, 0.085, 0.105 and 0,13 mm
From August 1987: 0.10, 0.12 and 0.15 mm

Differences in Cylinder Liners I: Liners have been changed, quote engine number

Cylinder Liner Bore Diameter:

	169B Engine	170 Engines
Class A — 1 ref. line:	84.000 - 84.011 mm	88.000 - 88.011 mm
Class B — 2 ref. lines:	84.012 - 84.022 mm	88.012 - 88.022 mm
Class C — 3 ref. lines:	84.023 - 84.033 mm	88.023 - 88.033 mm
Class D — 4 ref. lines:	84.034 - 88.044 mm	88.034 - 88.044 mm

Note: Pistons are marked with the same class sizes. Refer to Page 47 for piston sizes belonging to each of the cylinder liners.

1.4.3.1. General

The removal of the crankshaft is described in Section 1.2. The crankshaft runs in five shell bearings. Main bearing and crankpin journals can be re-ground to one undersize to fit oversize bearing shells.

The crankshaft end float is controlled by half thrust washers, fitted to the rear crankshaft main bearing. An oil seal is fitted to the front end of the crankshaft, inside the timing cover. The rear end of the crankshaft is sealed off by two side seals in the rear main bearing cap.

Note that the main bearing journals have different diameters. The bearing shells have, however, the same thickness.

1.4.3.2. Checking the Crankshaft End Float

Check the end float of the crankshaft before the shaft is removed from the crankcase. The resulting value can then be used to correct the end float during the installation of the shaft, by fitting oversize thrust washers. Check the end float as described below:

- Attach a dial gauge with a suitable bracket to the cylinder block end face and place the dial gauge onto the shaft as shown in Fig. 1.31 on Page 26. Push the crankshaft in the direction of the arrow, using a screwdriver, and set the gauge to "Zero".
- Push the crankshaft into the other direction and read off the value on the dial gauge. The standard value is between 0.08 - 0.20 mm (0.003 - 0.008 in.). Write down the value for installation reference. If the end float is outside the upper limit, fit new thrust half washers during assembly. The oversizes are given in Section. 1.4.3.0.
- Remove the dial gauge. The crankshaft can now be removed.

1.4.3.3. Inspection of Parts

Thoroughly clean the crankshaft, paying particular attention to the oilways. Check the crankshaft for visible damage to the journals (seizure, nicks, etc.). Use a micrometer to measure the main bearing and crankpin journals at various points. From the measurements evaluate if a particular journal is out of round or tapered. Each journal must be fully round, within a tolerance of 0.007 mm.

If facilities are available, the crankshaft should be inspected for run-out at the centre journal. To do this, place the two end journals into "V" blocks and apply a dial gauge to the centre bearing journals as shown in Fig. 1.71. Slowly rotate the crankshaft and read off

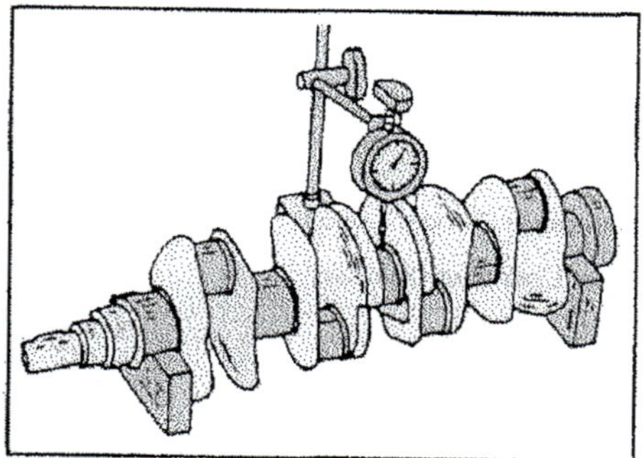

Fig. 1.71. — Checking the crankshaft for run-out. Place the two end journals into "V" blocks.

the dial gauge. Note that the value on the gauge must be divided by "2" to obtain the correct value. This must not exceed 0.02 mm (0.001 in.).

1.4.3.4. Crankshaft — Installation

The installation of the crankshaft is described in conjunction with the assembly of the engine in Section 1.3. Make sure that bearing shells with oil drillings are fitted to the correct locations (see Page 52). Both half thrust washers must have the same thickness.

1.4.3.4. Front Crankshaft Oil — Replacement

The front crankshaft oil seal is located in the timing cover and can be replaced with the engine fitted. Parts obstructing the access to the oil seal must be removed accordingly. To remove the oil seal, screw two self-tapping screws into the seal and withdraw it with a combination of screwdriver and pliers.

The engine must be supported from below as the engine mounting on the timing side must be removed to replace the oil seal. Remove the oil seal or the timing cover as follows:

- Disconnect the battery earth cable. Push the cable away from the terminal to prevent accidentaql "re-connection".
- Remove the alternator drive belt.
- Place the front end of the vehicle on chassis stands to gain access to the water pump drive belt. Remove the belt by inserting a screwdriver as shown in Fig. 1.72. Then turn the crankshaft pulley with a 35 mm socket until the belt slips off and can be taken off. Take care not to damage the belt.
- Slacken the crankshaft pulley nut. The crankshaft must be blocked against rotation. Either remove the cover below the flywheel and insert a strong screwdriver blade into the flywheel teeth or engage a gear. A 35 mm socket is required to slacken the nut.
- Jack up the engine with a jack (wooden block between jack head and oil sump) or lift the engine with a suitable tackle. Make sure the engine is well supported and remove the engine mounting shown in Fig. 1.58. Remove three bolts on the water pump and the nut (1) in the centre of the engine mounting. Take off the aluminium engine mounting carrier. Check once more the support of the engine before the mounting parts are removed.

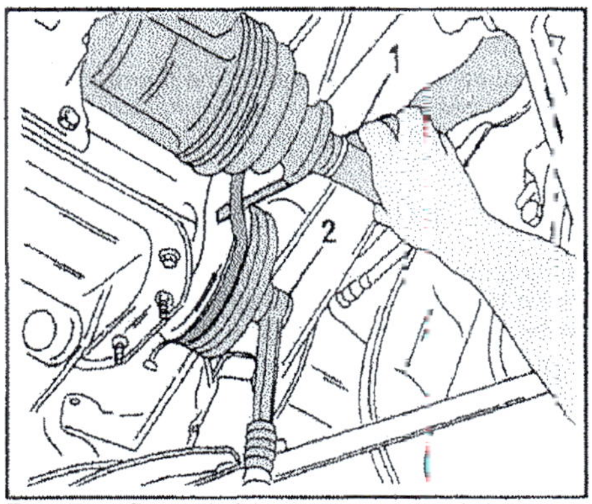

Fig. 1.72. — Removal of the water pump drive belt. Insert a screwdriver (1) below the V-belt and rotate the pulley with a socket (2) until the belt is free.

- Remove the crankshaft pulley. A tight pulley can be removed by inserting two tyre levers underneath the pulley.
- Unscrew the tming cover and remove the oil seal in conventional manner or use the two self-tapping screws as mentioned above to remove the seal without unscrewing the cover. The Woodruff key must be removed from the crankshaft (side cutter).

Note: The ignition timing plate must not be removed from the timing cover. Do not slacken the timing plate securing screws.

- Coat the outside of the oil seal with engine oil and knock the oil seal into the timing cover or into the timing cover and over the crankshaft end. If the cover has been removed, re-attach it loosely (with a new gasket) and drive the oil seal in position, at the same time centering the cover. A piece of tube, a large washer and the pulley nut can also be used to draw the seal in position. Tighten the timing cover when the seal is fitted.
- Fit the Woodruff key and slide the pulley in position. Place the drive belt behind the pulley to facilitate its installation.
- Raise or lower the engine to refit the engine mounting. Tighten the bolts t 5.0 kgm (36 ft.lb.) and the nut in the centre to 5.5 kgm (40 ft.lb.).
- Block the crankshaft against rotation and tighten the nut to 17.0 kgm (122.5 ft.lb.).
- Refit the water pump drive belt in a similar manner as during removal. Fit and tension the alternator drive belt.

1.4.3.5. Flywheel

If the flywheel teeth are damaged, check the teeth of the starter motor pinion. Both may have to be replaced.

The flywheel bolts are offset, i.e. the flywheel can only be fitted in one position. Coat the flywheel bolts with "Loctite". Always use new bolts. Tighten he bolts evenly to 6.8 kgm (49 ft.lb.). The flywheel must be blocked against rotation.

1.4.4. TIMING MECHANISM

A timing chain is used to drive the camshaft. The chain is held under its correct tension by means of a chain tensioner. The timing chain and the two timing gears can be replaced with the engine fitted. Remove and/or replace the parts as follows:

- Remove the timing cover as described in the last section.
- Drain the engine oil and remove the oil sump.
- Remove the chain tensioner, observing the different operations for the type fitted:

Sedis Chain Tensioner

- Insert a screwdriver as shown in Fig. 1.20 into the chain tensioner bore and press against the chain tensioner pad to release it from the chain. Lock the chain tensioner by turning the screwdriver in the direction of the arrow. The ratchet inside the tensioner will lock the pad in position. The tensioner is now free to remove (see next page).

Renold Chain Tensioner

- This type of chain tensioner has no locking mechanism. It must therefore locked mechanically, before it is removed. You require a piece of wire to lock the tensioner as shown in Fig. 1.21. Make sure the end is twisted securely.

All Chain Tensioners

- Undo the two securing screws and remove the chain tensioner. Treat the chain tensioner with care to ensure it can not unlock. Below the chain tensioner there is a filter which can now be withdrawn.
- In the given order remove the camshaft timing sprocket, the timing chain, the crankshaft timing sprocket and the camshaft. Before removing the chain check for timing marks. If none are visible mark the chain and the corresponding sprockets accordingly. The camshaft is held in position by a keeper plate and three bolts.

Attention: It is possible that there is no timing mark in the chain. In this case mark the chain and the two sprockets at opposite points to have a reference for installation (only if the same parts are refitted).

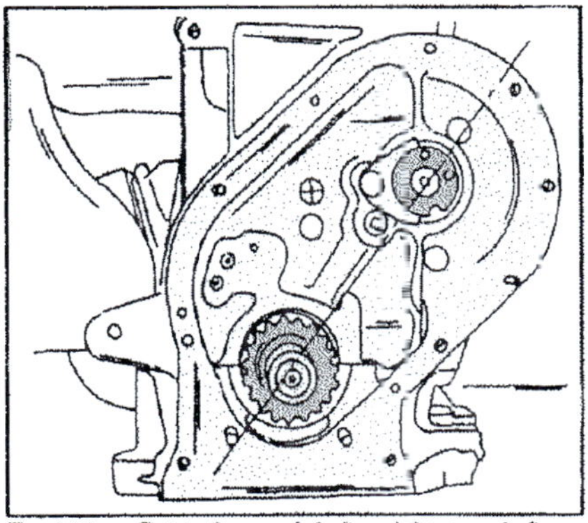

Fig. 1.73. — Rotate the crankshaft and the camshaft until the two timing marks are aligned as shown.

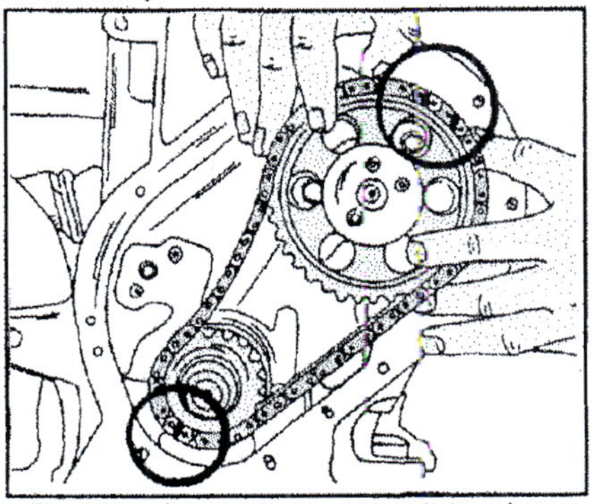

Fig. 1.74. — When fitting the timing chain make sure that the timing chain marks and the timing sprocket marks are aligned as shown.

Thoroughly clean and check all parts of the timing mechanism. Damage or wear can normally be found on the sprocket teeth. Shiny chain rollers are also signs of wear. The filter for the chain tensioner must be cleaned.

Refit the timing mechanism parts as follows:

- Fit a new paper gasket and attach the plate to the cylinder block. Tighten to 1.0 kgm (7.2 ft.lb.).
- Slide the double-row timing sprocket over the crankshaft end and drive it in position (tube). The key must engage, the timing mark must be on the outside.
- Rotate the crankshaft and the camshaft until the timing marks are aligned as shown in Fig. 1.73.
- Place the timing chain over the crankshaft timing sprocket and insert the

sprocket on the other side into the timing chain. Check that the timing marks are aligned as shown in Fig. 1.74 and bolt the camshaft sprocket to the camshaft. Timing chains without marks must be fitted in accordance with the marks made during dismantling.

- Place a new lockplate over the camshaft sprocket and fit the three bolts. Tighten the bolts to 2.3 kgm (17 ft.lb.). Fig. 1.75 shows the operation. The lock plate tabs must be bent over the sides of the three bolts.

Dismantling of the chain tensioner is described on Page 28. Follow the instructions for the chain tensioner in question until the tensioner is refitted to the cylinder block.

- Fit the timing cover with a new gasket The cover must be centred to draw in the oil seal. The operation is described on page 56 during the replacement of the front oil seal. Tighten the cover screws to 1.3 kgm (10 ft.lb.).
- Fit the Woodruff key and slide the pulley in position. Place the drive belt behind the pulley to facilitate its installation.
- Block the crankshaft against rotation and tighten the nut to 17.0 kgm (122.5 ft.lb.).

If the timing plate has been unscrewed from the cover, align it as follows:

- Rotate the crankshaft until the pistons of No. 1 and No. 4 cylinder are at top dead centre. The valves of No. 4 cylinder must be "rocking", i.e. one valve must be opening and the other one closing. The exact TDC point should, however, be set with a dial gauge, applied as shown in Fig. 1.41. Rotate the crankshaft until the dial gauge needle shows that TDC is obtained.

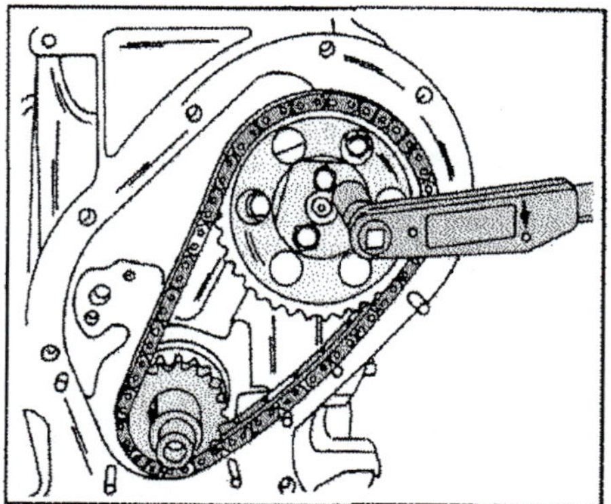

Fig. 1.75. — The camshaft spocket is secured with three locked screws to the camshaft.

- Fit the timing plate and rotate it until the "Zero" in the plate is opposite the timing mark on the pulley. Tighten the two nuts. One of the nuts and the plate should be marked with paint for future use of the timing plate.
- The remaining operations are carried out in reverse order to the removal procedure.

1.4.5. COMPRESSION CHECK

A compression check can be carried out as follows:

- Unscrew the spark plugs.
- Open the throttle valve flap and the starter plate.
- Insert the compression tester into the first plug bore.

- Ask a helper to press the throttle pedal fully down and operate the starter motor until the compression printer shows the highest valve.
- Check the remaining cylinders in the same manner.

Normaly the cylinder with the lowest compression should not be less than 80 % when compared with the cylinder with the highest compression. Worn piston rings could be a reason for low compression.

1.5. Engine — Tightening Torques

Cylinder Head Bolts:
169 B Engine to Engine No. 012625
170 B Engine to Engine No. 021874
170 B Engine from Engine No. 021875

First stage:	6.0 kgm (36 ft.lb.)
Second stage:	Slacken all bolts
Third stage:	2.0 kgm (14.5 ft.lb.)
Fourth stage:	Angle-tighten 90°

169 B Engine from Engine No. 0126261
170 B Engine from Engine No. 031999:
170 C engine

First stage:	5.0 kgm (36 ft.lb.)
Second stage:	Slacken all bolts
Third stage:	2.0 kgm (14.5 ft.lb.)
Fourth stage:	Angle-tighten 180°

Re-tightening of cylinder head bolts	Refer to Text (Page 34)

169 B, 170 B, 170 C Engines from April 1989 ("Torx" heaqd bolts)

First stage:	6.0 kgm (43.5 ft.lb.)
Second stage:	Slacken all bolts
Third stage:	2.0 kgm (14.5 ft.lb.)
Fourth stage:	Angle-tighten 300°
Re-tightening of bolts:	Refer to Text, Page 34

Cylinder Head Bolt Use:

To July 1985:	12 x 144 mm long, 19 mm hexagonal head
From April 1989:	11 x 1.5, 181 mm long, hexagonal head
From April 1989:	11 x 1.5, 175 mm long, "Torx" head, No. 55

Camshaft sprocket bolts:	2.3 kgm (17 ft.lb.)
Rocker shaft pedestal bolts:	1.5 kgm (11 ft.lb.)
Intermediate plate, timing side:	1.0 kgm (7.2 ft.lb.)
Keeper plate, camshaft:	1.7 kgm (12.2 ft.lb.)
Water pump to cylinder head:	
10 mm bolts:	2.3 kgm (20 ft.lb.)
8 mm bolts:	2.3 kgm (17 ft.lb.)
10 mm nuts:	4.3 kgm (31 ft.lb.)
Oil filter bracket:	1.3 kgm (9.5 ft lb.)
Oil pressure switch:	4.0 kgm (30 ft.lb.)
Main bearing cap bolts:	7.5 kgm (54 ft.lb.)
Big end bearing caps:	4.0 kgm (30 ft.lb.)
Flywheel bolts:	6.8 kgm (49 ft.lb.)
Clutch bolts:	1.5 kgm (11 ft.lb.)
Crankshaft pulley nut:	17.0 kgm (122 ft.lb.)
Oil pump:	1.0 kgm (7.2 ft.lb.)
Crankshaft counter weights:	6.8 kgm (49 ft.lb.)

1.6. Ignition System

1.6.0. Technical Data

Spark plugs
Type: .... In general Champion N281 YC or Bosch W7DC, check with manufacture
Electrode gap: .... 0.6 - 0.7 mm (0.024 - 0.003 in.)
Tightening torques: .... 1.0 - 1.3 kgm (7.2 - 9.4 ft.lb.)
Hexagon A/F: .... 21 mm

Ignition Distributor and Ignition System
Type: .... Transistorised ignition with ignition module

Fitted Distributor (typical examples):
169 B and 170 B engines: .... Ducellier 525 450 or Bosch 0237002 093
170 C engine: .... Ducellier 525 627

Ignition Timing Point:
169 B and 170 B engines: .... 10° before TDC at 800/rpm (retard by 4° with lead-free petrol)
170 C engine: .... 10° before TDC at 700 rpm (6° with lead free petrol)

Firing order: .... 1—3—4—2
Ignition timing point mark: .... Crankshaft pulley

Ignition Coil
Maker: .... Ducellier 520015 or Bosch 02 211 22 317) — typical

Primary Resistance:
Ducellier: .... 0.8 ± 5 % Ohm
Bosch: .... 0.82 ± 10 % Ohm

Secondary Resistance:
Ducellier .... 6000 ± 5 % Ohm
Bosch: .... 8250 ± 10 % ohm

Length of Spark Plugs Cables:
Cylinder No. 1: .... 700 mm (3900 ohm)
Cylinder No. 2: .... 525 mm (2900 ohm)
Cylinder No. 3: .... 450 mm (2500 ohm)
Cylinder No. 4: .... 300 mm (1700 ohm)

1.6.1. GENERAL DESCRIPTION

All engines operate with a transistorised ignition system with an electro-magnetic impulse trigger. Fig. 1.76 shows a diagram of the ignition system. The distributor (5) has no contact breaker points:

The contact breaker points are replaced by a magnetic feeler, which sends the ignition pulses to the electronic ignition module (75).The magnetic circuit has four fixed branches and four moveable branches driven by the distributor shaft. When the moveable branches during their rotation pass the xied ones, a flow variation takes place and the currect is induced into the pick-up coil.

This current in turn triggers the electronic module which builds up the current in the the primary circuit of the ignition coil (50) and then cuts it off, thereby creating a high tension current in the secondary circuit of the coil and providing a spark at the plug selected by the distributor rotor arm.

Fig. 1.76. — Layout of the ignition system. The numbers are identical with the unit numbers in the wiring diagram.

5 Ignition distributor
50 Ignition coil
114 Spark plugs
130 TDC sender unit
229 Ignition switch
720 Diagnostic socket

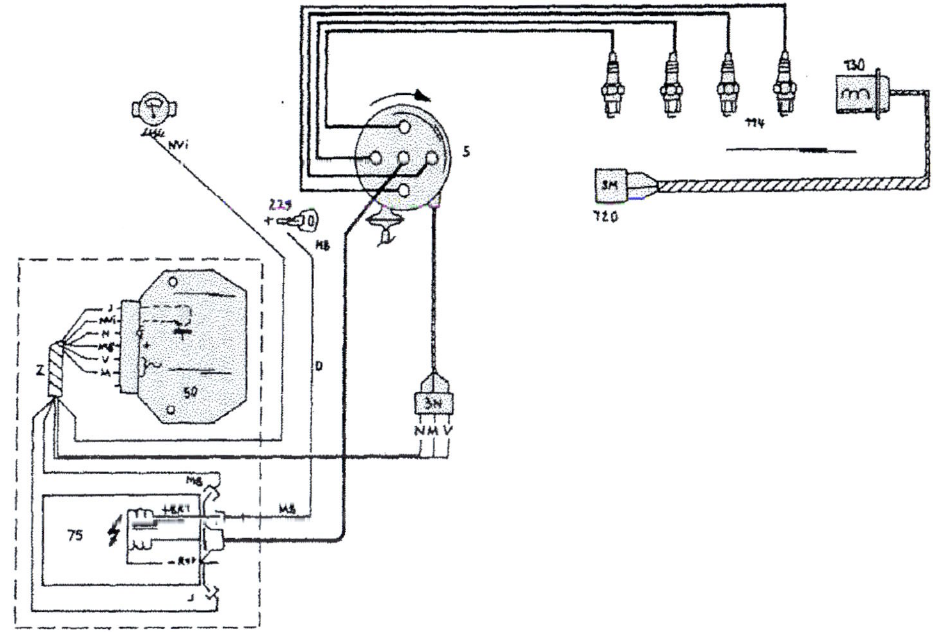

The following precautions must be observed when working on the ignition system:

- When checking the idle speed or the ignition timing point use a revolution counter compatible with the ignition system. Make sure you have the right instrument before you connect it.
- No starting aid must be used to start the engine. The battery must not be rechared with a quick charger.
- Always disconnect the battery before electric weldings are carried out.

1.6.2. Distributor

1.6.2.0. Maintenance

At regular intervals clean the distributor cap inside and outside to remove carbon, dust or moisture. Also clean the rotor tip. Use a rag moistened in petrol to wipe off the part. Check the distributor cap for cracks, if the ignition system has given problems.

Replace the distributor rotor if the contacts in the inside show signs of wear. Contacts must not be filed to clean themn.

With the distributor cap removed, luricate the inside of the distributor shaft with 2 or 3 drops of oil to lubricate the shaft.

The ignition cables (spark plug cables) must be kep clean and free from moisture. As a precaution withdraw the cables from the distributor cap and check the connecting ends. Never cut off cable ends to rectify any corrosion, always fit new cables, noting the length of aech cable (Section 1.6.0.)

1.6.2.1. Removal and Installation

If the distributor is to be removed, it is preferable that the engine should not be rotated with the unit removed. If this is possible, the replacement of the distributor is simply a question of aligning the drive slot in the camshaft with the drive dog of the distributor. If the engine is undergoing repairs, it will be necessary to reset the engine to the correct position to install the distributor.

The distributor is fitted to the side of the cylinder block and driven through a shaft from the camshaft. A a slot in the end of the shaft engages with the drive dog on the distributor. The distributor must be removed if you remove the oil pump. Remove the unit as follows:

- Disconnect the battery.
- Spring back the distributor cap clips and remove the cap. Disconnect the vacuum hose and the electrical lead leading to the ignition module.
- Rotate the crankshaft until the piston of No. 1 cylinder is at top dead centre position (ignition timing point) and mark the position of the rotor tip into the outside edge of the distributor housing. To rotate the crankshaft you can remove the plugs and apply a 35 mm socket to the crankshaft pulley nut. Otherwise jack up one of the front wheels, engage the highest gear and rotate the crankshaft by turning the wheel.
- Remove the distributor clamp and remove the dilstributor upwards.

The installation of the distributor is a reversal of the removal procedure. The following points should be noted:

- If no repairs have been carried out and the engine has not been rotated with the distributor removed, refit the distributor and tighten the clamp. If the engine has been rotated, proceed as follows:
- Rotate the crankshaft until the piston of No. 1 cylinder ist at top dead centre, i.e. both valves of No. 1 cylinder must be closes (if the cylinder head cover is removed) or the ignition timing marks on timing plate and crankshaft pulley are in line.
- Turn the distributor rotor until it points to the mark in the distributor housing (the one marked before removal).
- Shine a torch into the opening for the distributor and check that the drive slot in Fig. 1.77 is in the position shown by (2). The view shows the shaft with the distributor support housing removed. You will notice that the driv slot has a larger and s smaller segment. The larger segment must face towards the rear of the engine, if this is not the case, rotate the crankshaft by one turn and re-align the notch in the pulley with the index on the timing plate. Secure the clamp plate in this position.

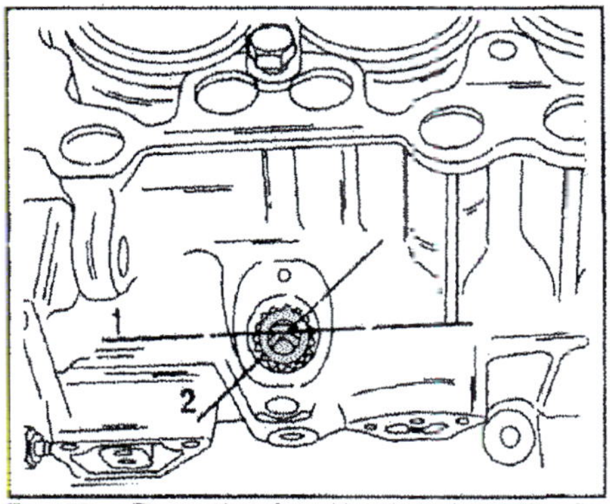

Fig. 1.77. — The position of the drive slot during the installation of the distributor. From the horizontal line (2) obtain the position (2) before you insert the distributor.

- Fit the distributor cap, connect the H.T. leads to the spark plugs and to the ignition coil and connect the pick-up connector to the wiring harness. Make sure that the H.T. cables are well secured to their attachments. Also re-connect the vacuum hose.
- Adjust the ignition timing as described in Section 1.6.3.

1.6.3. IGNITION TIMING

The ignition timing must be checked and/or adjusted by means of a stroboscopic timing light. A timing plate on the timing cover will give you the TDC position and the graduations for the ignition timing point. A notch in the crankshaft pulley must be aligned with the ignition timing point (for example 10° before TDC, but refer to Section 1.6.0 for exceptions). Check and/or adjust the timing point as follows. The vacuum hose must be disconnected from the distributor and plugged-up to carry out the check. Proceed as follows:

- Connect the stroboscopic timing light in accordance with the instructions of the manufacturer.
- Connect a suitable revolution counter in accordance with the instructions of the manufacturer.
- Start the engine and run at idle speed. Note the following differences: The 1.8 litre engine and the 2.0 litre 78 BHP engine must idle with more than 800 rpm, the 85 BHP engine must idle with more than 700 rpm.

The screw securing the distributor must be slackened. If the distributor has been refitted after removal, set the unit so that the securing screw is in the centre of the elongated hole.

- Direct the flash of the stroboscopic timing light at the crankshaft pulley/timing scale plate. The notch will be "stationary" and shows the timing point. If the notch cannot be seen immediately, stop the engine and mark the notch with a spot of white paint. Allow the pain to dry and re-check the setting.
- If the timing point is outside the value given, rotate the distributor at the same time observing the notch. It will "wander" under the influence of the timining light.
- Switch off the engine and secure the distributor clamp plate. Re-check the timing point as described. If necessary make further corrections after slackening the clamp.
- Disconnect the timing light and revolution counter and re-connect the vacuum hose.
- Start the engine and check that the correct idle speed is still there.

1.6.4. SPARK PLUGS

Some spark plugs for the different engines are given in Section 1.6.0.0., but note that not all manufacturers may recommend the same plugs. Always check with your parts supplier to obtain the recommended plugs for your engine. The electrode gap of all types is 0.6 - 0.7 mm (0.024 - 0.028 in.). Always make sure that the plug threads and seats are clean before the plugs are screwed in.

Plugs should be cleaned and their electrode gaps adjusted at regular intervals. Never attempt to bend the centre electrode as this will split the insulator. To reduce the plug gap, use the handle of a screwdriver and tap the side electrode towards the centre electrode. To increase the plug gap, insert a small screwdriver between the electrodes and carefully bend away the side electrode.

Inspect the condition of the insulator tip and the electrodes. Following there are a few examples to interprete the condition of plugs removed from the engine.

Normal Plug Face: The colour of the of the insulator should appear greyish-brown or tan-coloured. The electrodes should be black or sooted. These are signs of a plug which has been used under normal conditions with alternative short and long driving periods. White or yellow deposits mean that the car has been used for long periods at high speeds and can be ignored.

Worn Plug Appearance: Insulator tip and electrodes are burnt off. All plugs which show this condition must be replaced. Always replace the whole set and make sure to fit the correct plug.

Oiled-up Appearance: Normally this condition is recognised by wet oil deposits which have been left by excessive ingress of oil into the combustion chamber (worn piston rings or pistons, inlet valves or valve guides, worn bearings, etc.). Hotter plugs are normally able to overcome the fault, but in serious cases an overhaul of the engine is necessary.

Burnt or Overheated Appearance: Burnt or overheated plugs can normally be recognised by their electrodes being coloured white or being burnt, or by the presence of blisters on the insulator or the electrodes. Electrodes may also be burnt off. Faults can be traced to the cooling system or improper ignition timing.

To single out a faulty plug in the engine, proceed as follows:

- Remove the plug from the engine and push the plug cable connector over the plug.
- Place the plug on the cylinder head cover, ensuring that it cannot fall off when the starter motor is operated. An insulated pair of pliers can be used to hold the plug.
- Have a second person turn the starter switch and observe if there is a spark between the two electrodes. If a spark is visible, this is by no means an indication that the plug is in perfect condition, as it is possible that the spark cannot be produced under the compression of the engine. This can only be tested with a spark plug tester.
- If no spark is visible after several attempts, examine the plug. If the engine has been running with one of the plugs out of action this will be indicated by the fact that the spark plug will be saturated with petrol or oil and this is your confirmation that this particular cylinder has not been firing. This could be so for various reasons, with the extreme case that the piston rings are allowing oil to pass from the cylinder into the combustion chamber. There are, however, a few points which might be cured on the spot. The first remedy is, of course, to substitute the suspect plug with one known to be working to ensure that the plug is at fault. To do this, proceed as follows (let us assume that the No. 3 cylinder is the faulty one):

Unscrew one of the remaining plugs and check the appearance of the plug face. This will be dry and will most probably have a light brown colour. Screw this plug into the cylinder where the first plug has been removed and fit the faulty plug to the remaining cylinder. Re-connect the high-tension leads to the spark plugs and re-start the engine.

Check the firing of the engine by pulling off the H.T. leads between the ignition distributor and the plugs. If the suspected plug is faulty the engine should still run on three cylinders with the difference that the cylinder that was originally misfiring is now operating and that the good cylinder, where the suspected plug is fitted, is now out of action.

Example:

As already mentioned, it was assumed that the No. 3 cylinder (and thereby the spark plug) was faulty. Remove either Nos. 1, 2 or 4 spark plugs from the engine which should operate normally. For our example let us remove No. 1 spark plug.

Fit the No. 1 spark plug into the No. 3 cylinder and the No. 3 spark plug into the No. 1 cylinder. After the engine has been re-started it should now run on cylinders Nos. 2, 3 and 4 as the suspected plug is in the No. 1 cylinder this cylinder will, therefore, not be able to fire. This can be further confirmed by unscrewing the plug from the No. 3 cylinder which will now have a wet appearance, although it will not be the same as the plug face of the faulty plug because it has not been running for very long.

Remove the faulty plug (which is now in the No. 1 cylinder according to our example) and fit a new plug. It is still possible to rectify the fault if either of the two following cases apply:

1. The spark plug electrodes are too close together so that no gap exists.

2. The spark plug electrodes are too far apart so that the spark is not strong enough to jump from one electrode to the other.

Before the plug is refitted to the engine, wipe off the plug face with a clean cloth and make sure that no deposits are bridging the gap between the two electrodes. If the plug appears wet, blow in the inside of the plug. The plug insulator (the white centre part) must be wiped clean to prevent leakage of current between the end terminal and the plug body.

1.6.4. IGNITION COIL

The coil cannot be dismantled or serviced, but your dealer can check the resistance of the primary and secondary windings with special equipment. In the event of trouble with the coil, the easiest test is to borrow a known good coil and substitute it in the circuit. It is useful to remember that ignition coils sometimes do not show faults except when at their working temperatures. A "cold" test may, therefore, not always be a complete answer.

To check the cable between the centre of the ignition distributor cap and the centre of the ignition coil, withdraw the cable from the distributor cap and hold the blank end of the cable 10 mm (0.04 in.) away from a good earthing point. An insulated pair of pliers should be used for this check. Ask a second person to operate the starter motor switch. A clean spark should jump between the blank end of the cable and the earth (ground) point. If the spark is there, the fault should not be in the coil.

1.7. Lubrication System

1.7.0. TECHNICAL DATA

Engine Sump capacity:
- Without filter: .... 3.5 litres
- With filter: .... 4.0 litres
- "Dry" engine: .... 4.0 litres

Difference between "Low" and "High" on dipstick: .... 1.0 litres

Recommended oil grade: .... Follow recommendation of the various manufacturers (10 W40 or 15 W 40)

Oil Filter — Type (typical):
- With M18 thread: .... Purflux LS 152
- With M20 thread: .... Purflux LS 468 A

Oil pressure: .... Refer to Page 9

1.7.1. OIL PUMP

1.7.1.0. Removal and Installation

The removal of the oil pump can be accomplished with the engine fitted to the vehicle. The vehicle should preferably placed onto a lift; failing this, ramps can be used to lift the front end of the vehicle, but remember the height of the van. Proceed as follows to remove the oil pump:

- Unscrew the plug from the bottom of the oil sump and drain the engine oil into a suitable container (approx. 6.5 pints). The oil will drain easier, if the vehicle has been driven a short distance.
- Slacken the ignition distributor and remove it. If the engine is set to the TDC position for the 1st cylinder it will be a matter of reversing the removal installation later on.
- Remove the distributor support housing. The drive shaft for the oil pump and the distributor must be set to a specific position when the parts are refitted.
- Remove the oil sump bolts evenly and take off the oil sump. A sticking oil sump can be freed by tapping it with a hammer. Avoid to insert a screwdriver between the sealing faces, as this mau damage the sump.
- The oil pump can now be seen at the bottom of the crankcase. Fig. 1.78 shows the location with the engine removed. Unscrew the pump and withdraw it from the crankcase. The drive shaft can also be withdrawn from above.

If the pump has been removed because of low oil pressure, replace the complete assembly, as most probably the pump gearwheels and the housing bore is worn.

Before fitting the pump clean the face of the crankcase without using sharp tools. Refit as follows:

- Insert the drive shaft into the cylinder block with the drive slot in the position (1) in Fig. 1.79. The smaller of the two segments must face towards the cylinder block.
- Push the shaft fully in to engage the pinion on the other end with the skew gear on camshaft. The drive shaft will now rotate, as the teeth engage and the drive slot will move to the position (2). The larger segment of the drive dog will now be facing towards the rear of the cylinder block. If this is not the case, rotate the crankshaft by one full turn.
- Refit the distributor support housing and attach it with the single screw.
- At the bottom of the crankcase check that the dowel sleeve (1) in Fig. 1.78 is in posi-

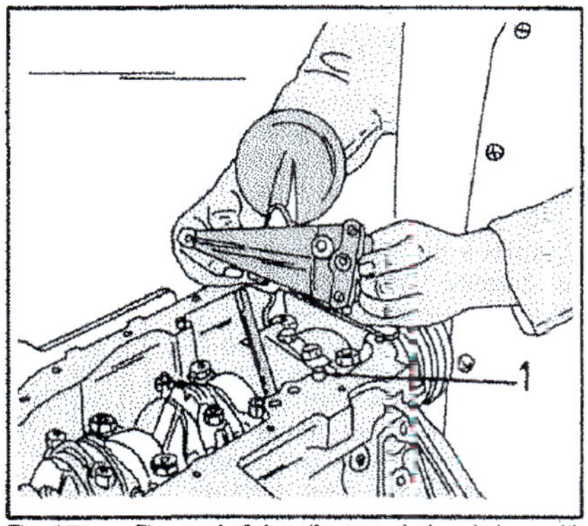

Fig. 1.78. — Removal of the oil pump. A dowel sleeve (1) locates the pump on the crankcase face.

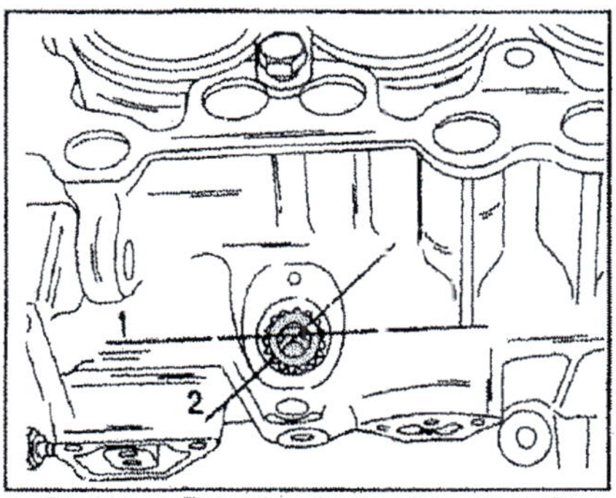

Fig. 1.79. — Fitting the oil pump/distributor shaft.

tion. Fit a new "O" seal. Fit the oil pump, engaging the shaft and push the pump over the dowel sleeve. Tighten the bolts evenly to 1.0 kgm (7.2 ft.lb.)

- Refit the oil sump with a new gasket. Tighten the screws evenly to 1.0 kgm (7.2 ft.lb.).
- Refit the ignition distributor. The ignition timing must be checked and if necessary adjusted as already described (Page 63).
- Fit the oil drain plug, tighten it to 3.0 kgm (21 ft.lb.) and fill the engine with the required amount of the recommended engine oil. Withdraw the centre lead from the distributor and crank the engine with the starter motor until the oil pressure warning light is "out". This ensures that the pump produces enough pressure to lubricate the engine. Re-connect the H.T. cable.
- Start the engine and allow it run at idle speed until the operating temperature is obtained. Check the oil sump joining faces for oil leaks. Also check the oil level and correct if necessary.

1.7.2. OIL FILTER

An oil filter with a by-pass valve is fitted after July 1983. The oil filter (Purflux LS 468 A) is specially designed for these engines and only a replacement of the same type must be fitted. You can recognise sich a filter by the threaded sleeve. It will have a diameter of 20 mm. The filter is fitted to the engine at the position shown in Fig. 1.80.

To remove the filter, disconnect the battery and use a filter wrench to unscrew the filter. If none is available, try a piece of emery cloth. Place this around the outside of the filter, with the abrasive side towards the filter housing and with the two hands, try to unscrew the filter. Another method is possible by driving the blade of a screwdriver through the side of the filter and using the handle to unscrew the filter.

Fig. 1.80. — Location of the oil filter.

Lubricate the seal of the new filter with engine oil and tighten the filter until it touches the cylinder block. From this position, and with the hands only, tighten the filter by a further ¾ of a turn.

- Check the oil level in the sum, if the engine oil has not been replaced at the same time. Otherwise fill the engine with the required amount of the recommended oil.

1.7.3. CHECKING THE OIL PRESSURE

If a suitable adaptor to screw into the thread for the oil pressure switch is available, the oil pressure can be checked as follows:

- Run the engine until the oil temperature has reached 90° C (temperature gauge shows normal). Then idle the engine for 5 minutes until the cooling fan has switched off.
- Check and if necessary correct the sump oil level.
- Switch off the engine.
- Disconnect the oil pressure switch lead and unscrew the switch. The switch is located at the bottom of the oil filter, on the R.H. side next to the alternator, below the large water hose.
- Fit the oil pressure gauge with a sealing washer and re-start the engine. Run the engine at idle speed and check the oil pressure indication, which should be around 2.7 kg/sq.cm. (38 psi.). Increase the engine speed to 2000 rpm and check that the oil pressure reaches at least 3.3 kg/sq.cm. (47 psi.).
- Once more increase the engine speed, this time to 4000 rpm. The oil pressure must now be 3.8 kg/sq.cm (54 psi.).
- If the oil pressure is below the values given, it may be necessary to carry out an oil change. Re-check the pressure. If the pressure is still low, the oil pump must be suspect and the pump must be removed for further investigation.
- Tighten the oil pressure switch to 2.2 kgm (16.0 ft.lb.).

The oil pressures given are valid for a good engine. If the engine has already a high mileage, it is possible that the pressure is lower as given during idle speed, must however, not drop below 0.2 - 0.4 kg/sq.cm. (3 - 5.5 psi.).

1.7.4. ENGINE OIL LEVEL

The oil level must be checked with the vehicle standing on level ground. Preferably the engine should be switched off for at least 10 minutes. Check the oil level in the conventional manner. From the mark on the dipstick decide the amount of oil missing. The difference between the "Low" and the "High" marks is 1.0 litres. Always check the oil level before any long journey.

1.8. Cooling System

1.8.0. TECHNICAL DATA

Type of system:	Sealed, with expansion tank
System capacity:	See Section 0.3.
Water pump:	Impeller, not repairable
Water pump drive:	"V" belt
Thermostat:	
Location:	Below water pump
Opening temperature:	Marked in thermostat
Fully open:	95° C
Water Temperature Switch in Cylinder Head:	
Opening temperature:	105 ± 3° C
Cooling Fan Temperature Switch:	
Opening temperature:	92 ± 2° C
Closing temperature:	87 ± 2° C
Filling capacity:	9 litres (3 Gallons)

Opening pressure of expansion tankl cap: . . . . 1.0 kg/sq.cm. (14.5 psi.)

Cooling Fan:
- Number of fans: 1
- Performance: . . . . 80 kW
- Speed: . . . . 2700 rpm
- Diameter: . . . . 280 mm
- Direction of rotation: . . . . Clockwise

1.8.1. DRAINING AND REFILLING

Two separate drain points are provided and both must be opened to drain the system. First unscrew the expansion tank cap, then remove the drain plug at the bottom of the radiator. Make sure the engine is not hot when the expansion tank cap is removed. The anti-freeze can be collected if still in good condition.

If new anti-freeze is to be filled in, place a suitable container underneath the drain point and collect it. It should not be emptied into the ground.

- Remove the drain plug from the side of the cylinder block to drain the remaining coolant.
- Remove the expansion tank from its attachment and empty the remaining coolant. Place the tank to one side.

Prepare the anti-freeze mixture in accordance with the temperatures you expect in your area. Manufacturer's charts will give you the correct ratio, but remember that the cylinder head is made of aluminium and only an anti-freeze which will not attack this type of metal is suitable.

Refit the cylinder block and radiator drain plugs and make sure that they are tight. Open the bleed screws in accordance with the cooling system diagram shown in Figs. 1.81. The expansion tank cap must not be fitted.

- Refit the expansion tank and fill it completely until the water, free of air bubbles, ermerges from the bleeder screw bore. Tighten the screw.
- Once more check that both drain plugs are tightened. Never start the engine with the bleeder screw opened.
- Start the engine and wait until the thermostat has opened fully, i.e. the fan has switched on. Re-check the coolant level and add more anti-freeze if necessary.

  When the engine has cooled down, waut approx. 10 minutes and re-check the level. The coolant must be at the "Max" mark on the expansion tank.

1.8.2. RADIATOR — REMOVAL AND INSTALLATION

The radiator is made of aluminium. Make sure that only anti-freeze suitable for aluminium is used in the cooling system. Remove the radiator as follows:

- Disconnect the battery earth cable.
- Drain the cooling system as described in the last section. Disconnect the upper and lower radiator hoses and withdraw all hoses between radiator and other parts.
- Remove the front section of the vehicle and disconnect the cables from the following connectors: Headlamps and flasher lamps, cooling fan motor, radiator temperature switch. Free the cable clamps as applicable (see also Fig. 1.9).

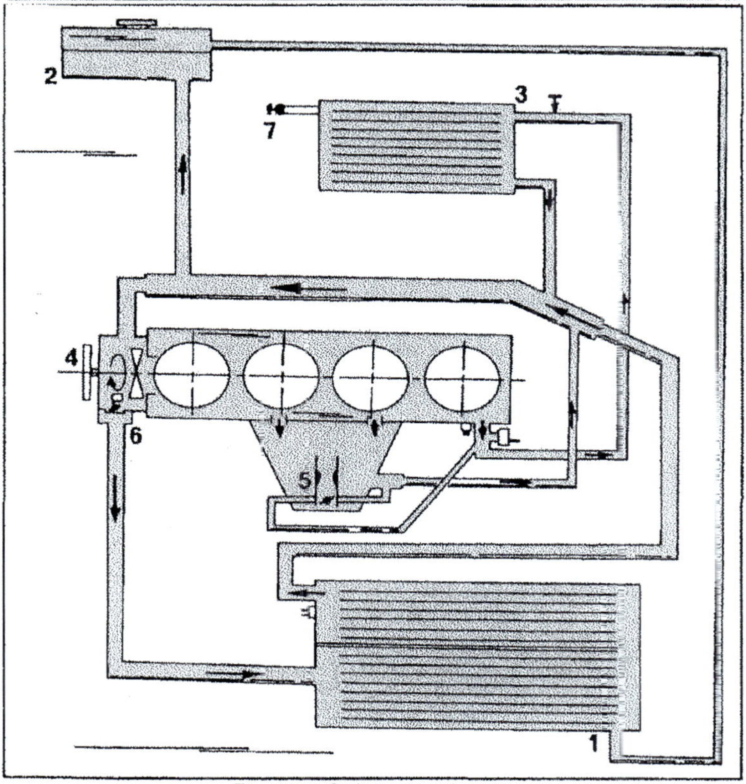

Fig. 1.81. — Cooling system diagram.

1 Radiator
2 Expansion tank
3 Heater radiator
4 Water pump
5 Manifold pre-heating element
6 Thermostat
7 Bleeder screw

- Disconnect a small hose leading to the expansion tank (R.H. side of engine compartment).
- Remove two screws securing the bonnet lock and remove the lock.
- Remove two bolts at the top and the further bolts at the bottom of the front panel and remove the complete radiator grille together with the radiator and the cooling fan assembly. The two water hoses are pulled at the same time from their connectors on the engine. The help of a second person could be appreciated. The radiator can now be removed from the front panel.

The installation of the radiator is a reversal of the removal procedure. Check all coolant hoses for porosity or other damage. Suspect hoses should always be replaced. Refit the drain plug. If the radiator has been replaced, transfer the rubber mountings to the new radiator. The thread of the temperature switch is coated with sealing compound.

The remaining installation is a reversal of the removal procedure. Finally refill the cooling system as described in 1.8.1.

1.8.3. WATER PUMP — REMOVAL AND INSTALLATION

The water pump cannot be repaired or serviced. If the pump is faulty or leaking, it should be replaced with a new unit.

The water pump is driven by a separate drive belt from the crankshaft pulley. The belt has no tensioning device, i.e. it must be "forced" off the pulleys and fitted in a similar manner. The layout of the belt is shown in Fig. 1.82.

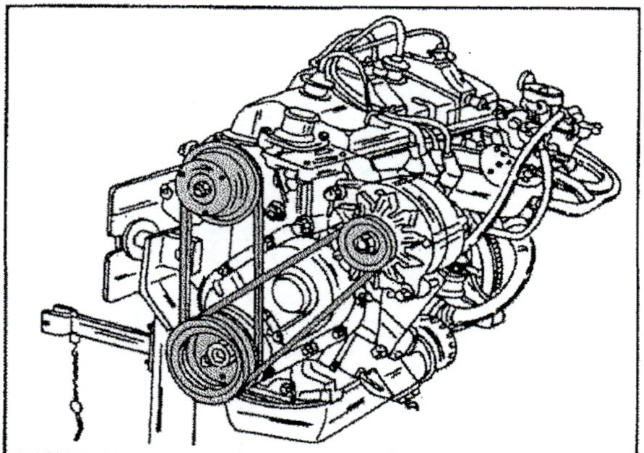

Fig. 1.82. — The water pump drive belt is fitted vertically between the crankshaft pulley and the water pump. The other belt drives the alternator.

As the water pump is connected to the R.H. engine mounting you will have to support the engine in suitable manner from below or use a lifting tackle and ropes or chains to lift the engine out of its mountings. Remove the water pump as follows:

- Disconnect the battery earth cable.
- Drain the cooling system as described in Section 1.8.1. If the anti-freeze is still in good condition, collect it in a container.
- Jack up the front end of the vehicle and place on chassis stands, to gain access to the water pump drive belt. First remove the alternator drive belt to have this one out of the way. To remove the drive belt, use a screwdriver and insert it underneath the drive belt as shown in Fig. 1.83. Apply a 35 mm socket to the crankshaft pulley nut and slowly rotate the crankshaft until the belt slips off the lower pulley (towards the inside). Take care not to damage the belt. Take off the belt after it is free.

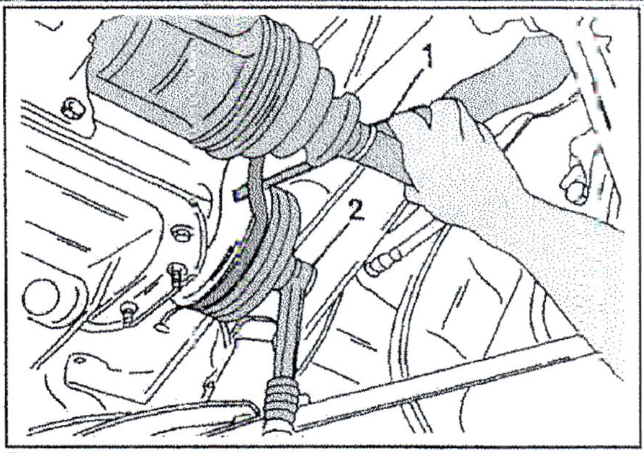

Fig. 1.83. — Insert a screwdriver (1) as shown and rotate the crankshaft with a socket (2) until the water pump drive belt is free.

- The engine must now be lifted out of the engine mountings. Either place a jack underneath the oil sump (wooden block between jack head and oil sump) or lift the timing side of the engine with a tackle or hand crane. Remember, however, not to obstruct the access to the cylinder head.
- Remove the nut (1) in Fig. 1.84, followed by the bolts (2) to remove the mounting carrier from the water pump. Remove the carrier. Make absolutely sure that the engine is well supported before the parts are removed.
- Remove the water pump securing bolts and lift off the pump at an inclined position as shown in Fig. 1.85. Not all nuts have the same size and must be tightened to the torque values given below. Remove the sealing rings from the sealing face. They must be replaced.

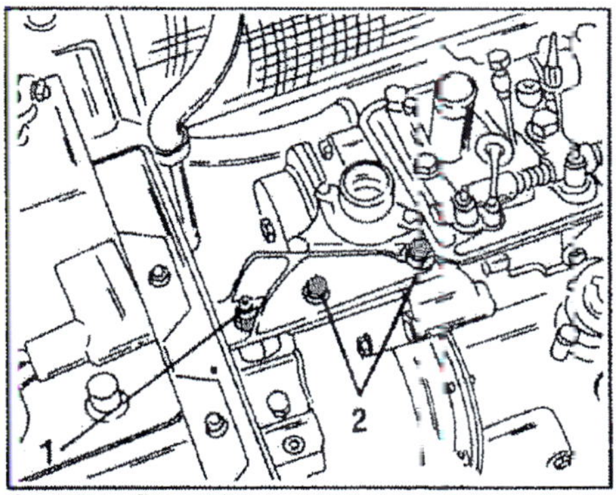

Fig. 1.84. — The engine mounting on the water pump side.
1 Nut, 5.5 kgm 2 Bolts, 5.0 kgm

The installation of the water pump is a reversal of the removal procedure, noting the following points:

- Fit new rubber seals to the pump sealing face and lift the pump against the cylinder head face. Observe the angle shown in Fig. 1.85, otherwise it may be difficult to fit the pump over the studs in the cylinder head. Tighten the nuts and bolts to the following torques, depending on the thread size:

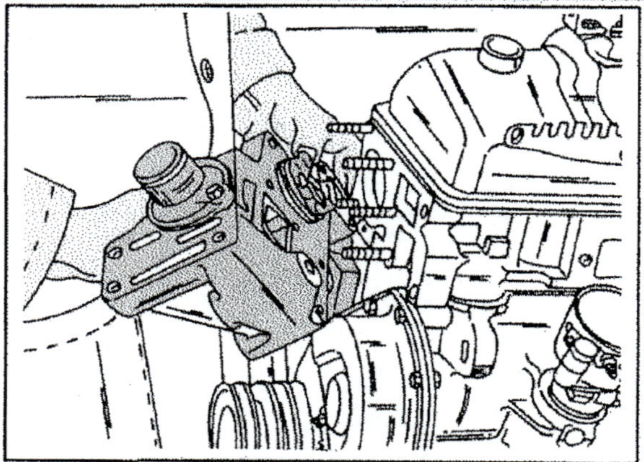

Fig. 1.85. — The water pump must be removed or installed at the angle shown.

M8 nuts: .... 2.3 kgm (16.5 ft.lb.)
M10 nuts: .... 4.3 kgm (31 ft.lb.)
M10 bolts: .... 2.8 kgm (20 ft.lb.)

- Place the water pump drive belt **behind** the crankshaft pulley and engage it with the water pump pulley. Now fit the belt at the bottom over the crankshaft pulley in a similar manner as shown in Fig. 1.82, again rotating the crankshaft pulley nut with a 35 mm socket and a ratchet until the belt jumps into the groove.
- Fit the alternator drive belt and tension it as described in the next section.
- The remaining operations are carried out in reverse order to the removal procedure. Finally fill the cooling system as described earlier on and check all refitted hoses and the water pump joining face for leaks after the engine has reached operating temperature.

1.8.4. ALTERNATOR DRIVE BELT TENSION

The layout of the alternator belt can be seen in Fig. 1.82. The adjusting point for the belt is located on the alternator. The workshop will use a special gauge to tension the belt, which is placed against the belt. Without this tension checking gauge proceed as follows:

- Check the deflection of the belt between forefinger and thumb. This should be around 5 mm (0.2 in.) or perhaps a little more.
- To tention the belt, slacken the alternator securing bolts and push the alternator towards the outside using a strong screwdriver or a tyre lever until the belt can be deflected on its longest run by the amount given above. Hold the alternator in this position and re-tighten the mounting bolts.

Note: A slipping alternator belt can normally be recognised by a squealing noise during quick acceleration.

1.8.5. COOLING FAN

To check the operation of the cooling fan disconnect the lead from the temperature switch in the side of the radiator and connect it with the electrical system, using a bridging wire. The fan must rotate.

The radiator cowling must be removed to replace the cooling fan or the cooling fan motor.

1.8.6. THERMOSTAT

The thermostat is located inside the water outlet on the cylinder head at the location shown in Fig. 1.81. To remove the thermostat, drain the cooling system and disconnect the hose from the water outlet. Unscrew the thermostat cover and lift out the thermostat.

The thermostat cannot be repaird or adjusted and must be replaced if faulty. The opening temperature of the thermostat is the same on all engines. The opening temperature is stamped into the thermostat and can be used as a guide during the following test.

A thermostat can be tested by immersing it in a container of cool water and gradually raising the temperature to check that it opens smoothly.

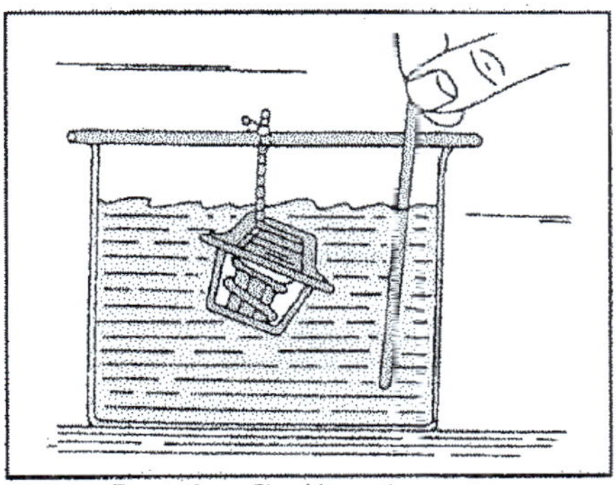

Fig. 1.86. — Checking a thermostat.

Suspend the thermostat on a piece of wire so that it does not touch the sides of the bottom of the container. A thermometer must also be suspended in the same manner. Check the temperature when the thermostat opens. A difference of plus or minus 1° C is permissible.

The installation of the thermostat is a reversal of the removal procedure. Check the condition of the hose before connecting it. Refill the cooling system.

1.8.7. ANTI-FREEZE

The cooling system is filled with an anti-freeze solution and this mixture should be left in the system throughout the year. If a fresh mixture is prepared, use anti-freeze and mix with water. 50% anti-freeze and 50% water will protect the system to very low temperatures. Use less anti-freeze if lower temperatures are anticipated. We advise you only to use the anti-freeze marketed by Citroën, Fiat or Peugeot Dealers, as this solution has been specially formulated for use with your engine. If the system is topped-up with plain water, remember that the anti-freeze solution will be diluted. Make sure to check the strength of the mixture before the cold temperatures are expected and correct if necessary.

1.9. Carburettor Fuel System

1.9.0. CARBURETTOR — TECHNICAL DATA

Carburettor type: .... Solex 34 PBISA 16
Fitted to:
169 B and 170 B engines: .... PEU A 315
170 C engine: .... PSA 425
Operation: .... Single-barrel downdraught carburettor with manually operated choke valve

Carburettor Jets and Settings

	PEU A 315	PSA 425
Venturi bore:	25 mm	25 mm
Main jet:	130	127.5
Air correction jet:	160	155
Idle air jet:	44	45
Constant CO fuel jet:	35	35
Accelerator pump injector:	50	50
Econostat calibration:	70	50
Float needle valve diameter:	1.6 mm	1.6 mm
Float weight:	5.7 g	5.7 g

Idle Speed:
169 B and 170 B engines: .... 800 ± 50 rpm
170 C engine: .... 900 ± 50 rpm
CO Content:
169 B and 170 B engines: .... 0.5 - 2.5 %
170 C engine: .... 1.0 - 2.0 %

Positive throttle valve opening:	0.9 mm	1.0 mm
End of pump stroke for a butterfly opening of	4.0 mm	1.0 mm

1.9.1. CARBURETTOR — REMOVAL AND INSTALLATION

The following instructions are applicable to the carburettor fitted to all models, but differences may be encoutered. Remove the carburettor as follows:

- Disconnect the battery earth cable.
- Disconnect the connecting hose for the air cleaner from the suction horn of the carburettor.
- Disconnect the throttle operating cable from the carburettor lever.
- Drain the cooling system to the height of the carburettor. The foot of the carburettor is surrounded by coolant to pre-heat the fuel/air mixture.
- Disconnect all water hoses from the carburettor.
- Disconnect the choke cable after slackening the two clamp screws on the carburettor.
- Disconnect the vacuum hose from the connection on the carburettor.
- Disconnect the fuel pipe from the carburettor. Plug the open end of the fuel pipe in suitable manner to prevent entry of dirt or other foreign matter.
- Withdraw the electrical lead from the idle speed cut-off valve.
- Unscrew the carburettor from the inlet manifold. Immediately place clean rag over the intakte opening to prevent anything dropping into the inlet manifold opening.

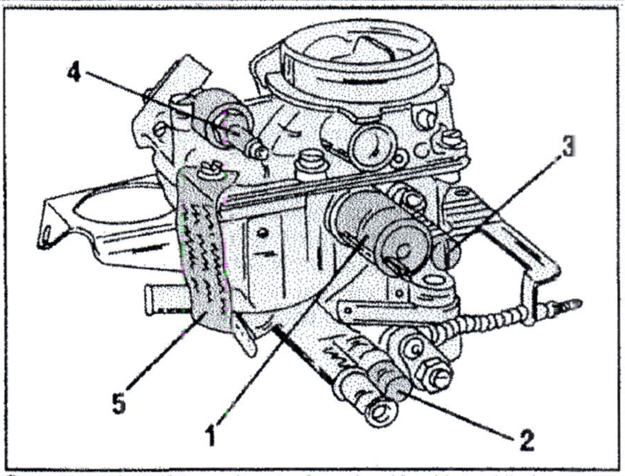

Fig. 1.87. — View of the carburettor from the side with the idle fuel cut-off valve.

1 Idle fuel cut-off valve
2 Mixture control screw with cap
3 Constant CO adjusting screw
4 Fuel line connector with filter
5 Carburettor No. marking

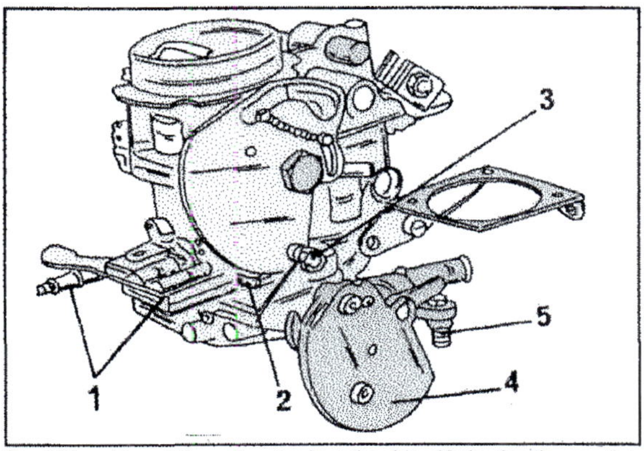

Fig. 1.88. — View of the carburettor from the side with the throttle operating lever.

1 Accelerating pump linkage
2 Throttle valve gap screw
3 Choke cable connection
4 Throttle valve segment
5 Throttle valve stop screw (idle speed adjustment)

The installation of the carburettor is a reversal of the removal procedure. Use a new gasket. After installation top-up the cooling system or refill it completely, depending in which manner it has been drained. Check the idle speed and CO content after installation.

1.9.2. SERVICING

If the carburettor is dismantled for cleaning or servicing it is essential that all gaskets are renewed. Clean the interior of the carburettor with fuel and use only clean, lint-free rags. Clear blocked jets with fuel and blow through them with compressed air. On no account should any wire or metal object (for example paper clips) be introduced into the jets in an attempt to clean them.

Take care that the jets are not damaged by the careless use of screwdrivers or tools. Any buurs or scratches will ruin the jets.

Figs. 1.87 to 1.89 show views of the carburettor and give the location of the jets and other parts. If jets are replaced, make sure that only jets of the same calibration are used. The jets have been carefully selected for the engine and fitting oversize jets will in most cases unbalance the engine performance, fuel consumption, starting, etc.

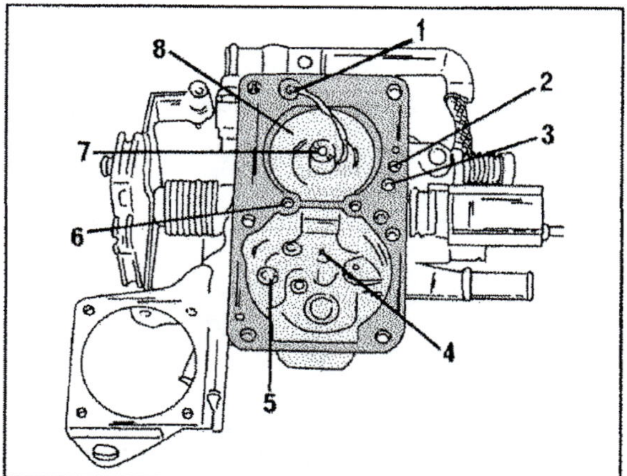

Fig. 1.89. — Top view of the carburettor.

1 Injection tube
2 Idle fuel jet
3 Idle air jet
4 Main jet
5 Suction valve (accelerating pump)
6 Econostat jet
7 Air correction jet with emulsion tube
8 Venturi

1.9.3. ADJUSTMENTS

1.9.3.0. Float Level

A special float level gauge must be used to check the float level on the single barrel **Solex 32 PBISA** carburettors. The carburettor cover is held upside down and the float level gauge is placed over the cover face, with the cover gasket fitted. The float should just touch the upper face of the float, with a tolerance of plus or minus 1.0 mm. If the gauge cannot be obtained, hold the carburettor cover as described and measure the distance from the cover face to the upper face of the float. The measurement is similar as shown in Fig. 1.90 and should be 38 mm.

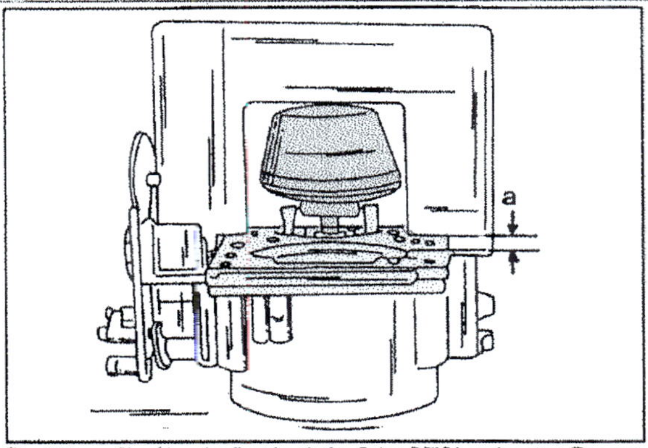

Fig. 1.90. — Checking the float level of a Solex PBISA carburettor. The gap "a" must not exceed 1.0 mm.

1.9.3.1 Idle Speed Adjustment

The idle speed of all engines covered in this manual is given in Section 1.9.0., but you must note the differences between the 78 BHP and the 85 BHP engines. The adjustment is the same for all models. Fig. 1.91 shows as you will see the carburettor on the engine. The adjustments are carried out by referring to this illustration.

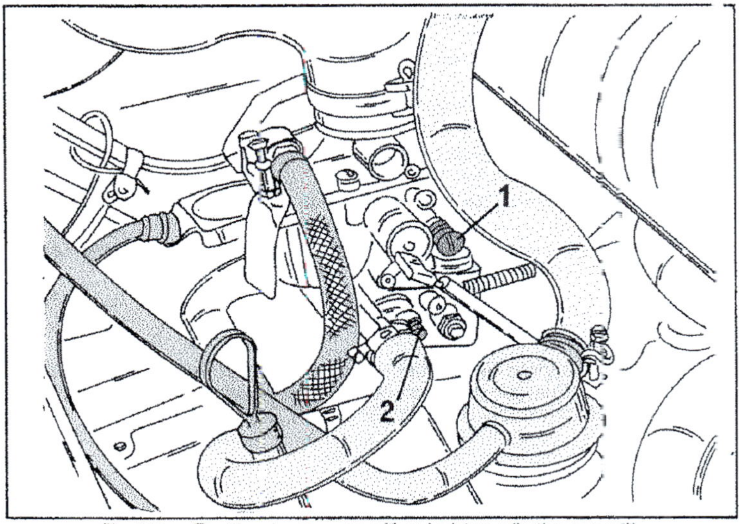

Fig. 1.91. — Throttle valve stop screw (1) and mixture adjusting screw (2).

The ignition timing point and the valve clearances must be correctly adjusted before a good idling speed can be obtained. A revolution counter and a CO content meter must be available, you may, however, be able to adjust the CO content without CO meter if you follow the instructions below.

With CO Meter

- Connect the revolution counter and the CO meter in accordance with the instructions of the manufaturer.
- Warm up the engine until the electric fan cuts in and then stops.
- Check that the choke cable is pushed fully in.
- Check the idle speed on the revolution counter and compare with the specified value.
- Check the CO content on the CO meter, which should be in accordance with the value given in Section 1.9.0.
- The adjustment of the idle speed is now carried out as follows:
- Turn the throttle stop screw (1) in Fig. 1.91, located at the throttle lever until the engine runs with the speed given.
- To adjust the CO content, remove the tamper-proof plug covering the volume control screw (2) in Fig. 1.91 and turn the screw until the value given above is obtained. A pointed instrument (for example a scriber) must be used to remove the plug. Note the different values for the various engines, given in Section 1.9.0.
- Re-adjust the idle speed again as described above and re- check the CO content.
- Fit a white tamper-proof plug over the volume control screw (2).

Without CO Meter

- Adjust the idle speed as described above until the engine has obtained the specified speed.
- Rotate the throttle valve stop screw (1) in Fig. 1.91 until the engine idle speed has increased by approx. 50 rpm above the value applicable to the engine.
- Try to obtain the highest possible idle speed by screwing the volume control screw (mixture control screw) in or out.
- Repeat the two adjusting steps until the engine idles as fast as possible by turning the screw (2).
- **Rotate screw (2) inwards** until the engine runs with the specified idle speed for the engine in question.

1.9.4 Fuel Pump

The fuel pump is supplied by different manufacturers, but their is no rule which pump can be fitted. Fuel pumps cannot be repaired or overhauled and must be replaced if faulty. Removal and installation is straight forward.

1.9.5. Air Cleaner

The air cleaner element should be replaced every 12,000 miles. Make sure all hoses are securely connected.

2. CLUTCH

2.0. Technical Data

Type: .... Single plate, dry clutch with diaphragm spring
Fitted type:
With 169 B engine to July 1984: .... 215 CP 450
With 169 B engine, July 1984 to Oct. 1985: .... 215 DBR 510
With 169 B engine, from Oct. 1985: .... 215 CP 4850
With 170 (2.0 litre engine), from Sept. 1989: .... 230 DBR 5500

Clutch Lining Dimensions::
With 1.8 litre engine: .... 215 x 145 mm
With 2.0 litre engine: .... 228.6 x 156 mm
With four-wheel drive: .... 228.6 x 153 mm
Clutch driven plate thickness: .... 7.7 mm (0.30 in.)

Driven Plate Identification:
1.8 litre engine: .... G 12 A
2.0 litre engine: .... M 33 AX

Colour of clutch driven plate springs:
1.8 litre engine to July 1984: .... 2 x pale green
1.8 litre engine, Oct. 1982 to Oct. 1987: .... 6 x green/white
2.0 litre engine, four-wheel drive: .... 2 x olive brown, 2 x dark green, 2 x light blue

Lining Material:
1.8 litre to Oct. 1985 to Oct. 1987: .... Ferodo F 755
1.8 litre from Oct. 1987 and 2.0 litre: .... Ferodo F 202

Release bearing (general guide line): .... Ball-type, constantly resting on diaphragm plate of clutch
Clutch operation: .... Mechanical, by cable
Clutch pedal clearance: .... 8 - 9 mm, manual adjustment

Clutch/Flywheel Bolt Tightening Torque:
Clutch bolts: .... 1.5 kgm (11 ft.lb.)
Flywheel: .... 6.8 kgm (41 ft.lb.)

2.1. Clutch Unit

2.1.0. CHECKING THE CLUTCH OPERATION

The clutch can be checked for proper operation when fitted to the vehicle. To do this, proceed as follows:

- Start the engine and allow to idle. Depress the clutch pedal and wait approx. 3 secs. Engage the reverse gear. If grating noises can be heard from the transmission, it can be assumed that the clutch or driven plate needs replacement, as the driven plate no longer connects the clutch pressure plate with the flywheel.
- To check the clutch for signs of slipping, drive the vehicle until the clutch and transmission have reached their operating temperature. Stop the vehicle, firmly apply the handbrake and engage the 3rd gear. Keep the clutch pedal fully depressed and accelerate the engine to approx. 3000 - 4000 rpm. Release the

clutch pedal suddenly. The clutch operates satisfactorily if the engine stalls immediately.

2.1.1. REMOVAL AND INSTALLATION

The transmission or the engine and transmission must be removed to replace the clutch plate and/or driven plate. Proceed as follows:

- Mark the clutch cover and flywheel face to ensure correct re-assembly. Remove the clutch bolts carefully, a little at a time. The engine must be prevented from rotating when the bolts are slackened. Otherwise use a ring spanner and place it over the bolt heads and hit it with a short, sharp blow to loosen the bolts.
- Remove the clutch and take out the driven plate. Do not allow grease or oil to get on the lining faces or any other part if there is a chance that the parts can be re-used. Make a note which way the driven plate is fitted.
- Clean out the inside of the flywheel and check the friction face for wear. If the clutch lining rivets have worn down to the height of the rivets there is a possibility that the rivet head have left marks in the flywheel. Replace the flywheel if necesary, but remember that new flywheel bolts must be used. The tightening torque is different for the two engine groups. Flywheels can be re-ground to a certain dimension. Your dealer should have all the necessary information.

The installation of the clutch requires normally the use of an alignment mandrel, which is inserted as shown in Fig. 2.1. If this is not available, a spare clutch shaft can also be used. If neither of the above is available, and tools cannot be obtained, it is possible to line up the clutch disc in the inside of the flywheel by inserting a drift of the diameter of the spline bore. The end of the drift should either have a spigot which fits into the crankshaft bearing bore or in emergency have a pointed end so that this can be centred in the bore. Note that the long end of the clutch driven plate hub must face towards you, away from the flywheel.

Offer up the clutch assembly to the flywheel and centre the disc by inserting the mandrel into the flywheel bearing. Tighten the bolts carefully, a little at a time, working in a diagonal manner, to the torque setting given in Section 2.0.

Coat the clutch drive shaft and the outer face of the clutch release bearing with a little graphited grease (Molycote BR2) and refit the gearbox to the engine.

Adjust the clutch cable free play. At the end of the clutch cable there are two nuts. The aim of the adjustment is to bring the height of the clutch pedal to the same height as the brake pedal. Slacken the outer nut and then turn the lower unit. Tightening the nut will raise the clutch pedal, slackening the nut will lower the pedal. After adjustment tighten the two nuts against each other.

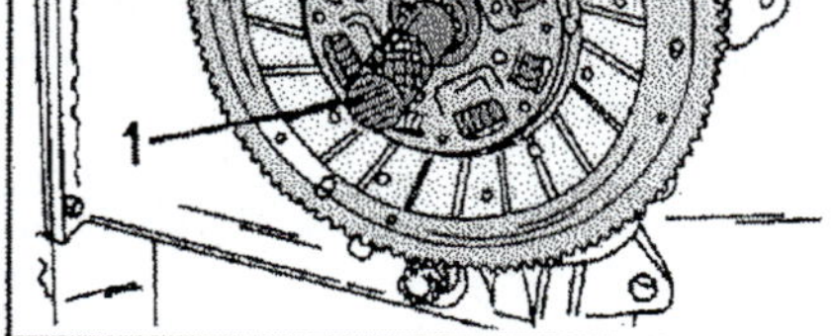

Fig. 2.1. — The centering mandrel is inserted into the fitted driven plate before the clutch unit is placed in position.

Measure the travel of the clutch pedal after adjustment. The should be a difference of 180 mm with the pedal fully released and the pedal fully depressed. First measure from the floor panel to the released pedal and then from the floor panel to the edge of the depressed pedal. The difference is the pedal travel.

2.2. Servicing

The cover assembly — pressure plate and diaphragm spring — must not be dismantled. Replace, if necessary with a complete assembly from your dealer, quoting the year of manufacture and the chassis number.

Inspect the driven plate and the linings, replacing the complete plate, if the linings are worn down close to the rivets. Again specify the engine type and model year as diffeerwnt clutch units and driven plates are used since the introduction of the vans. Again depending on the model year, clutch driven plates have different identifications. A driven plate with the linings contaminated with grease or oil cannot be cleaned successfully and should also be replaced. All rivets should be tight and the torsion springs should be sound and unbroken. Check the condition of the driven plate splines. Clamp the driven plate between the centres of a lathe and apply a dial gauge to the outside of the plate as shown in Fig. 2.2, at a diameter of 175.0 mm (6.4 in.).

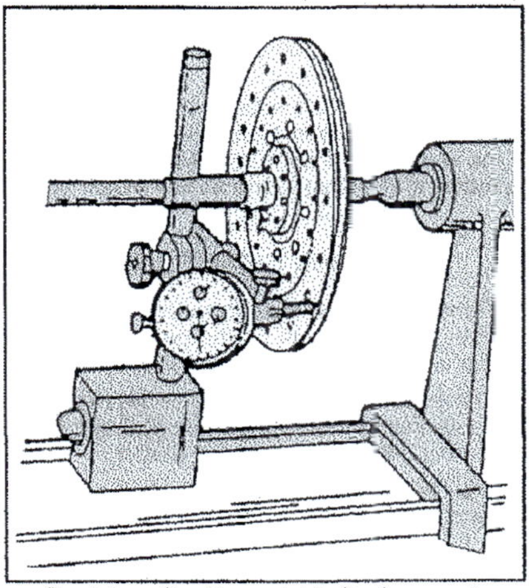

Fig. 2.2. — Checking a clutch disc for run-out.

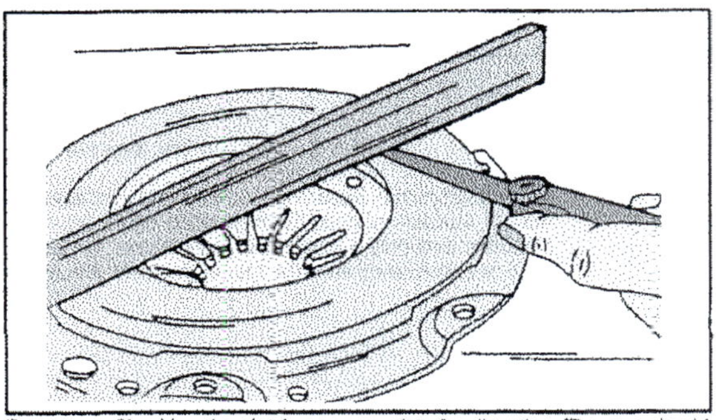

Fig. 2.3. — Checking the clutch pressure plate for distortion. The gap should be no more than 0.3 mm (0.012 in.) at the point shown. The max. run-out of the driven plate should be no more than 0.4 mm (0.016 in.).

Check the rivet fastening of the clutch pressure plate and replace the plate, if loose rivets can be detected.

Place a straight edge (steel ruler) over the friction face of the pressure plate and insert feeler gauges between the ruler and the surface. If the gap at the innermost spot of the friction face is no more than 0.3 mm (0.012 in.), the plate can be re-used. Fig. 2.3. shows this check.

2.2.1. REPLACEMENT OF RELEASE BEARING

The transmission must be removed from the engine to replace the release bearing. Remove the release bearing from the inside of the transmission bell housing and withdraw towards the front of the shaft. The release bearing is of the sealed type and must not be placed in any solvent. Check that the bearing revolves smoothly.

The installation of the release bearing is a reversal of the removal procedure. Coat the shaft and the bearing sleeve with Molycote BR2 grease. Grease the two sides of the release fork ends with M.P. grease. The release bearing should always be replaced at the same time as the clutch unit and clutch driven plate.

2.3. Clutch Cable Replacement

- Remove the two nuts from the end of the clutch cable, free the clutch cable from its attachment on the gearbox housing and push it towards the inside of the vehicle. Unhook the cable from the clutch pedal.
- The installation is a reversal of the removal procedure. All sliding portions of the cable must be lubricated with M.P. grease. Adjust the clutch cable as described during the instilation of the clutch.
- After adjustment start the engine and depress the clutch pedal. Engage reverse gear, If no grating noises can be heard, the adjustment should be OK.

3. GEARBOX

3.0. Technical Data

Type: .... 4- or 5-speed gearbox, together with final drive in one housing.

Gearbox Type: .... The gearbox has been changed several times since introduction of the various models. Each gearbox has a type identification number and only a gearbox with the same number must be fitted in accordance with the model year and the engine fitted.

Gear Ratios (typical):

1st gear: .... 3.727 : 1
2nd gear: .... 1.944 : 1
3rd gear: .... 1.250 : 1
4th gear: .... 0.829 : 1
5th gear: .... 0.767 : 1, 0.674 : 1 or 0.733 : 1
Reverse gear: .... 3.154 : 1

3. Transmission (Gearbox)

Lubrication:

Type: .... Transmission oil 75W/90

Capacity — with two wheel drive: .... 1.6 litres (1.25 litre to July 1989)

— with four-wheel drive: .... 2.5 litres

Final Drive Ratio: .... 5.167 : 1, 4.769 : 1 or 5.615 : 1, depending on engine and gearbox

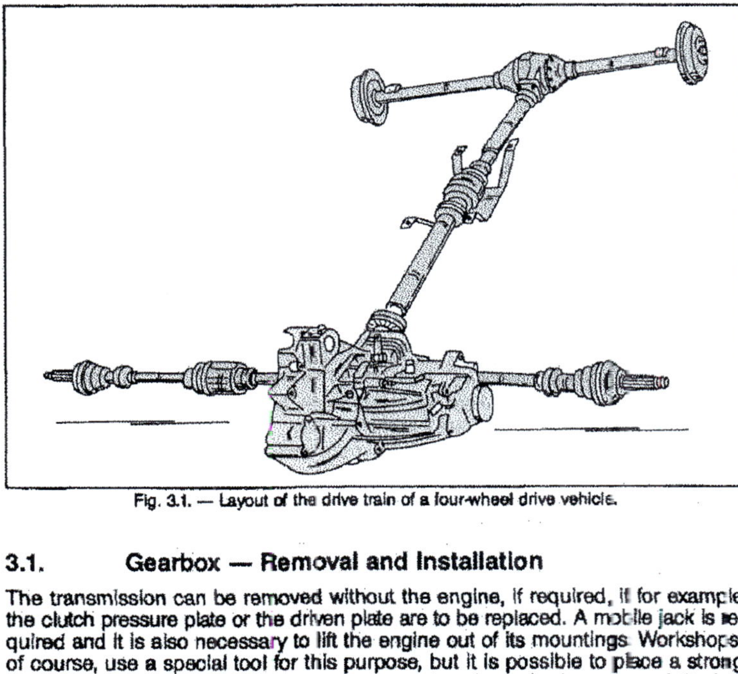

Fig. 3.1. — Layout of the drive train of a four-wheel drive vehicle.

3.1. Gearbox — Removal and Installation

The transmission can be removed without the engine, if required, if for example the clutch pressure plate or the driven plate are to be replaced. A mobile jack is required and it is also necessary to lift the engine out of its mountings. Workshops, of course, use a special tool for this purpose, but it is possible to place a strong metal bar across the engine compartment and to tie a wire loop around the bar and for example to the exhaust manifold. Use a tommy bar and wind the wire together, until the engine is under tension. Fig. 3.2 shows the arrangement used on a different engine. Proceed as follows to remove the gearbox, but note that there are differences in the removal and installation procedures, for two- and four-wheel drive vehicles and within the different manufacturers.

- Slacken the drive shaft nuts on boths sides of the vehicle whilst the wheels are resting on the ground.
- Remove the following parts: spare wheel, the complete air cleaner and the vacuum pump.
- Remove the upper bolts between engine and transmission. A strut is fitted under one of the bolts on some models.
- Disconnect the earth cable from the transmission.

- Disconnect the cables from the reversing light switch. Also disconnect the gearchange from the transmission and the speedometer cable.
- Suspend the engine and transmission as described above and remove the bolts securing the L.H. transmission mounting, but leave one bolt in position.
- Jack up the front end of the vehicle and place chassis stands under the sides of the body. Both wheels must be allowed to hang down under their own weight. Details of some of the following operations are given in sections "Front Suspension" or "Drive Shafts".
- Completely remove the mounting bracket for the L.H. reaction strut bar from the body or remove tyhe bar by removing the two nuts at the other end. On the same side disconnect the suspension arm either from the steering knuckle (swivel joint) or remove it at the inside.

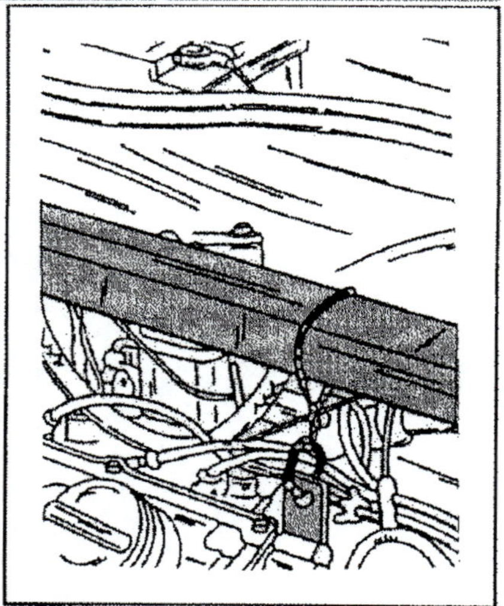

Fig. 3.2. — Lifting the engine out of its mountings with the home-made arrangement.

- Disconnect the L.H. drive shaft from the transmission as described in the relevant section.
- Disconnect the clutch cable from the clutch release lever and free it from the bracket on the transmission.
- On the R.H. side disconnect the complete ball joint from the bottom of the steering knuckle and push the suspension arm downwards, away from the steering knuckle.
- Remove the R.H. drive shaft as described in the relevant section.
- Remove the protective panel above the starter motor, disconnect the cables and remove the starter motor.
- Make sure that the engine is securely suspended and place a trolley jack underneath the gearbox.
- Lift the gearbox until it is just under tension and remove the last bolt from the L.H. gearbox mounting.
- Lower the transmission on the jack until the power unit is held by the lifting tackle only. Leave the jack in this position.
- Fully remove the L.H. gearbox mounting and the bolts between engine and gearbox at the bottom.
- With the gearbox supported on the jack withdraw it from the engine. Take care not to allow the clutch drive shaft to rest on the clutch driven plate as the gearbox is tasken out.

The installation of the transmission is a reversal of the removal procedure. Coat the clutch shaft splines, the guide sleeve for the release bearing with a little graphited grease. The gearbox mountings must be well centred.

Fill the transmission with the correct quantity of the recommended oil. The best way to fill the transmission may be to unscrew the reversing light switch. A funnel can then be inserted into the switch opening.

Models with four-wheel drive

The removal is carried out in a similar manner, with the difference that the propeller shaft must be disconnected at the rear of the gearbox.

3.2. Gearbox Repairs

Many special tools are required to dismantle, assemble and adjust the transmission. Additionally the transmission has been changed several times. For this reason it is practically impossible to describe the work involved.

A damaged or faulty transmission should be taken to a workshop for overhaul or try to obtain an exchange box. In the latter case you will need the usual chassis number, model year, etc. to ensure that the correct transmission is fitted.

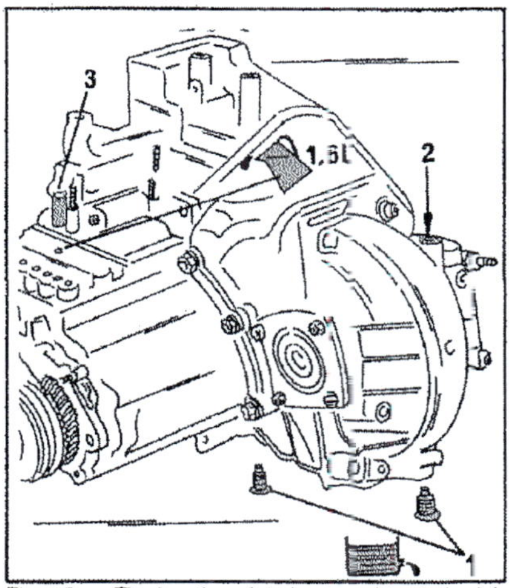

Fig. 3.3. — The location of drain plugs (1), oil dipstick (2) and oil filler plug (3).

3.3. Transmission Oil

An oil dipstick is fitted into the top of the transmission unit. After withdrawing the dipstick you will see a "Min" and a "Max" mark, showing you the level of oil in the gearbox. Fig. 3.3 shows a view of the transmission with the position of the drain plugs (1), the oil dipstick (2) and the oil filler opening (3). To top-up the transmission, unscrew the filler plug and, using a funnel, fill in the missing quantity of the recommended oil (75W 80W). Tighten the plug top 1.3 kgm (10 ft.lb.).

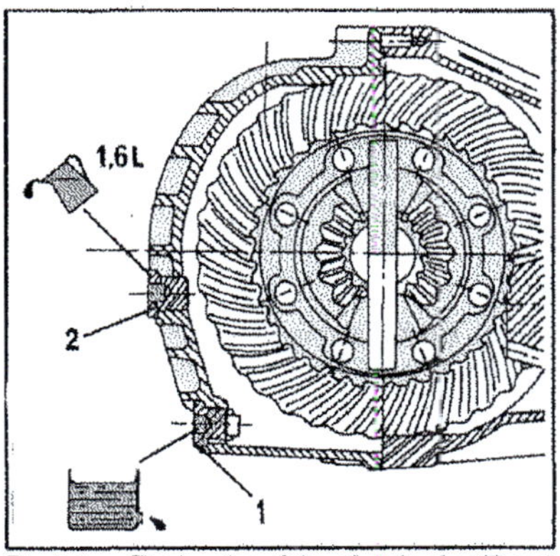

Fig. 3.4. — The location of the oil drain plug (1) and filler plug (2) of a 4WD vehicle.

Two drain plugs are fitted into the bottom of the transmission and both must be removed to drain the oil. Warm oil will facilitate the draining operations. Clean the plugs and fit and tighten them with 4.0 kgm (30 ft.lb.). Fill the gearbox with the quantity given in Section 3.0

Models with four-wheel drive have three drain plugs. The oil quantity is different, the tightening torque of the plugs is as given above.

3.4. Rear Axle Oil — 4WD Vehicles

A plug is inserted into the rear of the rear axle, as shown in Fig. 3.4 and must be removed to check the oil level. Insert the forefinger to reach the oil. If this is not the case, fill in additional oil, but note that special oil is used in the axle.

A drain plug (2) is fitted to the bottom of the rear axle drive housing. Unscrew the plug (2) to assist the draining of the oil. The rear axle will take 1.6 litres.

4. *DRIVE SHAFTS*

The drive shafts have a tri-axe constant velocity joint, sliding on inner splines, at the gearbox end and a non-sliding tri-axe constant velocity joint at the wheel end. An intermediate bearing is used to locate the R.H. drive shaft. Drive shafts have been changed at least once since production and cannot be interchanged. The nut at the end of the drive shaft is tightened with a high torque (50 kgm/360 ft.lb.) and is subsequently secured in position by peening the shoulder of the nut into a groove in the shaft. Fig. 4.1 shows a view of the two drive shafts and their main component parts.

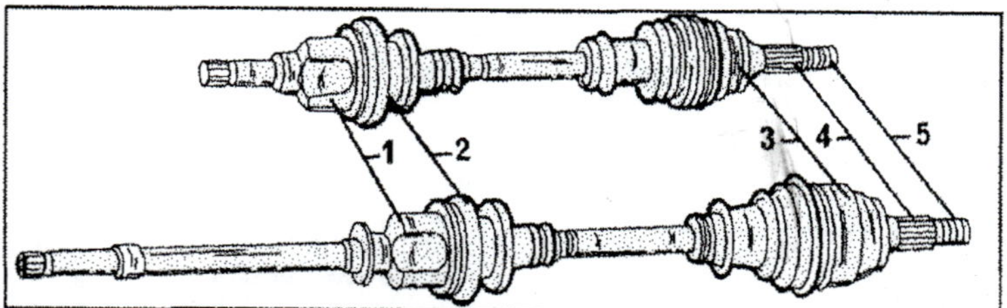

Fig. 4.1. — View of the two drive shafts.

1 Inner CV joint
2 Rubber boots (gaiters)
3 Outer CV joint
4 Shaft splines
5 Threaded end

4.0. Removal and Installation

It should be noted that the oil seal for the drive shaft in the gearbox housing must be replaced if a drive shaft is replaced, irrespective what type of repairs are carried out. Also note the following before proceeding with the work:

- You will need a flat chisel to remove the L.H. drive shaft out of the transmission. You will also need a supply of "Loctite" to secure the drive shaft nuts.
- The cap over the end of the wheel hub/axle shaft will be destroyed during removal, unless the puller used in the workshop is available.
- Gearbox oil will drip on the floor after removal of the shaft. Take care !

Remove a drive shaft as follows, noting the differences between the L.H. and R.H. shaft:

- Apply the handbrake and chock the rear wheels. Slacken the wheel nuts, jack up the front end of the vehicle and remove the wheel.
- Remove the hub grease cap by tapping with a small chisel into the gap around the cap. With a little luck the cap may come off without damage.
- Refit the wheel and lower the vehicle to the ground. Locate and remove the peening of the nut and slacken it with a suitable socket and a large extension bar.

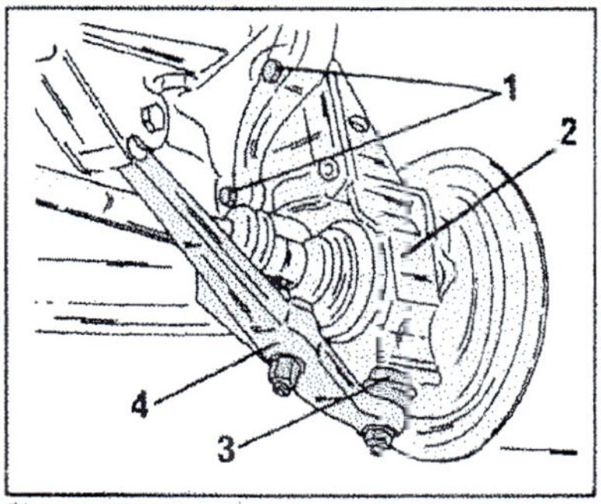

Fig. 4.2. The named parts must be removed when removing the R.H. drive shaft. The numbers are referred to in the text.

- Jack up the front wheel on the side to be worked on once more and remove the wheel. The steering knuckle must be able to hang down under its own weight, i.e. chassis stands must be placed underneath the body. Fully unscrew the drive shaft nut.
- Remove the gearbox oil drain plug and allow approx. 2 pints of oil to drain into a clean container. Alternatively drain the gearbox completely.
- Remove the two bolts securing the suspension ball joints (3) in Fig. 4.2 to the bottom of the steering knuckle and the bolts (1) securing the steering lever. Push the complete steering knuckle (2) towards the outside aqnd push the suspension arm (4) downwards until the ball joint is free of the steering knuckle. Pull the steering knuckle to the outside as far as it will go until the drive shaft is free of the steering knuckle. Push the shaft to one side.

Removal of a R.H. Drive Shaft

The removal of the drive shaft depends largely on the vehicle model and the type of attachment. On some models the shaft can simply be removed from the transmission. In most cases the shaft is, however, removed as follows:

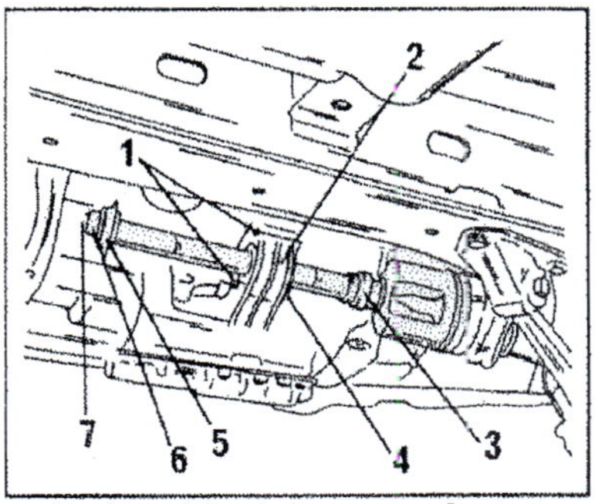

Fig. 4.3. — Drive shaft removal — See text.

- Refer to Fig. 4.3 and slacken the nuts (1) and swing down the attachments (4) by half a turn to disengage the outer cage. Remove the three bolts securing the support bearing (2) to the cylinder block and take out the shaft.

Removal of a L.H. Shaft

The small chisel mentioned on the previous page is now required. Take care when the given instructions are followed in order to avoid damage to the gearbox or drive shaft joint.

- Insert the chisel as shown in Fig. 4.4 between the CV joint housing and one of the bolts of the differential housing. Check that the chisel is correctly applied and hit the chisel in the direction of the arrow (1) with a hammer. After the chisel is wedged, hit against it sideways in the direction of arrow (2), until the shaft is free of the transmission.

- Grip the suspension arm as shown in Fig. 4.5. Pull the arm downwards, at the same time pushing the wheel towards the outside until the shaft is completely free.

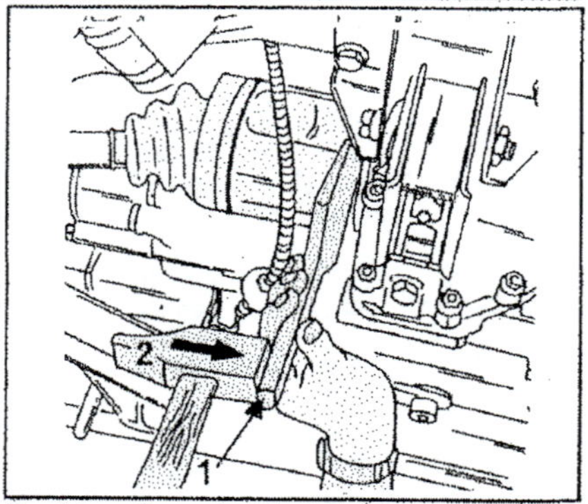

Fig. 4.4. — Removal of the L.H. drive shaft. Refer to text.

The installation of the drive shafts is carried out as follows:

- When fitting the L.H. shaft refer to Fig 4.4 and check that the "O" sealing ring (7) is fitted and secured with the circlip (6). It must be assured that the circlip is fully engaged into the groove in the differential side gear.
- When fitting the R.H. drive shaft insert the drive shaft at (2) into the support bearing (Fig. 4.4). At the protruding end of the shaft fit the dust seal (5), the circlip (6) and the "O" sealing ring (7).
- Fitg the bearing race (3), slightly greased, into the support bearing (2).

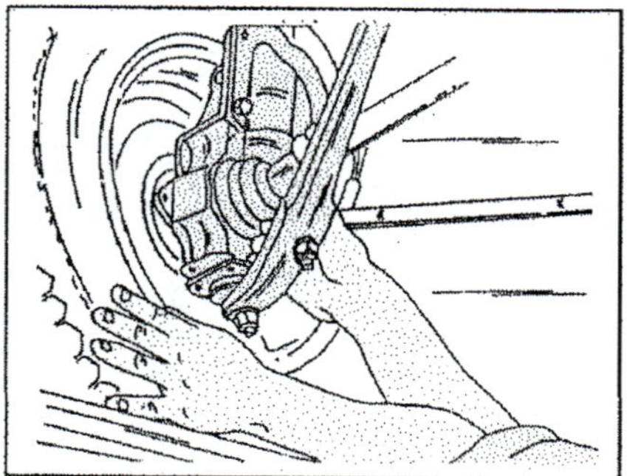

Fig. 4.5. — Pull the suspension arm downwards the push the wheel outwards to remove the L.H. drive shaft.

- Swing the tie rod (4) by half a turn so that they grip the outer track and tighten the self-locking nuts (1) to a torque reading of 1.0 kgm (7.2 ft.lb.).

In case of both shafts:

- Coat the area of the running face for the dust seal with grease and insert the drive shaft through the wheel hub.
- Lift up the suspension arm until the ball joint can be connected. Fit the bolts and secure the ball joint. Also refit the steering lever to the steering knuckle.
- Lower the vehicle to the ground and tighten the axle shaft nut(s) to 50 kgm (360 ft.lb.). The shaft threads must be smeared with "Loctite". After the nut has been tightened, use a small punch and peen the nut shoulder into the shaft at two opposite points.
- Check that the wheel nuts have been tightened before driving the vehicle and fill the transmission with oil.

4.1. Drive Shaft Repairs

Drive shaft repairs are always difficult. If the CV joint is worn or if the rubber gaiter is torn we recommend to take the drive shaft to a workshop and have it overhauled or fit a new drive shaft. If dirt has entered through a torn rubber gaiter it will have entered the CV joint, requiring the dismantling and greasing of the latter. Note that drive shafts have been changed during production of the models.

4.2. Replacing the Support Bearing

The support bearing is pressed over the R.H. drive shaft and a puller with long arms is required to remove the bearing. A piece of tube of 36 mm diameter and 450 mm length is used to press the new bearing over the shaft. We must stress that the rubber gaiter and the CV joint must be removed from the shaft in order to pull off the support bearing, i.e. we advise you to take the shaft to your dealer to have the bearing replaced if it has worn or is damaged.

5. FRONT AXLE AND SUSPENSION

5.0. Technical Data

Typ: .... independent suspension with McPherson spring struts, integral shock absorbers, coil springs, lower suspension arms and reaction strut bars

Spring Data (Citroën models given)

Wire Diameter:

Long wheel base, models 1000 - 1500: .... 16.8 mm (16.3 mm from model year 1991)
Model 1800: .... 16.8 mm (16.3 mm from model year 1991)
With 4WD: .... 16.8 mm

Free Length;

Long wheelbase, models 1000 - 1500: .... 383 mm
Model 1800: .... 373 mm
4WD: .... 389 mm

Fig. 5.1 shows a sectional view of one side of the front suspension, also giving the tightening torques of the individual elements. The reactions strut fitted between the lower suspension arm and a mounting bracket on the chassis (body) is secured with nuts on one end. Shims under the nuts are used to adjust the caster angle of the front wheel. Other things to note is the rating of the front springs, shock absorbers and the diameter of the wheel bearings. Only replace in accordance with the model and the chassis number.

5.1. Front Spring Struts

5.1.0. REMOVAL

The coil spring must be compressed with a suitable spring compressor before a spring strut can be dismantled. The wheel can eithe remain on the vehicle or is

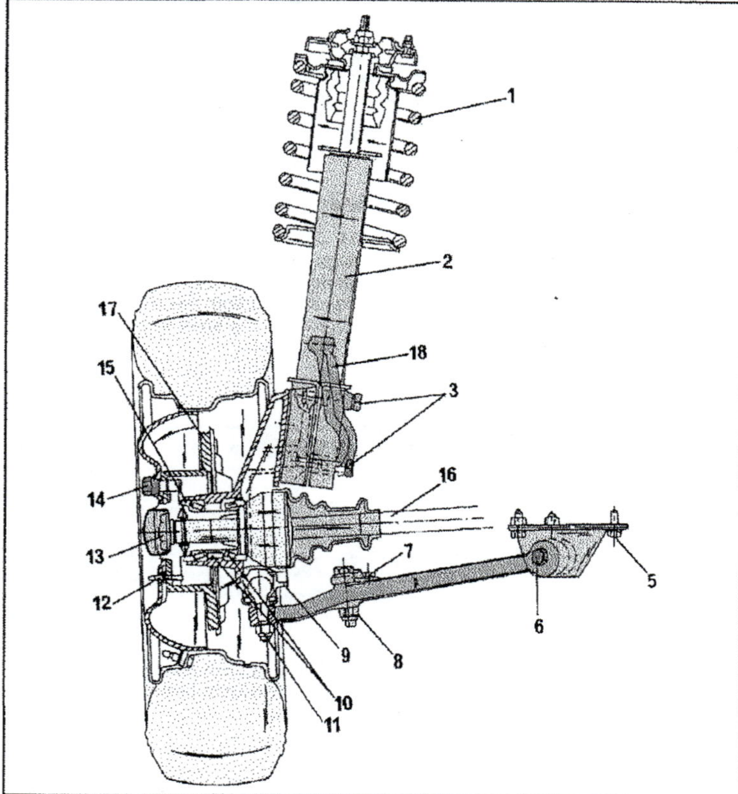

Fig. 5.1. — Sectional view of a front suspension strut.

1 Coil spring
2 Spring strut
3 Bolts, 12.5 kgm
4 Rubber mounting
5 Bolt, 5.0 kgm
6 Bolt, 9.0 kgm
7 Bolt, 2.5 kgm
8 Nut, 14 kgm
9 Bolt, 5.0 kgm
10 Wheel bearing adjusting shims
11 Nut, 10.0 kgm
12 Bolt, 1.5 kgm
13 Drive shaft nut, 50 kgm
14 Wheel bolt, 18 kgm
15 Wheel bearing (note diameter)
16 Drive shaft
17 Brake disc
18 Steering lever

removed. You have have more space to operate when the wheel is removed.

- Apply the handbrake, place chocks underneath the rear wheels, slacken the wheel nuts, place the the front end of the vehicle on chassis stands and remove the wheel. Place the jack loosely underneath the front suspension.
- In the inside of the vehicle remove the three nuts securing the nuts securing

the upper spring strut bearing to the body panel.

- Refer to Fig. 5.2 and remove the four bolts shown with the arrows.
- Slowly lower the jack until the upper end of the spring strut disengages from the body panel and release the strut from the steering knuckle. Withdraw the complete strut towards the rear. *Under no circumstances remove the nut in the centre of the spring strut, as it would "explode".* If the spring strut is to be dismantled, you can slacken the nut, but re-tighten it again before the strut is removed. The steering knuckle and suspension arm remain in the vehicle.

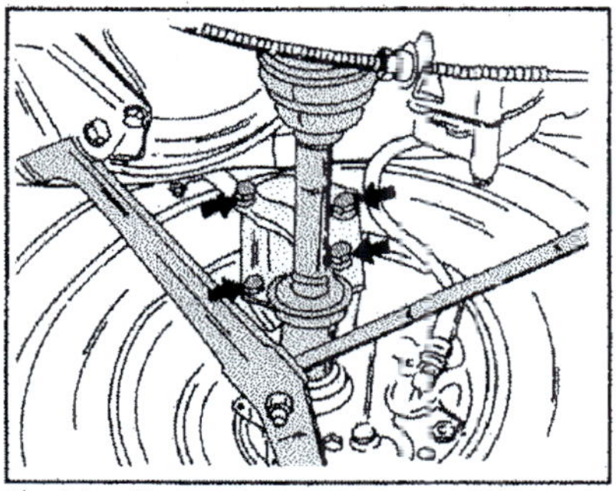

Fig. 5.2.— Remove the bolts shown by the arrows to remove the spring strut from the steering knuckle. Suspension arm, steering knuckle, etc. remain in the suspension when the strut is removed.

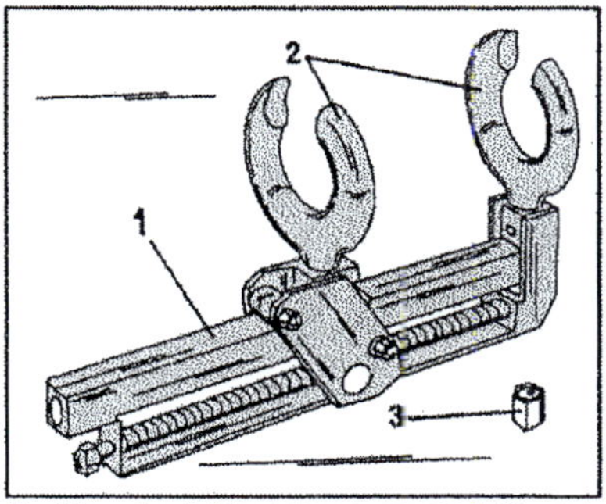

Fig. 5.3 — A suitable spring compressor to dismantle a spring strut. Anything similar is suitable.

5.1.2. DISMANTLING

Only the coil spring, the complete spring strut, the spring strut bearing and the sundry parts can be replaced. The spring strut cannot be dismantled. Never try to dismantle a spring strut without compressing the spring first. Fig. 5.3 shows a compressor as used in the workshop. A similar tool, available from tool hire companies for example, is suitable as long as the hooks can be replaced over 3 or 4 coils.

- Clamp the spring strut into a vice and fit the spring compressor. Fig. 5.4 shows the use of the compressor shown in Fig. 5.3. Make absolutely sure that the coils are securely retained in the compressor. Tighten the spring compressor until the spring can be rotated freely between the spring seats.
- Insert an Allenkey into the end of the piston rod as shown in Fig. 5.5 and slacken the piston rod nut, using a flat or ring spanner of suitable size. Fully unscrew the nut and remove the upper cup, the needle thrust bearing and the stop from the upper end of the spring strut. Remove the rubber rebound stop from the end of the piston rod and the strut from the compressed spring.

The rebound stop, the rubber protector and the washer, the needle thrust bearing, the seal, a second needle thrust bearing und the spring strut bearing must be replaced if no longer in good condition. If a spring strut is dismantled to replace a spring it is always adviseable to replace the items 3, 4, 5 and 6 in Fig. 5.6. Take care not to damage the smooth surface of the piston rod when the spring strut is stored for later assembly.

The shock absorber can be checked for correct operation by clamping the spring strut in upright position into a vice. Screw the nut back onto the piston rod and grip the nut with a pair of pliers. Move the piston rod up and down. The piston rod should move with even resistance. Any "dead play" indicates a faulty shock absorber.

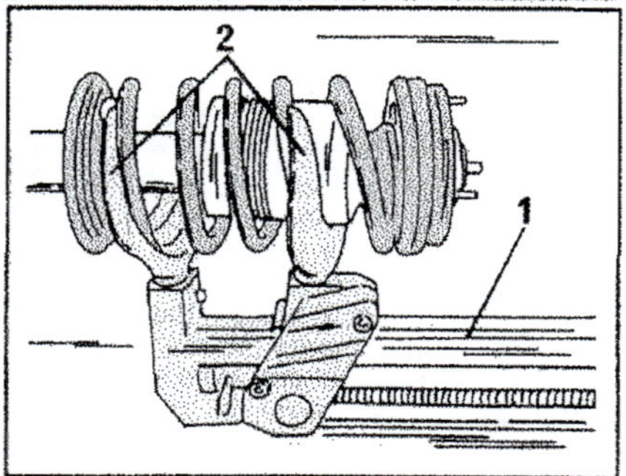

Fig. 5.4. — The spring compressor (1) can be clamped into a vice. The claws (2) are placed around the coils of the spring.

5.1.3. ASSEMBLY

Before assembly of the spring strut prepare the upper sring strut bearing.

- Place the upper spring cup onto its edge (upright position) and, using a small chisel or a screwdriver and knock the needle thrust bearing (6) in Fig. 5.6 out of the cup (7). Now place the spring cup with the smaller end onto a flat surface and drive out the bronze bush (3). A socket of suitable diameter is suitable for this operation.
- Clean the inside of the locating bore and drive a new bronze bush in position from the same side (use the socket).
- Push the new needle thrust bearing (6) into the spring cup, as shown in Fig. 5.7. If the bearing is difficult to fit in the manner shown, carefully use a rubber or plastic mallet to tap it in.

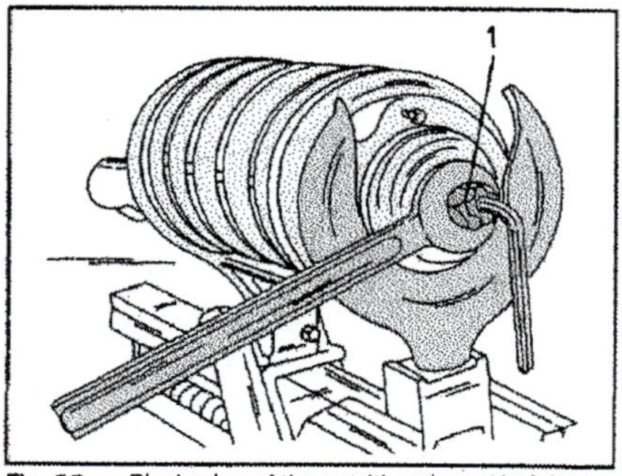

Fig. 5.5. — Slackening of the nut (1) at the end of the piston rod.

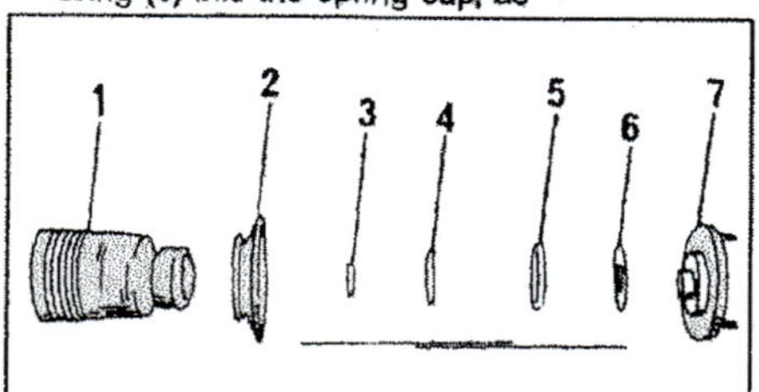

Fig. 5.6. — The parts on the upper end of a spring strut. Items 3, 4, 5 and 6 must be replaced when a spring strut has been dismantled.

1 Rebound rubber
2 Spring cup
3 Bronze bush
4 Needle thrust bearing
5 Seal
6 Needle thrust bearing
7 Upper spring bearing

- Insert the rebound rubber (1) into the inside of the spring cup and fit the seal (5) in a similar manner as shown in Fig. 5.7. Lubricate the sealing ring and place the needle thrust bearing locating washer (3) and then the strut bearing (7) over the assembled parts.
- Clamp the spring strut in upright position into a vice

and pull the piston rod out of the spring strut as far as it will go. Fit the compressed spring over the spring strut and, engaging the lower coil with its stop. Place the spacer over the end of the spring and the assembled strut bearing over the spring strut.

- Fit a washer and a new self-locking nut to the end of the piston rod and tighten the nut to 7.0 kgm (50.5 ft.lb.). The piston rod must be held against rotation as shown in Fig. 5.5 until it is possible to apply a socket with torque wrench to the nut. The latter should be tight enough to keep the piston rod in position.

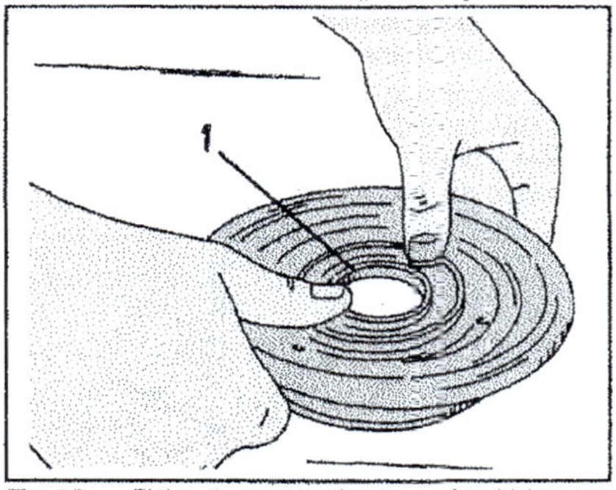

Fig. 5.7. — Fitting the needle thrust bearing (1) into the upper spring cup.

- Slowly release the spring compressor, at the same time checking that the spring coils enter their locations at top and bottom.

5.1.4. INSTALLATION

The installation of the spring strut is a reversal of the removal procedure. Note the following points:

- Insert the spring strut with the studs into the holes and fit the three nuts without tightening them. Always use new self-locking nuts.
- Lift the complete front suspension with the jack and fit the screw in the four bolts shown in Fig. 5.2. Tighten the bolts evenly alround to 12.5 kgm (90 ft.lb.).
- Tighten the three nuts securing the upper spring strut bearing to 1.5 kgm (11 ft.lb.).
- Lower the vehicle to the ground and tighten the wheel bolts to 18 kgm (130 ft.lb.).

5.2. Removal and Installation of a Front Suspension Unit on one Side

The following instructions must be followed when the complete steering knuckle together with the drive shaft is to be removed. It should be noted that the inner mounting of the suspension arm must be tightened when the weight of the vehicle is resting on its wheels. This will pre-tension the rubber mountings to their correct operating position.

Attention: The hub grease cap is normally removed with a puller to be suitable for re-fitting. A damaged cap must be replaced.

- Slacken the wheel bolts and remove the hub grease cap with a strong screwdriver or a small chisel. It may be easier to remove the wheel as you will be able to insert the chisel straight into the gap. In this case slacken the drive shaft nut before the wheel is removed. *Never attempt to slacken the nut when the vehicle is on chassis stands.*

- After slackening the drive shaft nut, place the front end of the vehicles on chassis stands and remove the wheel (as may be the case).

The front suspension will now look as shown in Fig. 5.8. The remaining operations are carried out by referring to this illustration.

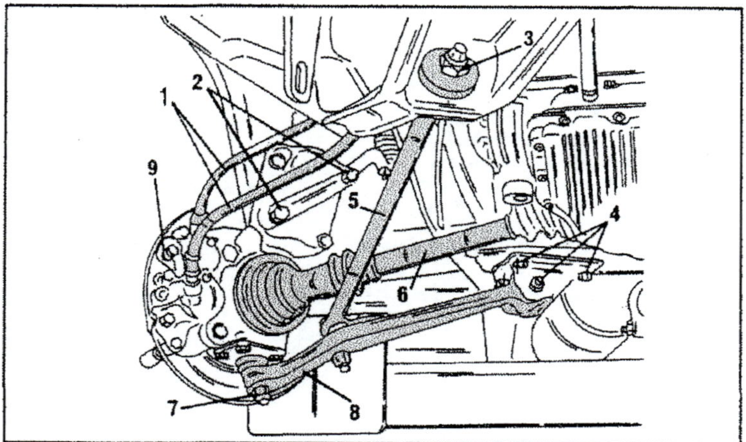

Fig. 5.8. — View of the front suspension on one side with the wheel removed.

1 Brake hoses
2 Steering lever bolts
3 Reaction strut bar nut, 10 kgm
4 Suspension arm bolts
5 Reaction strut
6 Drive shaft
7 Suspension ball joint
8 Suspension arm
9 Brake caliper

- Separate the connection between the brake hoses (1) and the metal pipes on the chassis. Plug the open ends of hoses/pipes in suitable manner. Sticky tape is useful for this job.
- Remove the bolts (2) securing the steering lever and remove the lever. The track rod can remain on the lever.
- Remove the nut (3) at the end of the reaction strut bar. Remove the washers, but keep them in the order of removal.
- Remove the bolts (4) of the suspension arm mounting at the inside (do not remove the fulcrum pin).
- In the engine compartment remove the three nuts securing the upper sring strut bearing. Support the suspension assembly from below as it will drop as soon as the last nut has been removed.
- Withdraw the steering knuckle towards the outside, guiding the drive shaft and the reaction strut accordingly. If the drive shaft is to be removed, follow the instructions in Section 4.1 for the side in question. Otherwise withdraw the steering knuckle from the end of the drive shaft. Retain the drive shaft with a piece of wire as horizontally as possible.

Install the removed assembly as follows:

- Insert the sporing strut from below, at the same time guiding the three studs into the upper spring strut mounting. Fit the nuts and tighten them to 1.5 kgm (11 ft.lb.).
- Swing the steering knuckle towards the outside and guide the drive shaft through the steering knuckle and the wheel hub.
- Fit the suspension arm mounting bracket, insert the bolts and tighten them to 5.0 kgm (36 ft.lb.).
- Insert the reaction strut into the chassis bracket (make sure the parts on the strut are fitted in correct order), fit the washer and screw on the nut. Tighten the nut (3) in Fig. 5.8 to a torque of 10.0 kgm (72 ft.lb.).
- Refit the steering lever to the steering knuckle. The bolts are tightened to 12.5 kgm (90 ft.lb.).
- Re-connect the brake pipes to the brake hoses. Bleed the brake system as described in Section "Brakes".
- Refit the wheel and lower the vehicle to the ground.
- Coat the drive shaft threads with "Loctite" and tighten the nut to 50.0 kgm (360 ft.lb.). You will obviously need a torque wrench of the necessary strength.
- Finally tighten the wheel bolts to a torque reading of 18.0 kgm (130 ft.lb.).

5.3. Dismantling and Aseembling a Front Axle Unit

After the front axle unit has been removed in the described manner you will be able to dismantle it to replace individual parts. All tightening torques are given in Fig. 5.1.

- If the suspension arm is to be removed together with the suspension ball joint, remove the bolts from the bottom of the steering knuckle. Otherwise remove the ball joint nut from the bottom of the steering knuckle and separate the joint stud with a suitable puller.
- Remove the reaction strut from the suspension arm. Keep the mounting parts with the strut, as the inserted shims will be required to obtain the correct castor. Depending on the model year, are up to three shims can be fitted.
- Unscrew the suspension arm from the mounting bracket. If a new suspension arm is fitted, tighten the bolt (6) in Fig. 5.1 to 9.0 kgm (65 ft.lb.) when the wheels are resting on the ground. Note that suspension arms are not the same for all models. Differences will be found in the diameter of the mounting bush.

5.4. Steering Knuckle and Wheel Bearings

The replacement of the wheel bearings is not a straight-forward operation, as a dioal gauge with a suitable holder are required to adjust the wheel bearing clearance. Required are also a puller and press mandrels, which can, however, be substituted by make-shift or conventional tools.

The steering knuckle must be removed, i.e. either the spring strut or the complete front axle unit must be removed as already described. A wheel bearing can then be removed as follows:

- Remove the wheel hub from the steering knuckle. Alternative methods are available. Either you place the steering knuckle under a press and remove the hub from the rear, using a suitable press mandrel or you use a puller, as shown in Fig. 5.9 and push out the wheel hub. The pressure of the centre spindle must be applied to the outer diameter of the hub, i.e. a suitable place must be placed over the hub before the puller is applied. The spindle can can then be tightened.

- Place the steering knuckle over a vice and drive the two bearings (2) and (5) in Fig. 5.10 out of the knuckle. The two grease seals (1) and (6) will come away together with the bearins.
- Remove the two outer bearing races from opposite sides of the steering knuckle. Collect the bearing spacer and the adjusting shims.

Thoroughly clean all parts and check them systematically for wear. Grease seals must always be replaced, once removed. Discolourated bearings are also due for replacement.

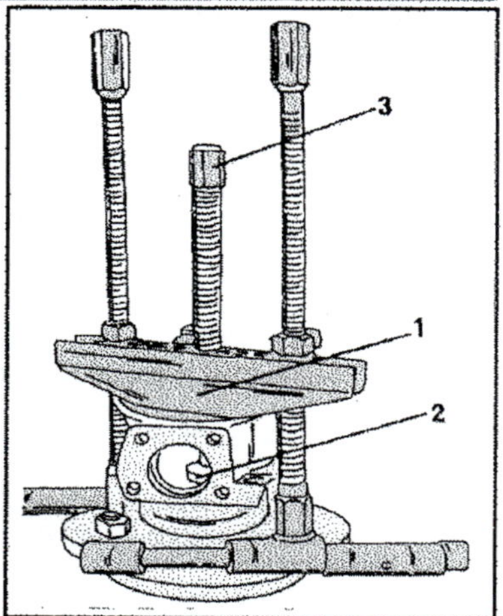

Fig. 5.9. — A wheel hub can be removed with a puller (1). Place thrust washer (2) over the wheel hub face. The spindle (3) is tightened to push out the hub.

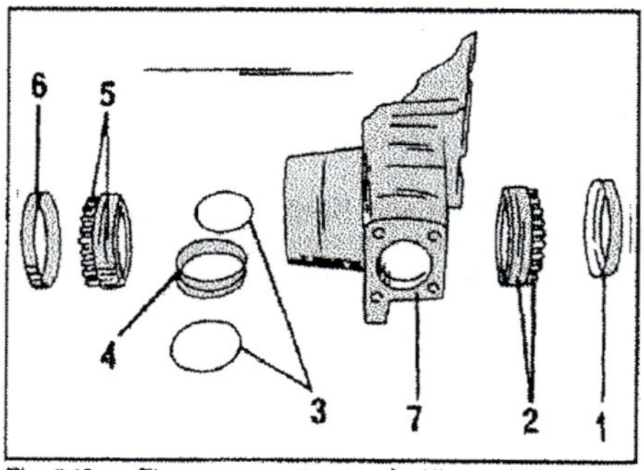

Fig. 5.10. — The component parts of a dismantled steering knuckle.

1 Inner grease seal
2 Inner wheel bearing
3 Adjusting shims
4 Bearing spacer
5 Outer grease seal
6 Outer grease seal
7 Steering knuckle

The wheel bearings are refitted in the following manner. The description is based on the use of the special tools, but suitable alternative tools can be used as applicable. Fig. 5.11 shows the press mandrels used to draw the bearings into the steering knuckle.

- Make sure that the inside of the steering knuckle is clean and drive the outer bearing races from opposite sides into the steering knuckle with the cone face towards the outside. Take care not to damage the bearing running surface.

The bearing clearance (play) must now be adjusted. The work must be carried out with great care, as badly adjusted wheel bearings will soon lead to failure. The bearing clearance must be adjusted to 0.025 - 0.10 mm and must be measured with a dial gauge.

- Clean the inside of the fitted outer bearing race, grease the bearing (6) in Fig.

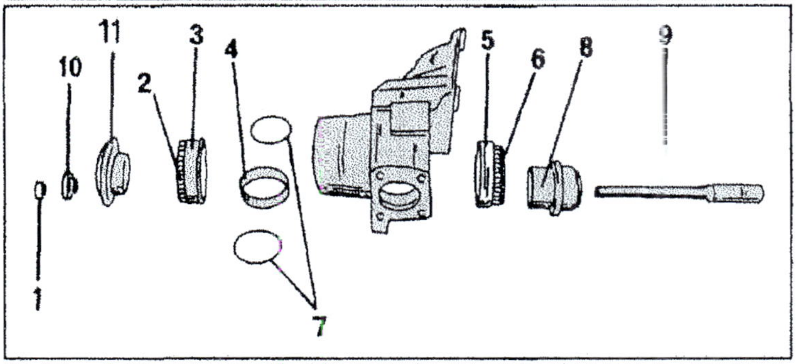

Fig. 5.11. — Details for the assembly of the steering knuckle and the wheel bearings, using the special tools.

1 Nut
2 Outer wheel bearing
3 Outer bearing race, outside
4 Bearing spacer
5 Outer bearing race, inside
6 Inner wheel bearing
7 Adjusting shims
8 Thrust piece
9 Assembly bolt
10 Thrust piece
11 Thrust piece

5.10 and tap the bearing in position.

- Insert the bearing spacer (4) from the outside into the steering knuckle, with a shim (7) on either side. The guide (8) will ensure that the parts are kept in the centre. Otherwise bring the knuckle in an upright position and place the parts in the centre of the bore.
- Grease the inner wheel bearing (2) and insert it into the other side. The two thrust pieces (11) and (10) are now inserted as shown. Fit a long bolt (9) through the bearing assembly and fit the nut (1) to the end. Tighten the bolt to 1.0 kgm (7.2 ft.lb.).
- Apply a ring spanner to the nut and rotate the wheel bearings a few times to settle them in position.

Note If the special tools cannot be obtained, use a long bolt. Suitable sockets can be used in place of items (8) and (11). Large washers and a nut complete the make-shift arrangement.

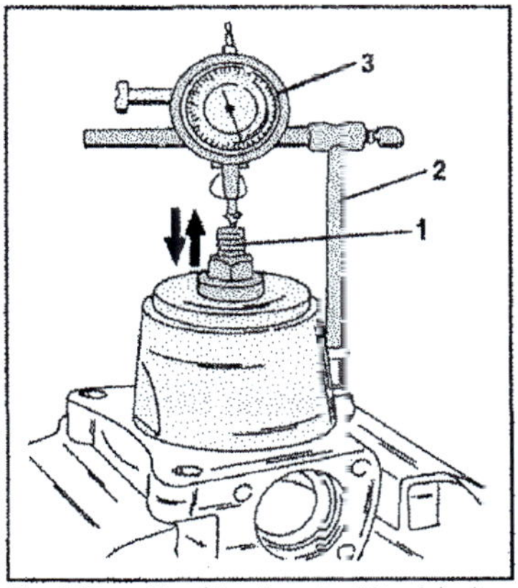

Fig. 5.12. — Checking the wheel bearing clearance. Place the stylus of the dial gauge (3) ont the end of the bolt (1). Moving the bolt up and down will indicate the clearance of the dial gauge. The dial gauge holder (2) is attached to the steering knuckle.

The pre-load of the wheel bearings must now be adjusted. Again the description is based on the special tools, but a suitable dial gauge, arranged as shown in Fig. 5.12, will do.

- Clamp the steering knuckle into a vice as shown in Fig. 5.12, attach the dial gauge holder and place the stylus onto the end of the bolt as shown in the illustration. Set the dial gauge to "Zero".
- Grip the end of the bolt (1) and move it to and fro, at the same time observing the dial gauge reading. The indication should be between 0.025 and 0.10 mm.
- If the clearance is not within the limits, shims (7) in Fig. 5.10 must be increase or descrased in their thickness. Shims are availabe in different sizes.
- Remove the used tools and take out the wheel bearings, if shims must be replaced.
- Grease the bearing (5) in Fig. 5.10 and drive it into the steering knuckle. Fit the grease seal (6) into the steering knuckle until the outside is flash.

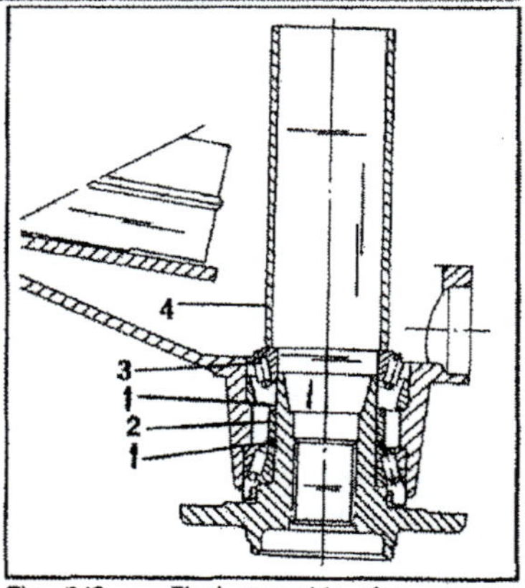

Fig. 5.13 — Final assembly of a steering knuckle.

1 Adjusting shim
2 Bearing spacer
3 Inner wheel bearing
4 Fitting tube

- Place the wheel hub with the flange onto the press table and drive the steering knuckle and the inserted bearing over the hub. A piece of tube of suitable diameter must be used. The tube must be placed against the inner bearing race. Drive the bearing fully over the hub.
- Place the selected shim, the bearing spacer and the second shim into the inside of the steering knuckle.
- Fit the well greased inner bearing race (2) into the steering knuckle, using a suitable piece of tube and fit a new oil seal (1). A sectional view of the final assembly stage is shown in Fig. 5.13.

5.5. Reaction Strut

The reaction sturt can be seen in Fig. 5.8 in fitted position. A reaction strut must, for example, be removed if the castor requires adjustment, as the adjusting shims at the rear of the strut may have to be replaced.

Remove a strut bar as follows:

- Remove the nut at the rear of the strut and withdraw the fitted parts.
- At the bottom of the suspension arm remove the nut securing the strut bar and remove the strut from the suspension arm and the chassis bracket. Note the installation order of all parts.

Installation is a reversal of the removal procedure. Shims removed during removal must be fitted to the original position. Tighten the strut to the specified torque. There may be no need to check the castor adjustment, unless the bar, the rubber bushes or the washers have been replaced.

If the front wheel geometry must be checked refer to the relevant section in the next Chapter.

6. STEERING

6.0. Technical Data

Type: .... Rack and pinion steering
Number of pinion teeth: 5
Number of rack teeth: 25
Steering Ratio:
 Mechanical steering: .... 25.2 : 1
 Power-steering: .... 16.0 : 1

Turning Circle between Kerb Stones:
 Wheelbase 2315 mm: .... 4.65 m
 Wheelbase 2923 mm: .... 5.70 m
 Wheelbase 3200: .... 6.15 m
 Wheelbase 3650: .... 6.95 m

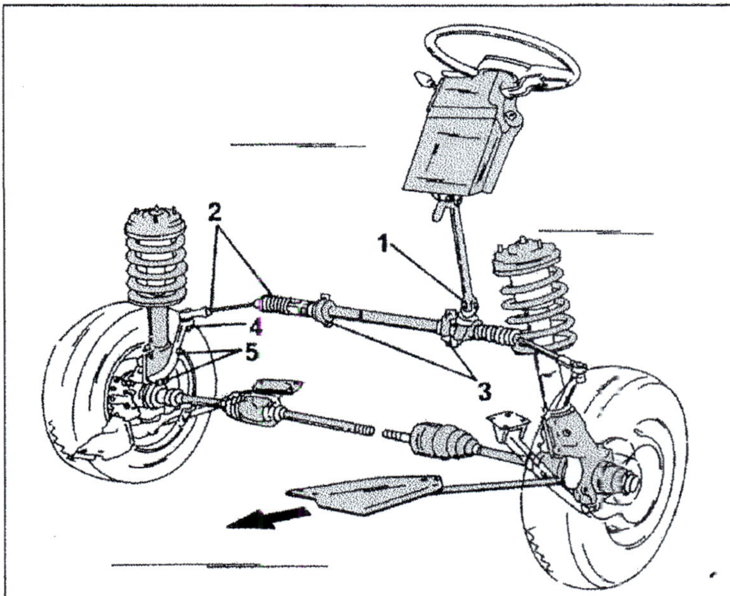

Fig. 6.1. — View of the fitted steering. The numbers refer to the tightening torques. The arrow points in the direction of drive.

1 = 2.5 kgm
2 = 6.0 kgm
3 = 5.0 kgm
4 = 5.5 kgm
5 = 12.5 kgm

Power Steering:
Manufacturer: .... Saginaw T.C.
Capacity of reservoir: .... approx. 0.3 litres
Capacity of system: .... 1.1 litres
Type of fluid: .... ATF fluid

6. Steering

Delivery of steering pump at 1500 rpm:	5.0 litres at 3.5 bar
Min. steering pressure:	3.0 bar
Max. steering pressure (steering in lock):	79 ± 4 bar
Diameter of crankshaft pulley:	140.0 mm
Diameter of steering pump pulley:	130.0 mm
Steering Lock Angles:	
Inner wheel:	38 - 41°
Outer wheel:	32 - 35°

Front Wheel Alignment:

Camber angle (depending on model):	1° 30' to 2° 30'
Caster Angle:	
To July 1990:	0 to 1°
From July 1990:	0° 15' to 1° 15'
1800:	0 to 0° 30'
Toe-in:	0.5 ± 1.0 mm (0.02 to 0.04 in.)
King-pin inclination:	9° 30' to 11° 30'

6.1. Steering Unit

6.1.0. REMOVAL

- Place the front end of the vehicle on chassis stands and remove the front wheels.
- Turn the steering into full lock to one side and remove the nut securing und track rod ball joint to the steering lever. Use a suitable puller, as shown in Fig. 6.2 and separate the ball joint connection.
- Turn the steering into the opposite lock and carry out the same operations on the other side.
- From the inside of the engine compartment remove the nut from the end of the clamp bolt (Fig. 6.3). The bolt secures the upper part of the steering column to the steering column universal joint. To separate the connection grip the steering wheel in pull it sharply upwards.

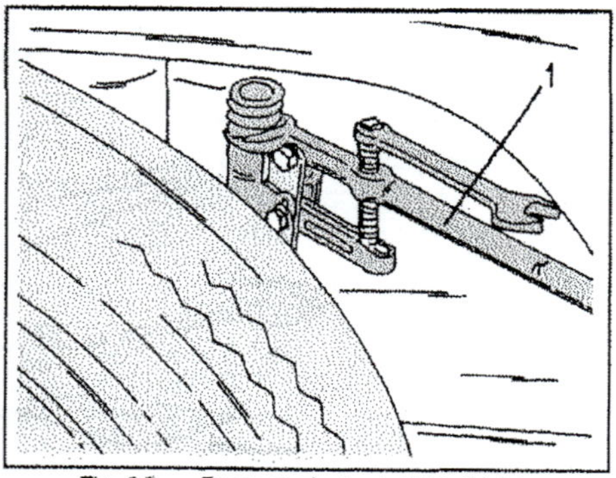

Fig. 6.2. — Removal of a track rod ball joint.

- Remove the screws securing the flior cover underneath the pedal assembly and remove the cover together with the rubber seal.
- In the now open floor board you will see a second universal joint. Remove the nut and the clamp bolt and remove the lower steering shaft together wuth the cover and the rubber seal out of the vehicle.
- Remove the two mounting clamps for the steering unit from below the vehicle. One clamp is situated at the position shown in Fig. 6.4. The second clamp is fitted to the opposite side of the steering box.

- Remove the steering box sideways out of the vehicle, guiding the track rods as necessary.

If the track rod ball joints are to be replaced, slacken the locknuts and unscrew the track rod ends, counting the number of turns and if apllicable half-turns necessary to fully unscrew a joint. Write the value down for each side for later fitting of the joint track rod end. If the new joint(s) are fitted in the same position they will set the track rods to the correct length for the adjustment of the toe-in.

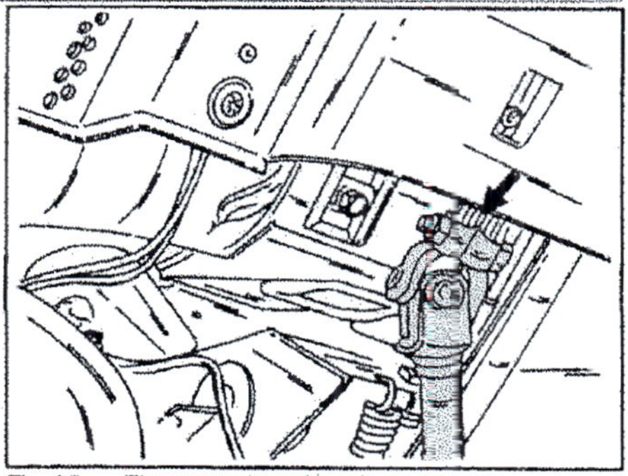

Fig. 6.3. — The arrow shows the clamp bolt of the universal joint between the upper and lower steering shaft.

6.1.1. INSTALLATION

The installation is a reversal of the removal, noting the following points:

- Check the condition of the steering rubber boots and make sure the boot clamps are tight.
- The securing bolts are tightened to 5.0 kgm (36 ft.lb.).
- If new track rod ball joints are to be fitted, screw them onto the end of the rod(s). After the end pieces have been fitted, measure the dimension "x" in Fig. 6.5. Correct the position of the end piece of the dimension is not exactly 322.0 mm. Tighten the locknut to 6.0 kgm (43.5 ft.lb.). Even if only one track rod end has been replaced or has been unscrewed set the rod to the specified dimension before the track rod is connected.

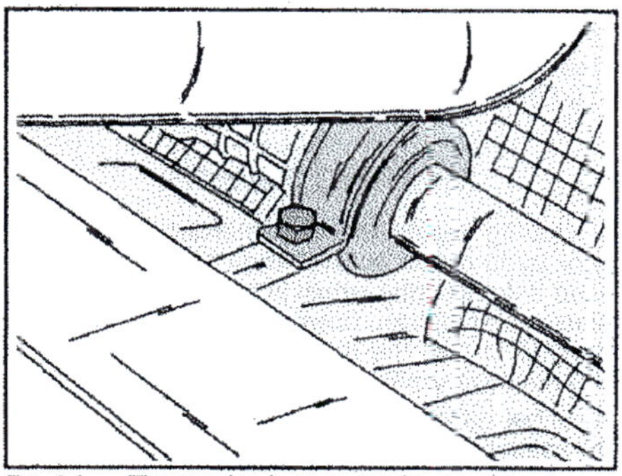

Fig. 6.4. — The steering is secured with mounting clamps on both sides. A similar attachment is on the other side.

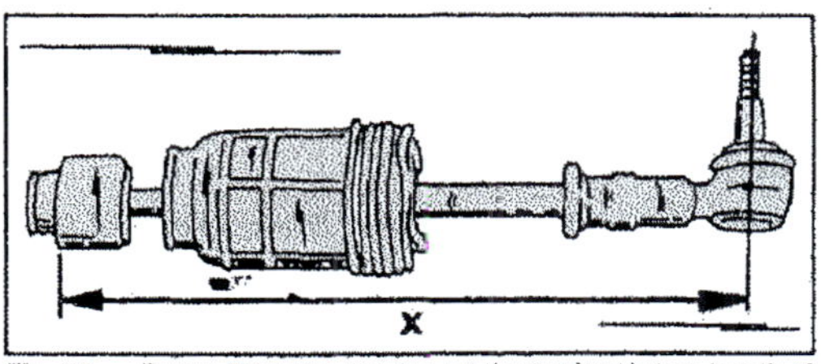

Fig. 6.5. — Before fitting the steering set the track rods to a length of 322.0 mm (dimension "X").

- Clean the ball joint stud(s) of oil or grease and connect with the steering lever(s). Tighten the nut(s) to 5.5 kgm (40 ft.lb.).
- Set the steering to the central position. To do this, undo the steering gaiter on

the L.H. side and pull it away from the steering box. Now turn the steering pinion until dimension "X" in Fig. 6.6 is exactly 76.0 mm. Use a ruler to measure. Without moving the steering rack, re-attach the steering gaiter.

- Set the steering wheel to the centre position and reconnect the two steering universal joints. This must be carried out without rotating the steering wheel or the steering pinion. Tighten the clamp bolts with 2.5 kgm (18 ft.lb.).
- Check the toe-in setting of the front wheels as described in Section 6.5.

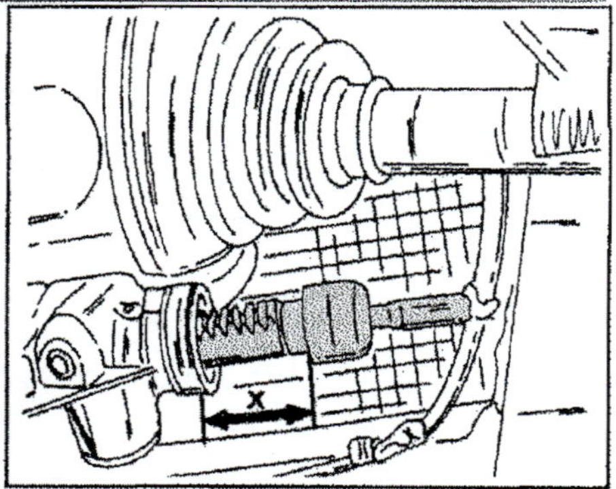

Fig. 6.6 — Turn the steering pinion until the end of the steering rack protrudes by 76.0 mm (dimension "X"). The rubber gaiter must be removed to measure.

6.1.2. STEERING REPAIRS

The steering should not be dismantled. In case of wear or damage fit a new steering or try to obtain an exchange steering. Steerings with excessive play (play is noticed if the steering wheel is turned from left to right or visa versa and before the wheels respond) can, however, be adjusted. For safety reasons, however, we recommend to take the removed steering to your dealer where it can be checked and if necessary adjusted professionally.

The rubber gaiters can be replaced after disconnecting the track rods. You will have to assess how long the gaiter is damaged, as dirt may have entered the steering housing/rack. Before fitting a new gaiter, turn the steering wheel to full lock and clean off all old grease as good as possible. Then re-grease the steering rack and fit the gaiter.

The replacement of the track rod ball joints is covered during the removal and installation of the steering unit.

6.2. Steering Centre Position

The steering must be in the centre position during checks and adjustments of the toe-in or other operations. Proceed as follows:

- Turn the steering wheel fully into one lock and attach a piece of sticky tape at the top of the steering wheel rim. Mark a line with a pencil into the tape.
- Turn the steering wheel into the opposite lock, counting the exact number of rotations.
- Divide the counted turns by 2 and turn the steering wheel towards the centre. The steering wheel must be in the centre position. If this is not the case, adjust the track rod on the side in question to set the wheel to the centre position. Check the position of the steering wheel and re-set it if necessary.

6.3. Replacing the Steering Shaft

The steering shaft can be replaced without removing the complete steering. First disconnect the steering shaft universal joint (see Fig. 6.3) by removing the clamp bolt and pulling the steering wheel upwards until the joint has disengaged.

Disconnect the lower universal joint from the steering pinion. To do this, remove the cover underneath the pedal assembly to gain access to the clamp bolt. Withdraw the shaft upwards to disengage it.

The installation is a reversal of the removal procedure. To set the steering rack to the centre position, remove the steering gaiter (rubber boot) on the L.H. side and pull it back. Turn the steering pinion until the rack protrudes by exactly 760 mm (dimension "X" in Fig. 6.6). Refit the gaiter and secure it.

Tighten the two clamp bolts at top and bottom to 2.5 kgm (18 ft.lb.). Make sure the rubber seal is fitted correctly under the floor panel cover.

6.4. Replacing a Track Rod

It is possible to replace a track rod when the steering is fitted, but it may be far easier to carry out the work when the steering is removed. This concerns mainly the locking of the new ball joint housing to the steering rack, as the access is rather difficult.

If the complete track rod is to be replaced replace it together with the ball joint housing as the old housing may have been damaged by peening the housing to the steering rack.

- Remove the rubber gaiter from the track rod and the side of the rack housing. Cut the old clamp band. On the other side roll back the two rubber rings securing the gaiter to the track rod. Move the gaiter towards the outside of the track rod.
- Clamp the steering box into a vice (soft-metal jaws) and unscrew the ball joint housing. Workshops use a special wrench, but a pair of pliers or grips can be used. The round-shaped ball joint housing is fairly tight and more than one attempt may be required. Definitely replace the ball joint housing if removed in the described manner.

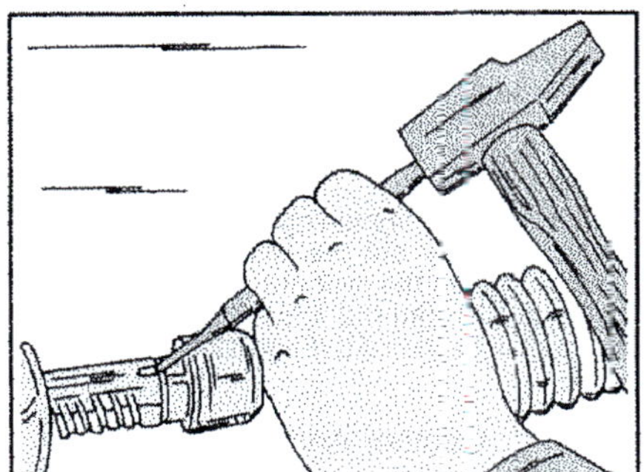

Fig. 6.7. — The track rod ball joint housing is secured as shown.

- Unscrew the track rod and clamp it into a vice. Slacken the track rod and unscrew the track rod end piece, counting the numbers of turns required to remove it.
- Screw the new track rod with the new ball joint housing to the rack and tighten it as much as possible with the grips.
- Secure the ball joint housing to the steering rack. The rack housing is clamped into a vice and the lug on the ball joint housing is peened into the groove of the

rack as shown in Fig. 6.7. Take care not to split the metal.

- Grease the steering rack and refit the rubber galter.
- Fit the track rod ball joint the same number of turns and measure the length of the track rod as shown in Fig. 6.5. Make the necessary corrections.
- Tighten the locknut to 6.0 kgm (43.5 ft.lb.). This may, however, be carried out after the toe-in of the front wheels has been checked and adjusted.

6.5. Front Wheel Geometry

The front wheel geometry must be checked when the engine has its kerb weight, i.e. unladen with coolant, oil and fuel.

6.5.0. Caster Angle

The caster angle can be adjusted by placing washers of 2.5 mm thickness at the position shown in Fig. 6.8 on the inside of the reaction strut rod mounting on the chassis. Between 1 and 3 washers are used. It should be noted that the caster angle has been changed over the years. Some values are given in Section 6.0, but we recommend to obtain the latest values from your workshop.

The castor angle can be measured with conventional equipment, but an optical measurement by a specialist is prefered. If the obtained values are outside the limits check the front suspension for distortion or better still have it checked professionally before you start fitting or removing additional shims.

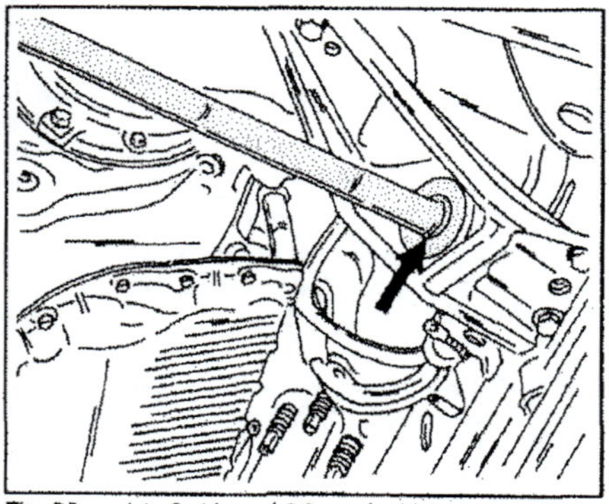

Fig. 6.8 — 1 to 3 shims of 2.5 mm in thickness can be inserted at the position shown by the arrow in order to adjust the castor angle of the front wheels.

Note the following tightening torques if you carry out the work yourself: Tighten the rear nut of the reaction strut to 14.0 kgm (101 ft.lb.) and the front nut to 10.0 kgm (7.2 ft.lb.). The removal and installation of the reaction strut is described in Section 5.5 (Page 122).

6.5.1. Camber Angle

The camber should be checked optically. If a mechanical camber gauge is used, follow the instructions of the manucturer. The difference between the two sides must not exceed 30'. The camber cannot be adjusted. Incorrect values are mainly due to distortion in the front suspension.

5.5.2. Toe-in Adjustment

The front wheel toe-in can be measured with a mechanical tracking gauge. The toe-in is set to 0.5 ± 1.0 mm, i.e. the front wheels have toe-in. Measure as follows:

- Check the tyre pressures and correct as necessary.
- Place the vehicle on level ground and turn the front wheels into the straight-ahead position.
- Place the tracking gauge with the pins against the wheel rims (level of wheel hubs) and set the gauge to "Zero". Mark the contact points with chalk or a spot of paint.
- Push the vehicle forward by half a turn of the wheels, i.e. the marked spot must now be at the rear, again level with the wheel hubs.
- Push the tracking gauge underneath the vehicle and place one pin against the marked spot. The pin on the other side will most probably not reach the rim. Unlock the moveable pin and pull it towards the outside until it can be placed against the rim. Lock the pin in position.
- Remove the tracking gauge and read off the measurement. The indication should be 0.5 mm higher or within the tolerance of 1.0 mm more or less.
- If an adjustment is necessasry, slacken the locknuts at the inside of the two track rod ball joints und turn the track rods by the same amount on both sides. Note that there must be a gap of at least 2.0 mm (0.08 in.) between the track rod ball joint and the locknut face. Make sure that the rubber gaiters cannot twist when the rods are turned. Slacken and re-tighten the gaiter clamp bands if necessary.
- Finally tighten the two locknuts to 6.0 kgm (43.5 ft.lb.). The track rods must be held against rotation.

6.6. Power-Assisted Steering

6.6.0. REMOVAL AND INSTALLATION

- Disconnect the battery.
- From the inside of the passenger compartment remove the cover for the steering universal joint and lift it up.

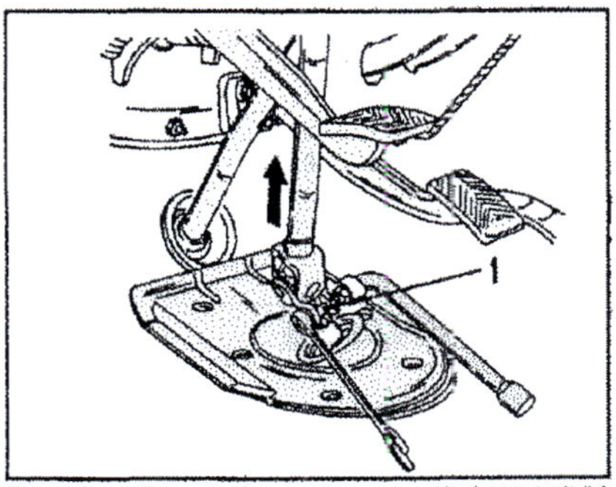

Fig. 6.9. — After slackening the nut and clamp bolt (1) and removing the bolt, push the steering shaft in the direction of the arrow to disengage it from the steering pinion. Tie the shaft to one side.

- Remove the clamp bolt and the nut securing the universal joint as shown in Fig. 6.9. The clamp bolt is driven out and the steering shaft pulled upwards until the joint if free of the steering pinion. Secure the shaft with a piece of wire in this position to have it out of the way.
- Remove the union nut immediately behind the steering pinion. The nut connects the fluid return pipe.
- Jack up the front end of the vehicle and place chassis stands underneath the body. The wheels can be removed to cre-

ate more working pace.

- Remove the fuel filler tube from the crossmember and the tank and withdraw it, as shown in Fig. 6.10.
- Turn the steering into full lock to one side and remove the nut securing und track rod ball joint to the steering lever. Use a suitable puller, as shown in Fig. 6.2 and separate the ball joint connection.
- Turn the steering into the opposite lock and carry out the same operations on the other side.

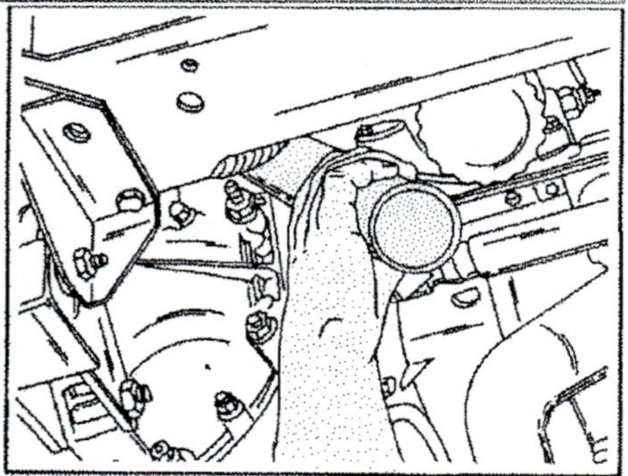

Fig. 6.10. — Removal of the fuel filler tube.

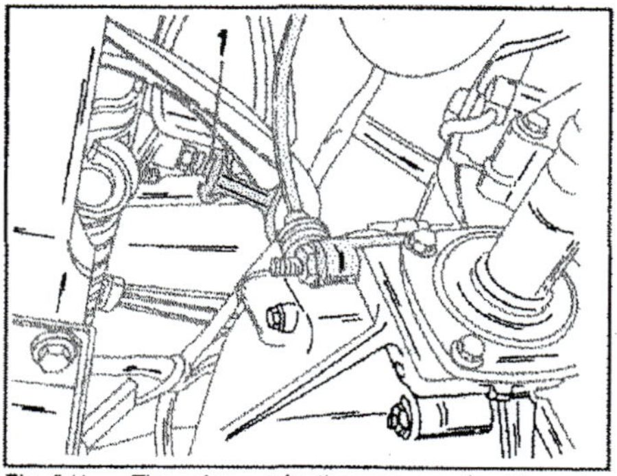

Fig. 6.11. — The union nut for the pressure pipe (1) can be found at the location shown.

- Unscrew the union nut (1) from the rotary valve of the steering box (Fig. 6.11) and withdraw the pipe.
- Suspend the engine on a hoist and remove the rear engine mounting bolt.
- Remove the steering mounting bolts on the L.H. and R.H. side of the steering. Push the R.H. front wheel (if still fitted) to one side and withdraw the steering.

The installation is a reversal of the removal procedure. After filling the steering system (1.1 litres/2 pints) move the steering wheel a few times to and fro, with the engine switched off. This will bleed the steering system of air. Correct the fluid level in the container if necessary. Dexron II fluid, as used for automatic transmission, also known as ATF, is used in the power steering.

7. REAR AXLE AND SUSPENSION

The rear suspension consists of two leaf springs, fitted in longitudinal direction to the chassis. Each spring consists of two main leaves and two auxiliary leaves. It is obvious that due to the different capcities of the various makes and models there are differences in the carrying capcity of the springs. Whenever a spring is replaced, quote the model and the chassis number.

Models with four-wheel drive have different springs.

7. Rear Axle and Suspension

The springs are secured at the centre by two "U" bolts to the rear axle tube. A spring pin with a detachable bracket secures each spring at the front. A spring shackle arrangement with welded-in bolts and detachable shackles is used to attach the springs at the rear. Spring pins and spring shackle pins are rubber-mounted (silent-block mounting).

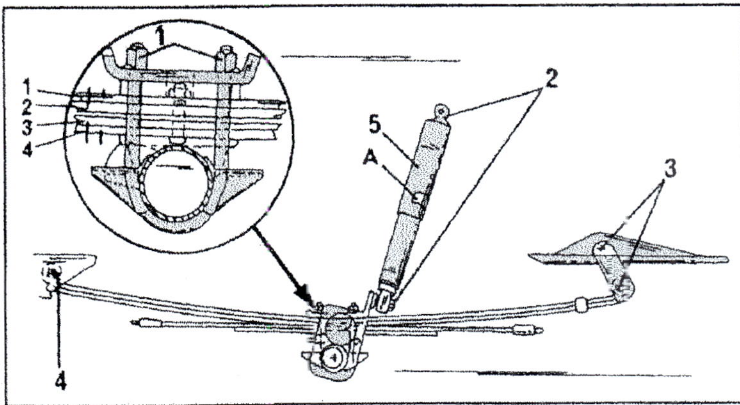

Fig. 7.1. — Side view of the rear suspension on one side in the case of two-wheel drive vehicles. The shock absorber itentification can be found at (A).

1 "U" bolts nut, 8.0 kgm
2 Shock absorber bolts, 5.0 kgm
3 Spring shackle nuts, 12.0 kgm
4 Spring pin nut, 15.0 kgm
5 Shock absorber

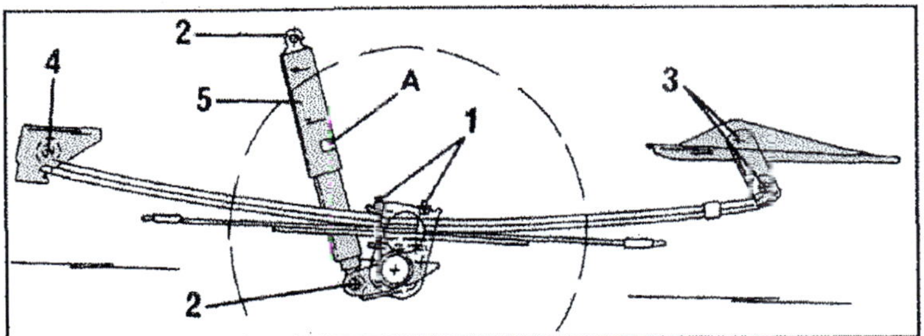

Fig. 7.2. — Side view of the rear suspension on one side in the case of a foor-wheel drive vehicle. The shock absorber identification can be found at "A".

1 "U" bolts nuts, 8.0 kgm
2 Shock absorber nuts, 5.0 kgm
3 Spring shackle nuts, 12.0 kgm
4 Spring bolt nut, 15.0 kgm
5 Shock absorber

Two-way acting telescopic shock absorbers complate the rear suspension, but have different mounting arrangements at the lower mounting. In the case of vehicles with two-wheel drive you will find the dampers secured above the leaf springs, in the case of 4WD vehicles the mounting takes place below the leaf springs. The mounting bolts are also governed by the type of mounting. Figs. 7.1 and 7.2 shows side views of the two rear suspensions used within the vehicle range. Note that different shock absorbers are fitted to the various makes and models. You will find an identification at "A" in the two illustrations.

There also differences in the rear wheel bearings, again depending on the model and capacity of the vehicle.

7.1. Removal and Installation of e Rear Spring

- Slacken the wheel bolts, jack up the rear end of the vehicle and place chassis stands under the side of the body. Remove the wheel. The jack is required later on to lower the axle.
- Follow the brake pipe and separate it at the brake hose connection. First unscrew the pipe union nut and withdraw the pipe. Suitable protect the pipe end (wrap sticky tape around). Drive the spring place out of the hose bracket and withdraw the hose. Again protect the open hose end in suitable manner.
- Place the jack underneath the axle on the side where the spring is to be removed.
- Slacken and remove the nuts (1) in Fig. 7.3 from the ends of the "U" bolts and carefully drive the bolts out of position. To prevent damage to the threads, tap each side of the bolt alternatively until the "U" bolt drops out. Remove the second "U" bolt in the same manner.
- At the rear of the spring unscrew the two nuts shown by the arrows, at the front of the spring remove the nut and the spring pin. The nut is at the inside.
- Unscrew the two spring shackle bracket. At the front unscrew the bolts to free the bracket, at the rear, i.e. near the spring shackle mounting, remove the four bracket mounting bolts.
- Lower the rear axle a few inches on the jack, drive out the spring pin at the front and remove the complete mounting bracket.
- At the rear of the spring take off the spring shackle plate, drive out the two mounting bolts and take off the bracket. The spring can drop during this ope-

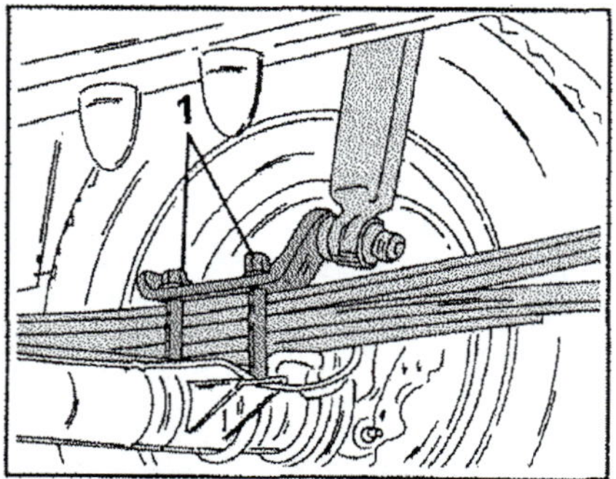

Fig. 7.3. — Attachment of a rear spring to the rear axle tube. The nuts (1) are secured by lock plates. Always replace the latter.

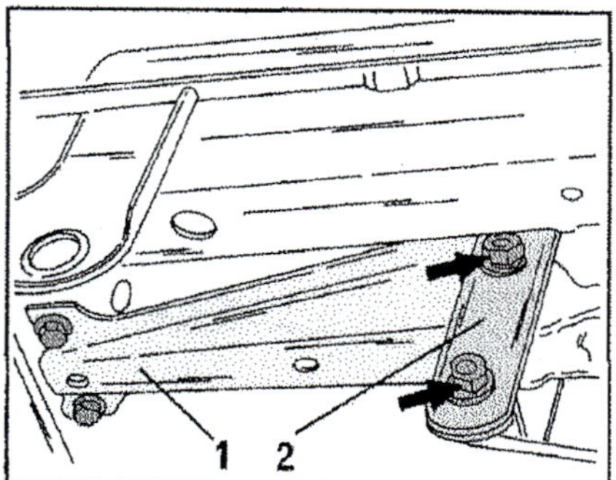

Fig. 7.4. — The arrows show the nuts securing the spring shackle plate (2) which is secured to the spring bracket (1) and the spring.

ration and the necessary care must be taken to keep it "balanced". The spring can now be removed.

The installation of the rear spring is carried out as follows:

- Fit the rear mounting bracket to the spring. To do this, insert the spring shackle pins from the rear, place the shackle plate in position and fit the nuts without tightening them.
- In a similar manner fit the front bracket to the spring, i.e. insert the spring pin and fit the nut. Again tighten the nut finger-tight only.
- Locate the spring underneath the frame and fit the rear bracket with the spring shackle mounting in position on the chassis. The mounting bracket must be centred. In Fig. 7.5 you can see two bores "a" and "b". Two metal drifts are required to centre the holes in the bracket with the holes on the locating pad, but note: a drift of 16 mm diameter must be used for hole "a", a drift of 12 mm diameter must be used for hole "b". After the bracket is in the centred position, tighten the bolts (1) to 5.0 kgm (36 ft.lb.).

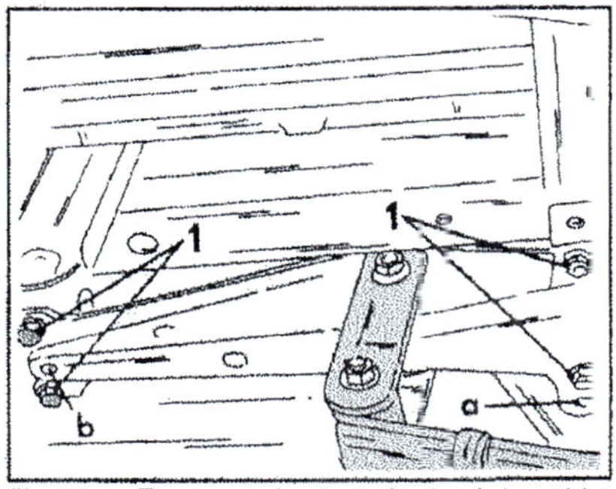

Fig. 7.5. — The rear spring mounting bracket must be centred before tightening the bolts (1). Bores "a" and "b" have different diameters.

- Fit the loosely attached front spring bracket to the chassis and insert and tighten the bolts to 5.0 kgm (36 ft.lb.).
- Lift the axle on the jack and guide the centre bolt of the spring into the hole of the axle. Jack up further until the hole assembly is under tension.
- Drive the "U" bolts from below into the axle. If they won't fit with a slight tap, check them for distortion. When both bolts are in position, fit the spring plate aver the bolt ends and new lock plates. Screw on the nuts and tighten them evenly to 8.0 kgm (58 ft.lb.). Secure the lock plate tabs over the nuts after final installation.
- Guide the brake hose through the bracket and insert the spring plate. Drive the plate in position. Screw the union nut into the hose end asnd tighten it without allowing the brake hose to twist.
- Refit the wheels and lower the vehicle to the ground.
- The rear suspension must now be weighted down to tighten the front and rear of the spring with the correct load. Place enough weight into the rear of the vehicle until the dimension "h" in Fig. 7.6, between the contact area "a" for the rebound rubber (1) and the stop "b" is exactly 107 mm. With the vehicle resting on its wheels this will of course be rather difficult, compared to carrying out the measurement when the vehicle is on a ramp.
- In the set position tighten the remaining spring mounting nuts. Tighten the nuts on the spring shackle mounting to 12.0 kgm (86.5 ft.lb.) and the nut securing the front spring pin to 15.0 kgm (108 ft.lb.).
- Remove the additional weights out of the vehicle and tighten the wheel nuts to 18.0 kgm (130 ft.lb.). *The brakes must be bled of air.*

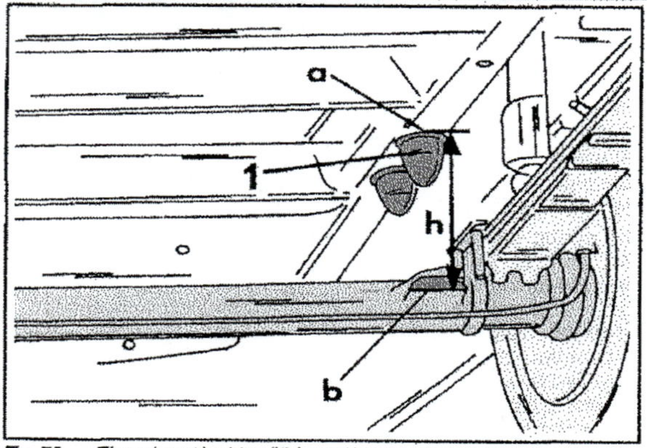

Fig. 7.6. — The rebound rubber (1) is used to measure the height of the rear axle when tightening the springs. Measure between points "a" and "b".

7.2. Removal and Installation of the Rear Axle

- Slacken the wheel bolts, lift up the rear end of the vehicle and place chassis stands in position. The vehicle must be high enough to roll out the rear axle with the wheels attached.
- Follow the routing of the brake pipe and separate the connection between brake line and brake hose. First unscrew the union nut and pull out the pipe end. Immediately protect the open end in suitable manner (sticky tape). Knock out the spring plate and remove the hose fitting out of the metal bracket. Again protect the open hose end by closing it off. Fig. 7.7 shows the fitted hose.
- Also referring to Fig. 7.7 disconnect the operating linkage for the brake pressure regulator (4) from the lever (5) at the position shown.
- Unscrew the nut from the end of the handbrake cable at the equaliser lever connection and disengage the cable at all attachment points.
- Place a mobile jack underneath the rear axle and lift the axle until the shock absorbers are slightly compressed. Remove the shock absorber mountings at the top and the bottom and take out the units.
- Check that the axle is secu-

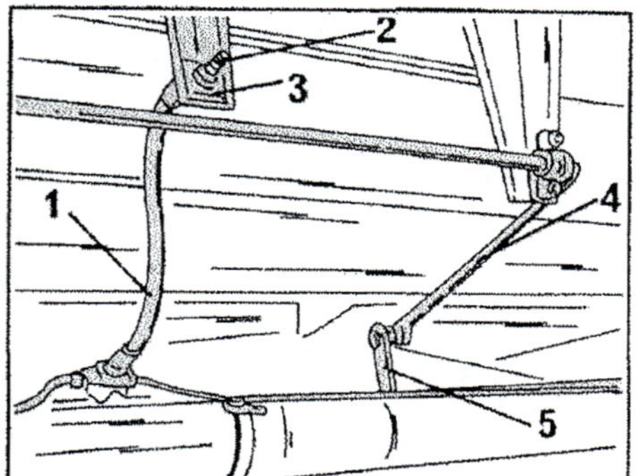

Fig. 7.7. — The items shown must be disconnected during removal of the rear axle.

1 Brake hose
2 Brake pipe
3 Spring plate
4 Operating linkage for brake pressure regulator
5 Operating lever

rely supported on the jack and remove the bolts securing the front spring mounting bracket and the spring shackle mounting at the rear. There is no need to slacken and/or remove the spring pin or the shackle pin nuts.

- Remove the exhaust system where it is attached near the rear axle and push it to one side. Alternatively remove the sections of the system near the rear axle.

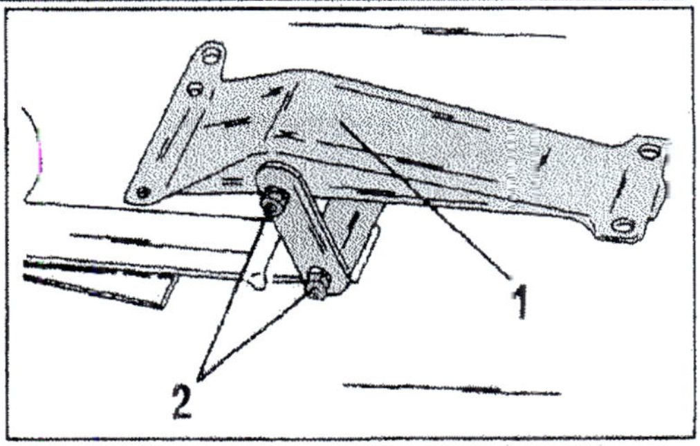

Fig. 7.8. — The rear spring mounting bracket (1) and the spring shackle mounting (2).

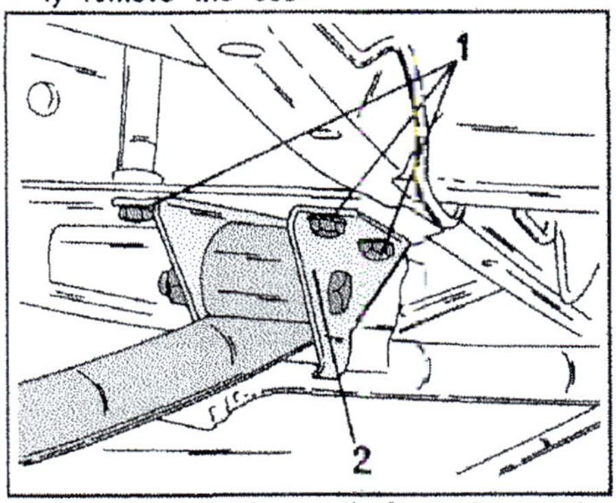

Fig. 7.9. — The bolts (1) secure the front spring mounting bracket (2) to the chassis.

- Slowly lower the rear axle on the jack until the wheels touch the ground. Withdraw the axle towards the rear. It is obvious that help is required, as the axle must be held in position on the jack until it is free of the chassis.

The installation of the rear axle is made more easy when the spring pin and the shackle pin nuts are slackened before the axle is lifted in position.

- Roll the axle underneath the vehicle and lift it in position until the rear mounting bracket (1) in Fig. 7.8 is snug against the mounting face on the chassis. Fit the mounting bolts without tightening them fully.
- Centre the mounting bracket as described during the installation of the rear springs, i.e. the bracket must be centred as shown in Fig. 7.5, utilising the centering bores "a" and "b" and suitable drifts. Tighten the bolts to 5.0 kgm (36 ft.lb.).
- Lift the axle further, as required until the front spring mounting bracket is against the chassis. Fit the bolts (1) in Fig. 7.9 without tightening them fully. Check that all bolts are situated in the centre of the elongated holes and then tighten them to 5.0 kgm (36 ft.lb.).
- Refit the shock absorbers without tightening the bolts and nuts.
- Re-connect the brake hose to the brake pipe, the linkages for the pressure regulator and the handbrake cable. The handbrake must be adjusted as described later on.
- The rear suspension must now be loaded down as described during the installation of the rear springs. Refer to Page 133 and Fig. 7.6.

- Tighten the spring shackle bolt nuts to 12.0 kgm (86.5 ft.lb.) and the spring pin nut to 15.0 kgm 108 ft.lb.). The shock absorber mountings are tightened to 5.0 kgm (36 ft.lb.) at both ends.
- Remove the weights out of the cargo room. Finally adjust the handbrake and bleed the brake syste.

7.3. Shock Absorbers — Removal and Installation

- Place the rear of the vehicle on chassis stands and place the jack underneath the centre of the rear axle. Lift the axle until the shock absorbers are compressed, i.e. they are not longer under tension from the springs.
- Remove the shock absorber mountings at the top and at the bottom. Fig. 7.10 shows how a shock absorber can be fitted, i.e. either directly next to the wheel or further towards the centre.

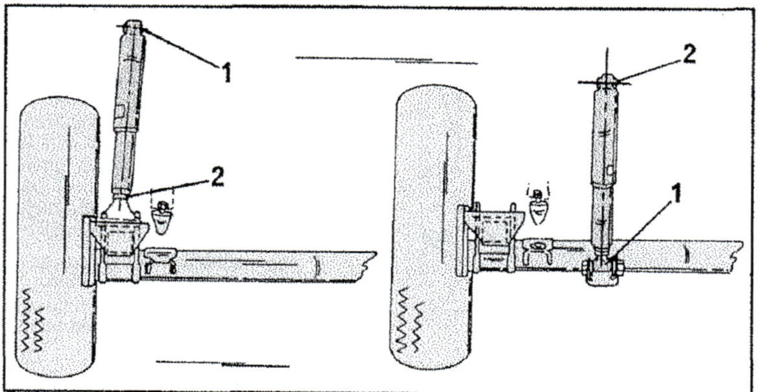

Fig. 7.10. — Fitting arrangement of the shock absorbers. Bolts (1) have a diameter of 10 mm, bolts (2) are 16 mm in diameter.

A shock absorber can be tested as follows: Clamp the unit in upright position into a vice and slowly "pump" it up and down. The resistance must be even through the travel. "Dead" play indicates a faulty shock absorber. Make sure that the shock absorber you obtain is the correct one for the vehicle in question, i.e. model year, carrying capacity, etc.

The installation is a reversal of the removal procedure. Note that the shock absorber bolts have different diameters (see Fig. 7.10). The tightening torque, however, is the same (50 kgm/36 ft.lb.).

7.4. Rear Hubs and Wheel Bearings

The rear wheel bearings must be adjusted after the brake drums have been fitted. The workshop uses a special template to reset the wheel bearing nut by the correct amount to obtain the necessary bearing clearance (play). The following description refers to the special tool, but by studying the illustrations you will see that the adjustment can be carried out without the appliance, mainly if you have some experience with motor cars. A wheel hub is removed as follows:

- Slacken the wheel bolts, place the rear of the vehicle on chassis stands and unscrew the wheel or the wheels.
- Unscrew the guide pin for the wheel (1) and the screw (2) in Fig. 7.11 and remove the brake drum. The drum will be very tight and you will need three M10 x 1.25 bolts to withdraw it. Screw the bolts into the threaded bores "a" and tighten them alternatively until the drum can be taken off.

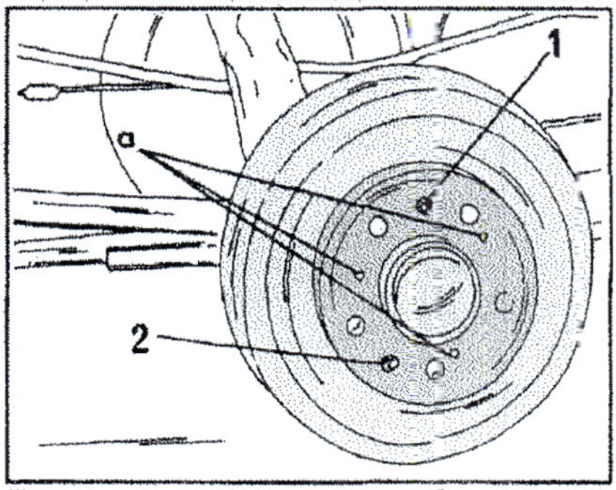

Fig. 7.11. — Removal of a brake drum. Remove the guide pin (1) and the securing screw (2). The extractor bolts are fitted into bores "a".

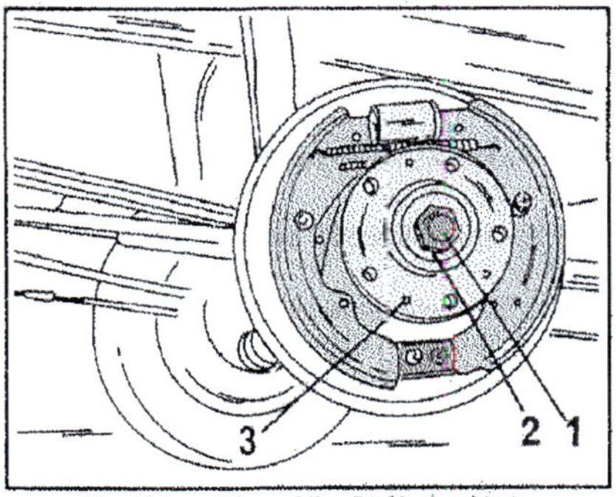

Fig. 7.12. — View of the fitted wheel hub.
1 Hub nut 2 Thrust washer Wheel hub

- Remove the hub grease cap with a small chisel. We must warn you, that the cap could be damaged.
- Find the peening of the wheel bearing nut (2 places) and knock it back. The wheel bearing nut must now be slackened, but note: The nut on the R.H. side has a **left-hand thread**, the nut on the L.H. side has a **right-hand thread**. Unscrew the nut in the applicable direction. To refresh your memory: The nut with left-hand thread is slackened in the direction normally associated with the tightening of a nut or bolt. Remove the wheel hub together with the wheel bearing. Fig. 7.12 shows what you will find at this stage.

If the axle stump must be removed, remove the bolts (2) in Fig. 7.13. Depending on the bolt diameter you will find lock plates (knock them back first) or not. The axle stump (1) can now be removed. Quote the chassis number if a new axle stump is purchased to make sure it is suitable for the bolt diameter of 12 or 14 mm.

- From the inside of the wheel hub remove the wheel bearing. The outer wheel bearing race is driven out of the wheel hub (only if the bearing is to be replaced).
- From the outside of the wheel hub remove the oil seal, take out the bearing and drive out the wheel bearing outer race (only if the bearing is to be replaced).
- Thoroughly clean all bearing parts. If the bearing requires replacement, dismantle the wheel hub as described above.

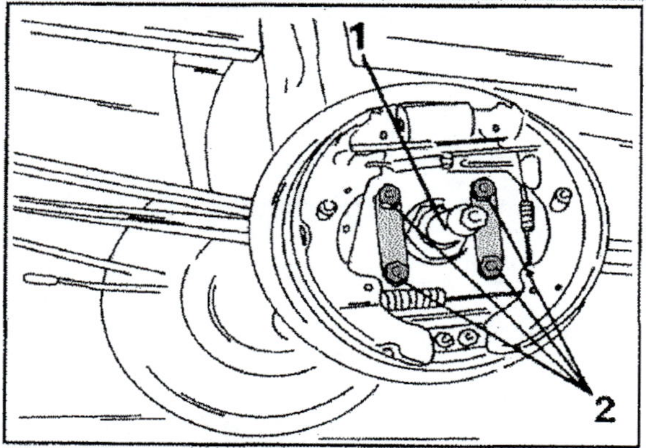

Fig. 7.13. — View of the brake back plate without brake drum. The axle stum (1) is secured with four bolts (2), but note the different diameter which can be found.

Assemble and refit a wheel hub as follows:

- Fill the inside of the wheel hub with heat-resisting grease (wheel bearing grease).
- Drive the two outer wheel bearing races from opposite sides into the wheel hub. Use a good drift to avoid damage.
- Insert the inner wheel bearing cage and fit a new oil seal.
- If the axle stump has been removed, refit it with or without lock plates. Bolts must always be replaced, but note that 12 mm bolts are fitted **with** lock plates and tightened to 10.0 kgm (7.2 ft.lb.), 14 mm bolts are fitted **without** lock plates and tightened to 17.0 kgm (122 ft.lb.).
- Slide the wheel hub over the axle stump and drive it in position, using a soft-metal hammer or plastic mallet. Grease the outer bearing cage, insert it into the wheel hub and place the washer in position. Fit a new wheel bearing nut finger-tight.
- Fit the brake drum and tighten it in position by means of the guide pin and the securing screw (see Fig. 7.11).

The wheel bearing must now be adjusted. Important is the bearing clearance of 0.025 - 0.10 mm. The following description refers to the use of the special template. Otherwise adjust the nut until a check with a dial gauge reveals the correct bearing clearance. *Remember that the R.H. side has a L.H. thread, i.e. the nut must be turned into the opposite direction.* Read the instructions below twice to make sure "you are on the correct side".

- Tighten the wheel bearing nut to 2.0 kgm (14.5 ft.lb.). Rotate the brake drum during the tightening process to settle wheel bearings into their races.
- Completely slacken the nut and then re-tighten it to 0.7 kgm (5 ft.lb.).
- Fit the adjusting gauge with the hexagonal opening over the wheel bearing nut and tighten it to the brake drum as shown in Fig. 7.14. One of the wheel bolts is used to fix the gauge. The bolt is not tightened fully.

The side with the **right-hand thread** is now adjusted as follows:

- Hold the gauge in position and move the bolt (4) in Fig. 7.14 towards the left, as shown by the arrow in Fig. 7.15. Apply the handbrake.
- Slacken the wheel bearing nut by moving the gauge completely towards the left, until the elongated hole of the gauge is stopped by the bolt. This operation can be seen in Fig. 7.16. Tighten the bolt (4) in Fig. 7.14 in this position to 1.0 kgm (7.2 ft.lb.). If the gauge is not used, you will see from the illustration how far the nut is released.
- Secure the nut in this position at two opposite points by peening the shoulder into the axle stump. If the gauge is not used, apply a dial gauge in suitable manner to the brake drum and rest the stylus onto the axle stump. Move the brake drum to and fro and check that the indicated clearance is between 0.025 - 0.10 mm. If this is the case, secure the nut as described.

The side with the **left-hand thread** is adjusted as follows:

- Hold the gauge in position and move the bolt (4) in Fig. 7.14 and with it the brake drum towards the right, i.e. not as shown in Fig. 7.15, but to the other side. Apply the handbrake.
- Slacken the nut by moving the gauge to the opposite side shown in Fig. 7.16.
- Peen the wheel bearing nut to secure it. If the gauge is not used, follow the instructions given above.
- Remove the gauge and release the handbrake. Fit the hub grease cap and the wheel and lower the vehicle to the ground. Tighten the wheel bolts.

7.5. Rear Drive Shafts (Four-wheel Drive)

Note: Never remove both drive shafts at the same time.

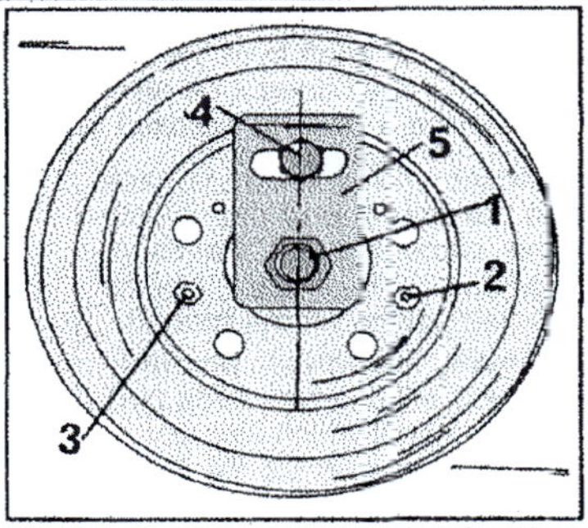

Fig. 7.14. — Fitted gauge to adjust the wheel bearing clearance.
1 Wheel bearing nut
2 Guide pin
3 Brake drum screw
4 Fitted wheel bolt
5 Adjusting gauge

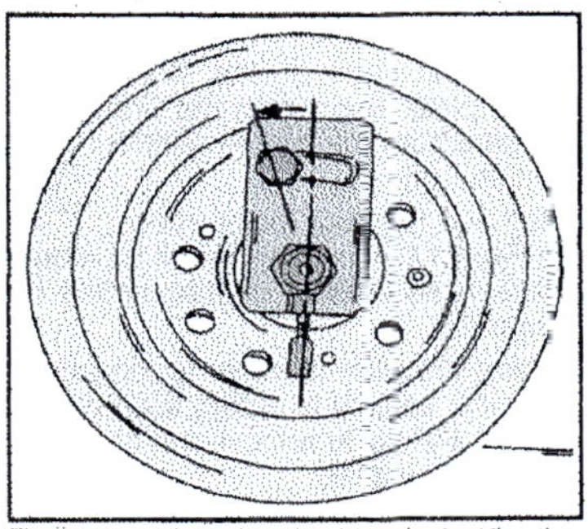

Fig. 7.15. — Move the wheel bolt in the direction of the arrow (R.H. thread).

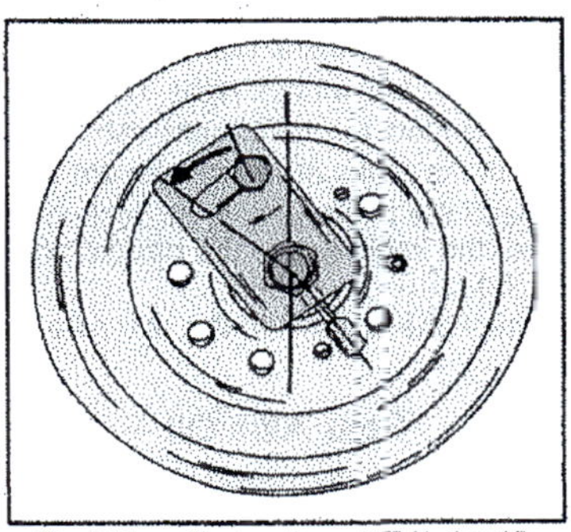

Fig. 7.16. — Slacken the nut (R.H. thread).

You will need an impact hammer (slide hammer), attached to the axle shaft flange to withdraw the shaft from the axle tube and the inside of the differential. The bearing on the shaft cannot be replaced with ordinary tools and we strongly recommend to have a bearing replaced in a workshop. Remove a drive shaft as follows:

- Slacken the wheel nuts, jack up the rear end of the vehicle and place chassis stands in position. The rear wheels should just be off the ground.
- Remove the wheel. Underneath you will see two guide pins for the wheel which also act as securing screws for the brake drum. Unscrew the pins and remove the brake drum.
- Disconnect the end of the handbrake cable from the lever and drive the outer sleeve of the cable out of the brake back plate. Use a cylindical drift.
- From the rear of the brake back plate disconnect the brake pipe from the wheel cylinder (union nut).

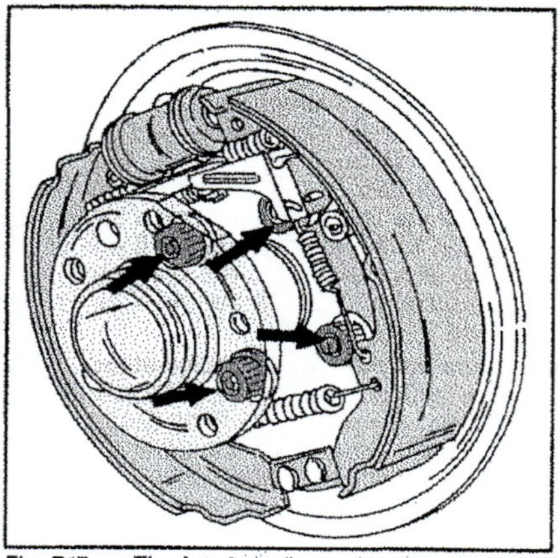

Fig. 7.17. — The four bolts (arrows) secure the brake back plate to the rear axle tube.

- Remove the four bolts shown in Fig. 7.17. An Allen key will be required to remove the bolts. Remove the brake back plate without contaminating the brake shoe linings with oily or greasy fingers.
- Attach the slide hammer to the axle shaft and pull out the shaft. If you are sure that the vehicle is sitting solid on the chassis stands, you may try to refit the wheel and try to remove the shaft by rocking and pulling on the wheel until the shaft is released.

Before fitting the shaft clean the locating bore for the bearing and coat it with sealing compound.

- Insert the shaft into the axle tube, turn it until the engagement takes place inside the differential and then push it fully in.
- Refit the brake back plate. The bolts are tightened to 17.0 kgm (122 ft.lb.).
- Re-connect the handbrake cable and the brake pipe.
- Refit the brake drum and secure with the two guide pins.
- Bleed the brake system as described in Section "Brakes". Refit the wheel, lower the vehicle onto the ground and tighten the wheel bolts to 18.0 kgm (130 ft.lb.).
- Check the oil level in the rear axle and correct if necessary.

7.6. Rear Axle Oil — 4WD Vehicles

The checking of the oil level in the rear axle case and the replacing of the oil has already been coverd in Section 3.. Page 110 should be referred to for further information.

7.7. Running Gear (Chassis) Tightening Torques

Steering

Steering wheel nut: .... 5.0 kgm (36 ft.lb.)
Steering to chassis: .... 5.0 kgm (36 ft.lb.)
Track rod ball joints to steering lever: .... 5.5 kgm (40 ft.lb.)
Track rods to steering rack: .... 6.0 kgm (43.5 ft.lb.)
Track rod locknuts: .... 6.0 kgm (43.5 ft.lb.)
Universal joint clamp bolts: .... 2.5 kgm (18 ft.lb.)
Steering lever to steering knuckle: .... 12.5 kgm (90 ft.lb.)
Steering column to body: .... 4.0 kgm (30 ft.lb.)
Power Steering:
  Hydraulic connections to steering: .... 2.6 - 3.3 kgm (19 - 24 ft.lb.)
  Hydraulic connections to steering pump: .... 2.5 kgm (18 ft.lb.)

Front Axle and Front Suspension

Spring strut to body: .... 2.0 kgm (14.5 ft.lb.)
Piston rod nut: .... 7.0 kgm (50.5 ft.lb.)
Steering lever to steering knuckle: .... 12.5 kgm (90 ft.lb.)
Reaction strut (upper face): .... 2.5 kgm (18 ft.lb.)
Reaction strut (nut at bottom): .... 14.0 kgm (101 ft.lb.)
Inside suspension arm attachment: .... 9.0 kgm (65 ft.lb.)
Suspension arm mounting bracket to body: .... 5.0 kgm (36 ft.lb.)
Suspension ball joint plate: .... 5.0 kgm (36 ft.lb.)
Suspension ball joint to suspension arm: .... 10.0 kgm (72 ft.lb.)
Brake disc to hub: .... 1.0 kgm (7.2 ft.lb.)
Axle shaft nut: .... 50.0 kgm (360 ft.lb.)
Wheel bolts: .... 18.0 kgm (130 ft.lb.)
Steering tightening torques: .... See above
Brake tightening torques: .... See Section "Brakes"

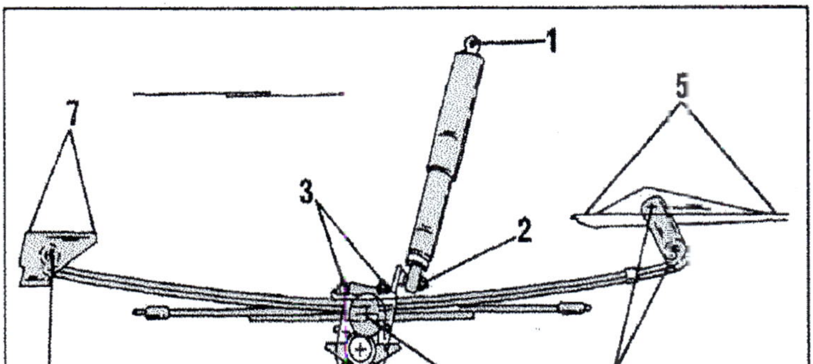

Fig. 7.18. — View of the rear suspension. The numbers are referred to below.

Rear Suspension (see Fig. 7.18)

Upper shock absorber mounting (1): .... 5.0 kgm (36 ft.lb.)
Lower shock absorber mounting (2): .... 5.0 kgm (36 ft.lb.)
Spring "U" bolt nuts (3): .... 8.0 kgm (58 ft.lb.)
Spring shackle bolt nuts (4): .... 12.0 kgm (86.5 ft.lb.)
Spring shackle mounting bracket (5): .... 5.0 kgm (36 ft.lb.)

8. Brakes

Front spring pin nut (6): .... 15.0 kgm (108 ft.lb.)
Front spring mounting bracket bolts (7): .... 5.0 kgm (36 ft.lb.)
Axle Stump Nuts (8):
20 mm thread: .... 10.5 kgm (75.5 ft.lb.)
22 mm thread: .... 17.0 kgm (122.5 ft.lb.)
Not shown in Fig. 7.18:
Wheel bolts: .... 18.0 kgm (130 ft.lb.)
Brake backplate and axle stump to axle tube:
12 mm bolts: .... 10.0 kgm (72 ft.lb.)
14 mm bolts: .... 17.0 kgm (122.5 ft.lb.)
With four-wheel drive: .... 17.0 kgm (122.5 ft.lb.)

8. BRAKE SYSTEM

8.0. Short Description

All models covered in the manual have disc brakes at the front. The brakes are made by Girling. Eazch front disc brake assembly has two pistons, supplied independently by separate brake circuits. Sliding callipers are employed, i.e. the pressure is applied to the pistons on one side and the complete brake caliper is moved sideways on slide bolts to press the brake pad on the opposite side against the brake disc.

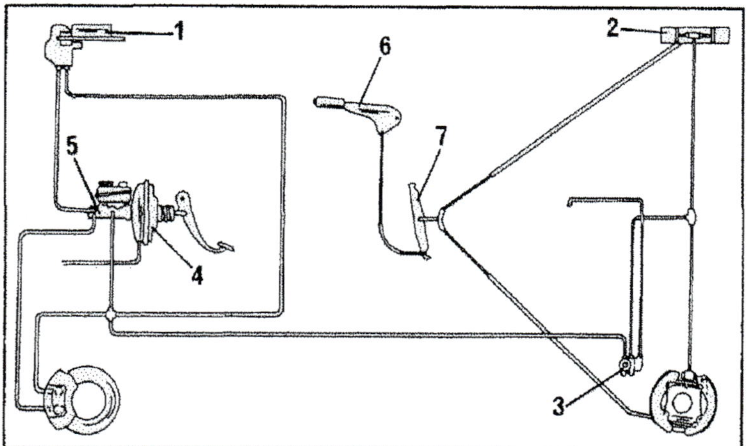

Fig. 8.1. — Brake circuit diagram.

1 Front disc brakes
2 Rear drum brakes
3 Brake pressure regulator
4 Brake servo
5 Master brake cylinder
6 Handbrake lever
7 Handbrake cable equaliser bracket

The tandem master cylinder works on the dual-line principle. The rear circuit of the cylinder supplies the upper piston of each front caliper and the rear brakes. The front circuit of the cylinder supplies the lower pistons of each caliper. Not all models in the range covered have the same master cylinder, as the diameter has been selected to be suitable for carrying capacity, version, etc. Fig. 8.1 shows how the various components are connected with each other.

A brake servo unit is fitted, the vacuum being supplied by a separate vacuum pump, driven by the engine. Not all pumps are of the same make. A brake pressure regulator regulates the brake pressure to the rear wheels.

The handbrake operates the rear wheels. The rear wheels should be locked when the handbrake lever is pulled 4 to 5 notches.

8.1. Technical Data

Type fitted:

Front brakes: .... Girling sliding-type calipers

Rear brakes: .... Girling self-adjusting drum brakes

Front Brakes

	Models 1000-1500	*1800-Turbo*
Brake disc diameter:	255.0 mm	290.0 mm
Brake Disc Diameter:		
To May 1984:	13.0 mm	16.0 mm
From May 1994:	16.0 mm	16.0 mm
Min. Disc Diameter through Wear:		
To May 1984:	11.8 mm	14.8 mm
From May 1984:	13.5 mm	14.8 mm
Max. disc run-out:	0.15 mm	0.15 mm
Measuring point on discs (from edge):	2.0 mm	2.0 mm
Min. thickness of brake pad material:	2.0 mm	2.0 mm
Caliper Cylinder Diameter:		
Upper piston:	38.0 mm	42.8 mm
Lower piston:	48.0 mm	48.0 mm
Number of pistons:	2	2
Braking area:	194.8 sq.cm.	269.6 sq.cm.
Brake Pad Material:		
To Jan. 1985:	Textar T 252	Galfer 3100
From Jan. 1985:	Energit 394 to Jan. 87 Galfer 3100 from Jan. 87	

Rear Brakes

	1000/1500/Turbo	*1800*
Manufacturer:	Girling	Girling
Drum diameter:	254,0 mm	254,0 mm
Max. drum diameter:	254,8 mm	254.8 mm
Max. diameter through wear:	255.6 mm	255.6 mm
Wheel brake cylinder — To Feb. 1983:	22.2 mm	———
— From Feb. 1993:	25.4 mm	———
Wheel brake cylinder:	———	27.0 mm
Min. brake lining thickness:	1.0 mm	1.0 mm
Braking area:	537.0 sq.cm.	554.0 sq.cm.
Brake lining material:	Ferodo, Ferit, Energit AM14 FF 339 550	Energit 550

Master Brake Cylinder

Diameter, 1000, 1500: .... 22.2 mm

Diameter, 1800: .... 25.4 mm

Stroke of piston — 1000/1500 to Feb. 1993: .... 19 + 17 mm

Stroke of piston — 1000/1500 from Feb. 1983:	21.5 + 12.5 mm
— 1800:	19.5 + 13.5 mm

Brake Servo Unit

Diameter of servo unit — 1000, 1500:	8 in. to Jan. 1992, then 9 in.
— 1800/Turbo:	8 in.

Note: The above dimensions are given for the Citroën version.

8.2. Front Disc Brakes

8.2.0. REPLACING THE BRAKE PADS

To check the remaining thickness of the brake pad material remove the front wheels and check the two brake pads through the inspection "window". Always check on both sides, as uneven wear is possible. If this is the case, check the brake caliper on the side with increased wear thoroughly, as the caliper could be sticking. If the thickness is less than approx. 2 matchsticks, replace the brake pads. The specified thickness is 2.0 mm (0.08 in.).

If the brake pads are removed for other reasons than replacement, mark each pad as you take it out, i.e. L.H. and R.H. side and inner and outer pad. Incorrect fitting could lead to brake pull to one side.

After you have removed a caliper you will find that it consists of two parts. **Never separate the caliper.**

Replace the brake pads as follows:

- Slacken the wheel bolts on both sides, jack up the front end of the vehicle and remove the wheels. The suspension must be allowed to hang down under its own weight.
- Disconnect the cables from the pad wear indicators.
- Insert a pair of pliers between the caliper and the inner brake pad (1) in Fig.

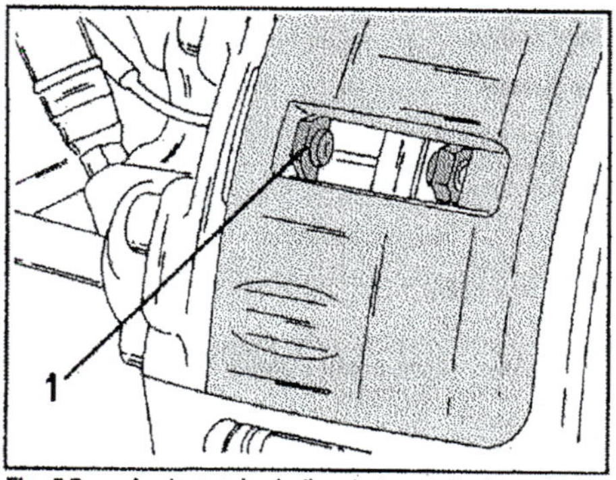

Fig. 8.2. — Apply a pair of pliers between the inner brake pad (1) and the caliper housing to push the piston into the bore.

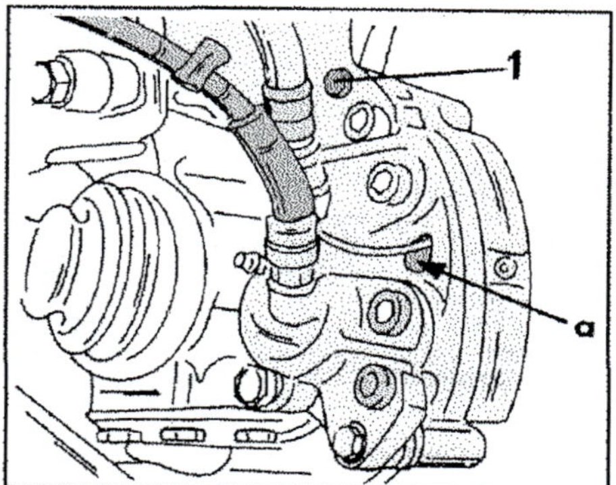

Fig. 8.3. — Details for the removal and installation of a brake caliper.

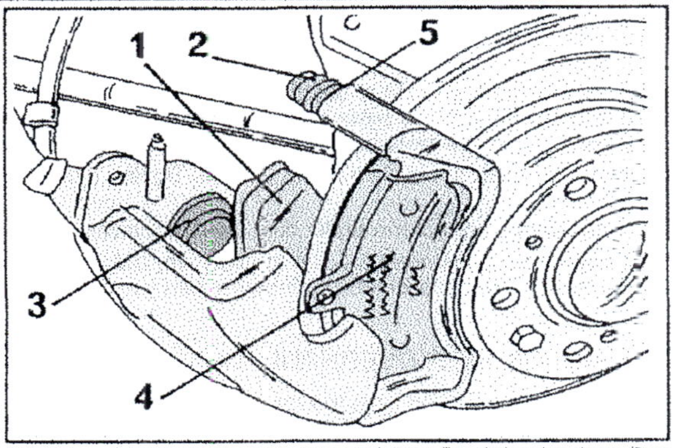

Fig. 8.4. — After removal of the upper bolt (see Fig. 8.3) swing the caliper downwards to expose the brake pads.

1 Inner brake pad
2 Guide bolt
3 Cylinder dust seal
4 Outer brake pad
5 Guide bolt rubber seal

8.2 and close the pliers. The pistons will be forced back into the cylinder. You may, of course, employ a different method to reset the pistons.

- Refer to Figs. 8.3 and 8.4 to remove a brake caliper. Remove the bolt (1) in Fig. 8.3 with a ring spanner, counterholding the guide bolt (2) in Fig. 8.4 with a second ring spanner or open-ended spanner. The guide bolt must not rotate.
- Swing the caliper downwards into the position shown in Fig. 8.4. The brake pad (1) at the inside and the pad (4) at the outside can now be removed from the caliper.

Clean the inside of the brake caliper opening with a stiff brush to remove brake dust. The pistons must now be pressed into their bores, if they appear to be protruding more than the caliper bore. Use a hammer handle, but have a helper observing the fluid level in the reservoir, as the fluid will rise, as the pistons are pushed in. If necessary remove some fluid out of the reservoir or open the bleed screw whilst the first piston is pushed in. Careful handling will not allow air into the system — otherwise the brake system must be bled of air.

If the sealing rubbers (5) in Fig. 8.4 are in bad condition, unscrew the guide bolt (2). Clean the bolt and refit it with the new rubber part. The guide bolt is fitted with rubber grease.

The installation of the brake pads follows the description below:

- Insert the inner brake pad (1) and the outer pad (4) in Fig. 8.4. The inner pad has the cable for the pad wear indication and must be routed through the opening "a" in Fig. 8.3.
- Check once more that the pads are fitted correctly and swing the caliper upwards, until the bolt at the top can be fitted. New bolts are normally included in the brake pad repair kit. *If none are supplied, coat the threads with "Loctite".*
- Hold the guide bolts (2) in Fig. 8.4 with an open-ended spanner and tighten the bolt (1) in Fig. 8.3 to 3.4 kgm (25 ft.lb.).

- Re-connect the cable to the brake pad wear indicator. Check that the cables cannot touch other parts of the front suspension when the wheels are moved from lock to lock.
- Operate the foot brake a few times to set the new pads against the brake disc. You will also find out if the brake systems requires bleeding. Pump the pedal with quick strokes. Air in the system is normally indicated by a rising pedal.
- Refit the wheels and lower the vehicle to the ground. Tighten the wheel nuts to 18 kgm (130 ft.lb.).
- Check and if necessary correct the brake fluid level in the reservoir.

Remember that new brake pads need a while to "bed" in, before the brakes obtain the full performance. Treat the brakes with care when you first drive off.

8.2.1. BRAKE CALIPER OVERHAUL

The brake caliper must be removed from the steering knuckle. Two bolts hold the caliper in position. As two brake hoses are fitted separate the connection between the hoses and the pipes, i.e. it is not possible to remove the brake caliper and then the brake hose. Brake pipes/hoses are connected with union nuts and spring plates. Close the ends of the brake pipes in suitable manner to prevent entry of dirt.

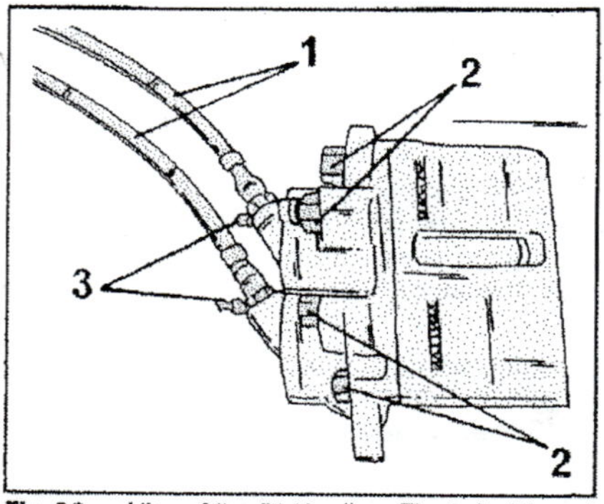

Fig. 8.5. — View of the fitted caliper. The bolts (2) must not be slackened or removed, as they keep the caliper halves together.

1 Brake hoses 2 Bolts 3 Bleeder screws

Note the following general rules when overhauling brake calipers or for that matter any other hydraulic part:

- The work must be carried out on a clean workbench.
- All rubber cups and seals must be replaced if the part has been dismantled. even if rubber parts still look useable, replace them.
- Never refit a piston or caliper if corrosion or other blemishes can be found. Always replace the part in question. Only use alcohol, white spirit or brake fluid to clean parts. Eeven small amount of petrol can damage the rubber parts sooner or later. Any marks left by the use of white spirits can be cleaned-off with a lint-free cloth.

Fig. 8.5. shows the fitted caliper. The illustration shows the four bolts (2) which hold the caliper together. *These are the bolts which must not be slackened or removed.*

- Unscrew the two brake hoses (1) from the the caliper and remove the two bleeder screws (3).
- The pistons are blown out with air. Place a piece of hartwood into the caliper opening to allow the piston to "hit" the wood and not the metal. Remember that you have two pistons, it may be necessary to deal with one piston at the time. Keep the fingers away from the area of the piston opening when the caliper is dismantled. Fig. 8.6 shows the removal of a piston. You may be able to

carry out the operation at a petrol station.

- From the inside of the cylinder bore remove the cylinder sealing ring(s) with a blunt, pointed instrument. Do not damage the bore(s).
- Clean all parts in clean brake fluid or alcohol. All parts in the repair kit must be used, i.e. do not use any of the old parts.
- Coat the cylinder seal(s) with clean brake fluid and insert them into the groove(s), using the fingers only.
- Fit the dust seals to the pistons and slowly insert the piston into the caliper bore. Insert the deal lip into the cylinder groove and push the piston fully in. Check that the dust seals are correctly fitted.

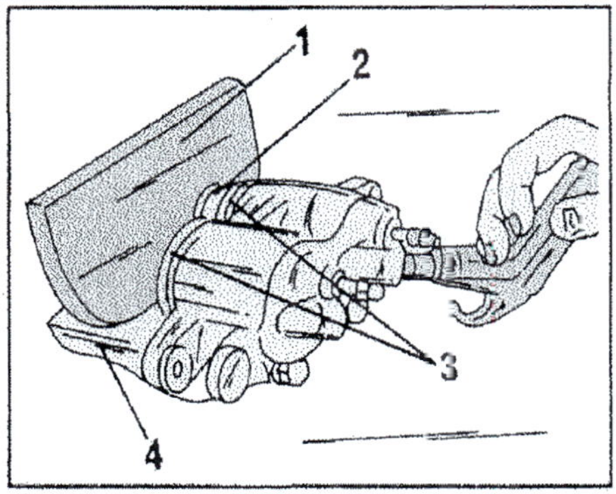

Fig. 8.6. — Removal of a caliper piston. Insert the piece of hardwood (1) into the caliper opening (4) to protect the piston (2) during removal. Each piston has a dust seal (3).

- Fit the brake hoses to the caliper body and tighten them to 1.3 kgm (11 ft.lb.).
- Thoroughly clean the mounting face of caliper and steering knuckle, coat the caliper bolts with "Loctite", fit the caliper assembly in position and fit the bolts. Tighten the bolts in several stages to a final torque of 14.5 kgm (105 ft.lb.).
- Fit the brake pads (Section 8.1.2).
- Insert the brake hoses into the bracket and secure with the spring plates. Fit the brake pipes and tighten the union nuts. Move the wheels from one lock to the other and check that the brake hoses cannot rub against other parts of the front suspension. If necessary, slacken the union nuts and rotate the hose(s) accordingly.
- Finally bleed the brake system as described later on.

8.2.2. BRAKE DISCS

Brake discs must be replaced if the friction faces show grooves or other damage. Grooves can develop if the brake pads have been allowed to wear down to the metal plates. Measure the thickness of the brake discs with a micrometer or a caliper and compare the results with the dimensions given in Section 8.1. If in doubt, you may be able to get information for your particular vehicle from your dealer. If the discs shows slight wear, you may have yhem re-ground.

Replace brake disc as follows:

- Slacken the wheel bolts, place the front end of the vehicle on chassis stands and remove the wheel.
- Remove the brake pads as described.
- Remove the two bolts from the outside of the wheel hub. One is used to guide the wheel, the other one secures the disc. The brake disc has a tight fit on the hub. Three M10 x 1.25 bolts can be screwed into the visible threaded bores and

used as extrator bolts to pull off the disc. Tighten the bolts evenly in small stages until the disc is free. Be careful, it can easily drop.

- During installation fit the disc over the hub and tap it in position with a rubber or plastic mallet. Fit the bolts and tighten them alternatively to 1.0 kgm (7 ft.lb.).

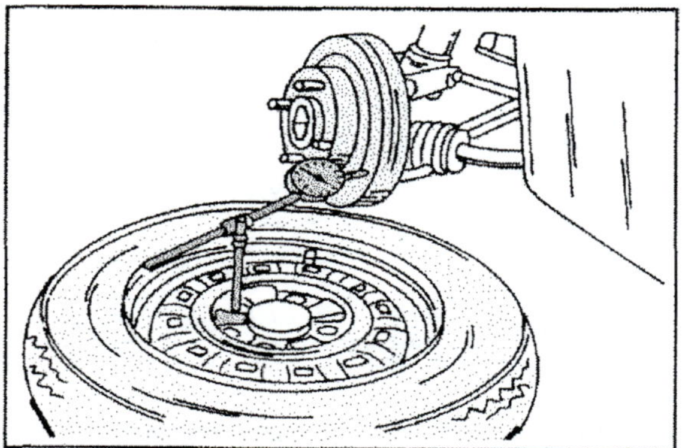

Fig. 8.7. — Checking a brake disc for run-out. The wheel can be used to mounting the dial gauge.

- Arrange a dial gauge with a suitable holder (a good solution is shown in Fig. 8.7) and apply the stylus approx. 2 mm from the outer edge of the disc. Slowly rotate the wheel hub/disc and observe the dial gauge reading. The highest run-out is 0.15 mm (0.006 in.). Higher readings can be due to dirt between disc and hub. In this case remove the disc once more and check the surfaces.
- Fit the wheel, lower the vehicle to the ground and tighten the wheel bolts.

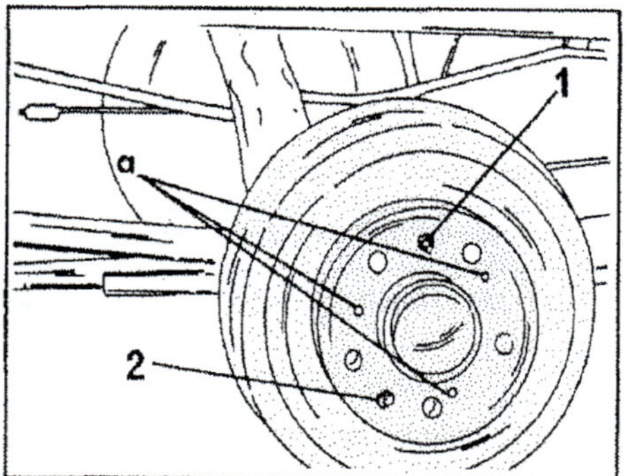

Fig. 8.8. — Removal of a brake drum. The drum is secured with the wheel guide pin (1) and a single screw (2). The threaded bores "a" are used to fit the extractor bolts.

8.3. Rear Brakes

8.3.0. REPLACING THE BRAKE SHOES

- Slacken the wheel bolts, jack up the rear end of the vehicle and remove both wheels.
- Refer to Fig. 8.8. and remove the brake drum and the wheel hub. In the outside

of the brake drum you will see a screw and a guide pin. Remove them to free the drum from the hub. The drum is very tight and three M10 x 1.25 bolts must be screwed into the three bores "a". By tightening the bolts evenly one after the other, the drum should come away. There are, however, cases that you may encounter a sticking drum. This is due to the self-adjusting mechanism inside the brake drum which must be freed. To do this, apply the handbrake and push the plunger (1) in Fig. 8.9 towards the inside. Free the stop for the handbrake operating lever inside the brake drum by pulling out the plastic part (2). Release the handbrake and remove the drum.

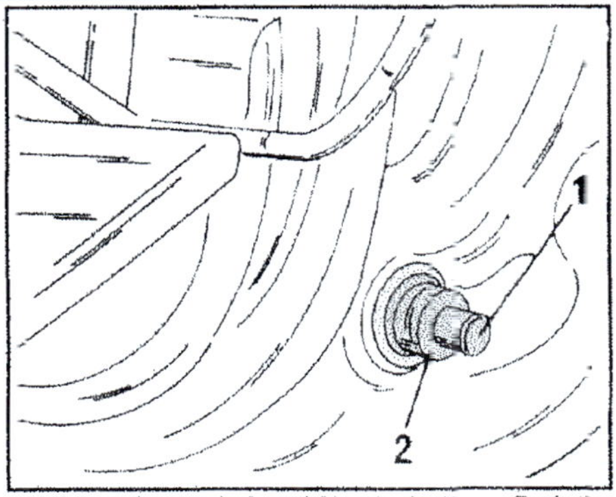

Fig. 8.9. — Removal of a sticking brake drum. Push the plunger (1) towards the inside and pull the plastic part (2) towards the outside. The handbrake lever must be pulled before the operation is carried out.

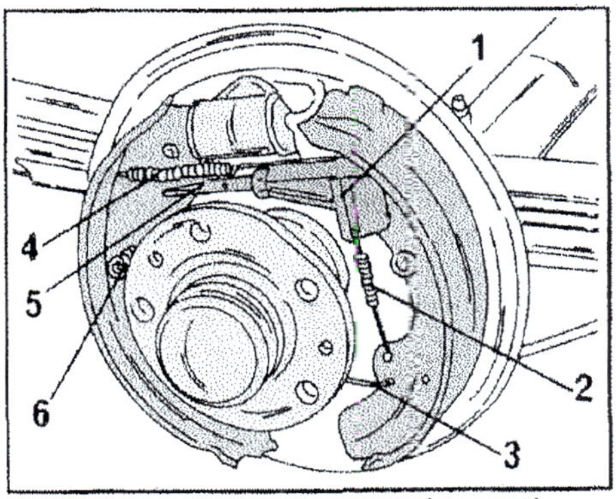

Fig. 8.10. — View of a fitted rear brake assembly.

1 Adjuster lever
2 Adjuster lever spring
3 Lower return spring
4 Upper return spring
5 Adjuster strut
6 Shoe hold-down pin

- Referring to Fig. 8.10 remove the adjuster lever (1) and the unhook the return spring (2). The upper return spring (4) and the lower spring (3) must be removed with a pair of pliers or use a scsrewdriver and carefully lift the spring hooks out of their anchorage. The thrust piece (5), i.e. the strut for the self-adjustment of the brakes shoes, in the centre will be released and can be taken out.
- Remove the shoe hold-down springs. Normally a special tool is available, which is used as shown in Fig. 8.11, but a pair of pliers is suitable. Push with a finger from the rear of the backplate against the hold-down pin and rotate the spring seat on the outside with a pair of pliers until the end of the pin can be guided through the slotted hole in the spring seat. Remove the spring seat and the spring and withdraw the pin from the rear.
- Carry out the same operations on the other side of the vehicle.
- Lift the brake shoes off the brake backplate. The handbrake cable must be dis-

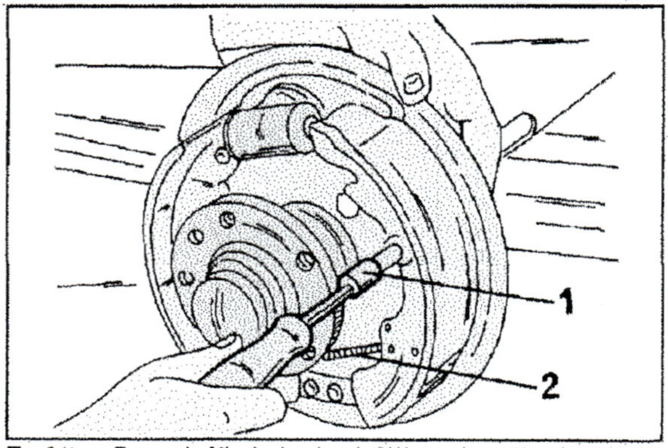

Fig. 8.11. — Removal of the brake shoe hold-down pins and springs, in this case shown with the special tool (1). The handbrake cable (2) must be disconnected from the rear brake shoe.

connected from the rear brake shoe. To do this, push back the spring until the cable end can be unhooked.

- If necessary remove the wheel brake cylinder (disconnect the brake pipe).

Thoroughly clean all parts, including the backplate. If petrol is used make sure it cannot come to the wheel cylinder (if still fitted). The brake linings can have a min. thickness of 2 mm. Otherwise replace the brake shoes as a set. Wheel brake cylinder can be overhauled, but first ensure that a repair kit is available. You will also need some experience with hydraulic cylinders.

8.3.1 INSTALLATION OF BRAKE SHOES

- Refit the wheel brake cylinder to the brake back plate and connect the brake pipe at the rear.
- Fit the brake shoes to the brake backplate, engaging the end of the handbrake cable with the rear shoe.
- Insert the brake shoe hold-down pins from the rear and place the spring and the spring seat over the pin at the front. Apply pressure to the pin from the rear, grip the spring seat with a pair of pliers and push it over the pin. As soon as the pin head appears above the sprign seat, turn the spring seat to lock the pin in position. Attach both brake shoes in this manner.

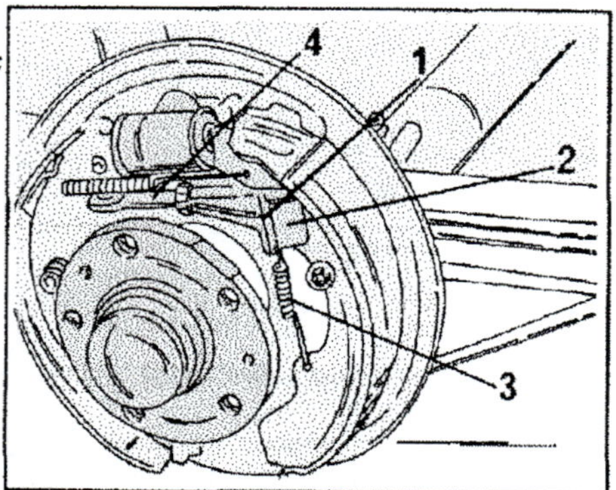

Fig. 8.12. — Details for the installation of the brake shoes.
1 Adjuster lever engagement 3 Return spring
2 Adjuster lever 4 Adjuster strut

- Insert the strut between the two brack shoes.
- Fit the upper and lower return springs between the brake shoes. First engage the spring hook on one side and then stretch the spring with a pair of pliers until the other end can be engaged. The spring hooks are inserted from the outside towards the inside.
- The next operations are carried out by referring to Fig. 8.12. Engage the spring (3) with the brake shoe and the other end with the adjuster lever (1).

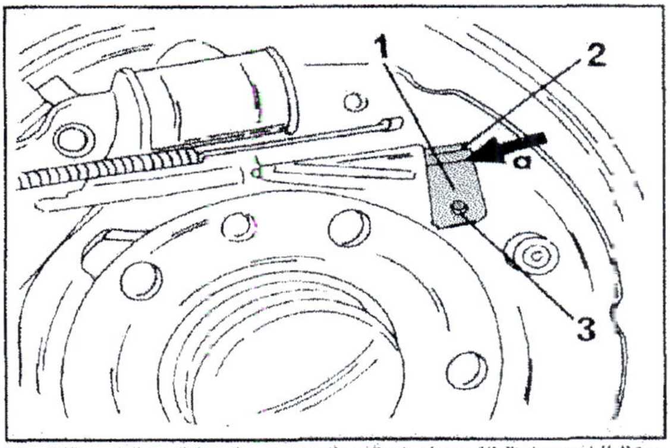

Fig. 8.13. — When fitting the automatic adjuster lever (1) fit the end "a" below the link (2) and above the pin (3).

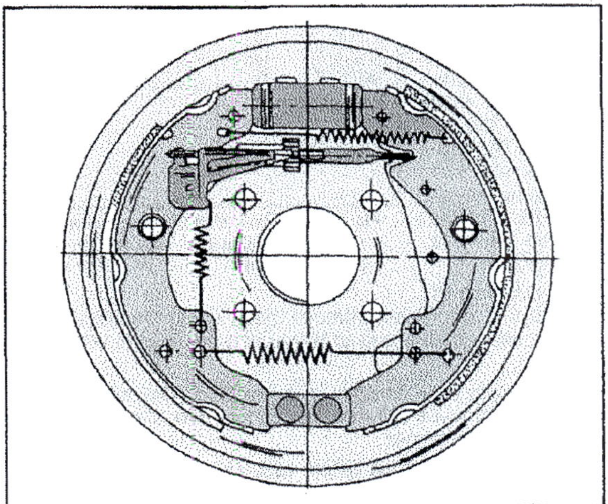

Fig. 8.14. — Before fitting the brake drums compare the fitted brake shoes with the illustration to make sure all parts are fitted as shown. This mainly concerns the return springs.

- Fit the adjuster lever (1). Fig. 8.13 shows more details of the installation. The end "a" of the lever must be placed under the the link (2) and above the pin (3).
- Centre the brake shoes on the brake backplate. Have a last look at the fitted brake shoes by comparing the assembly with Fig. 8.14 to make sure that all parts have been fitted correctly.
- Fit the brake drum and attach with the securing screw and the guide pin for the rear wheel.
- Operate the handbrake and the footbrake a few times to set the self-adjusting mechanism into operation. This will also centre the shoes inside the drum.
- If the wheel brake cylinder has been removed, i.e. the brake pipe disconnected, bleed the brake system as described later on. Remember that each front calliper has two bleed screws.
- Refit the wheels and lower the vehicle to the ground. Tighten the wheel bolts. Treat the brakes with the necessary care for the first few miles.

8.3.2. WHEEL BRAKE CYLINDERS

Before you attempt to overhaul a wheel brake cylinder check if a repair kit is available. You will need some experience with hydraulic cylinders, mainly to evaluate the condition of the cylinder bore and the two pistons. Otherwise it may be better to replace the cylinder.

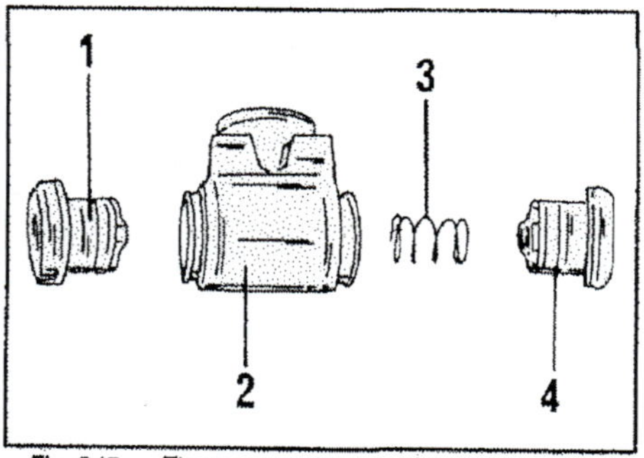

Fig. 8.15. — The component parts of w wheel cylinder.
1 Piston and dust cap
2 Cylinder body
3 Return spring
4 Piston and rubber cap

To dismantle the cylinder, remove the retaining rings from the rubber dust boots at the outside of the cylinder and remove one of the rubber dust caps. The piston is under spring pressure and may "jump" out. Remove the piston and the spring. The rubber cap on the other side can now be removed and the piston withdrawn. The cylinder is now dismantled into the parts shown in Fig. 8.15.

Check the fitting direction of the rubber cups on the pistons and remove them, using the fingers only. A small screwdriver can be used to lift a cup until you can get hold of with forefinger and thumb.

Clean all parts thoroughly in white spirit or brake fluid. The cylinder bore must be checked for corrosion, grooves or other blemishes. Very slight indents can be removed with fine-grain sand paper.

Coat the parts with clean brake fluid before assembly. Fit the rubber cups with the sharp edges towards the inside, again using the fingers only. Fit one of the pistons with the rubber dust cap attached into the cylinder bore and fit the cap to the cylinder. Insert the spring and fit the second piston from the other side. Attach both rubber dust caps with the metal band.

8.4. Master Brake Cylinder

Master cylinders of different diameter are used within the range covered. Always make sure that the correct cylinder or the correct repair kit for the cylinder in question is used.

8.4.0. REMOVAL AND INSTALLATION

The removal and installation of the cylinder is a fairly easy operation. The cylinder is bolted to the front face of the brake servo unit.

- Remove the two connector plugs from the brake fluid warning switch.
- Unscrew the brake pipe union nuts, withdraw the pipes and carefully bend the pipes to one side. Fig. 8.16 shows a view of the fitted cylinder. The shape of the cylinder can be different, depending on the vehicle model. To reach some of the connections it may be necessary to remove the spare wheel.
- Remove the two nuts securing the cylinder to the front face of the brake servo unit and carefully remove the cylinder. Take care not to drip brake fluid on painted surfaces. Hold a rag underneath the cylinder and lift it out at the angle shown in Fig. 8.17.

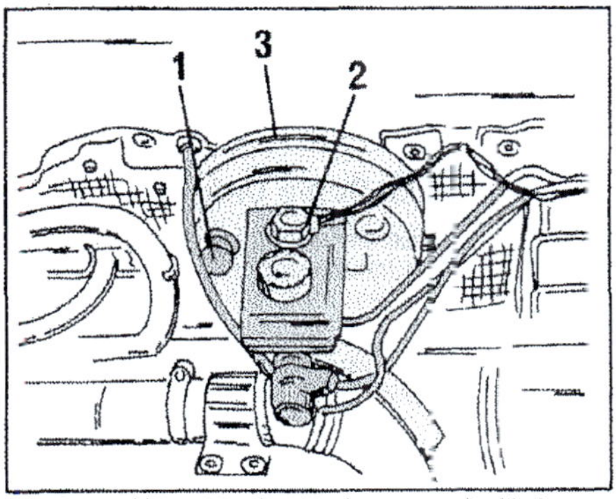

Fig. 8.16. — View of the fitted brake servo unit with the master brake cylinder.
1 Vacuum hose 2 Cable connection 3 Servo unit

Fig. 8.17. — Remove the master cylinder at the angle shown.

The installation of the cylinder is a reversal of the removal procedure. The nuts are tightened to 2.0 kgm (14.5 fft.bl.).

Fill the fluid reservoir with clean brake fluid and bleed the brake system as described later on.

8.4.1. CYLINDER REPAIRS

Master cylinders can be overhauled but we recommend to fit a new cylinder if the original one has developed a fault. The reservoir can be removed from the cylinder. It is just pushed into rubber grommets in the cylinder. To remove the reservoir, take a good hold of it and "rock" it to and fro, at the same time pulling it upward. The new cylinder will come with the grommets fitted and the reservoir is pushed in position. Coat the inside of the grommets with brake fluid before installation of the reservoir.

8.5. Brake Servo Unit

Repair of the brake servo unit should not be attempted. Loss of the brake servo assistance will not influence the operation of the brakes, but you will find that the pedal pressure necessary to brake the vehicle will be substantially higher.

The brake servo unit is not the same for all models. A unit with one chamber or one with a double-chamber (for example in turbo diesel vehicles) are used. The diameter of the brake servo unit has been changed around the beginning of 1992.

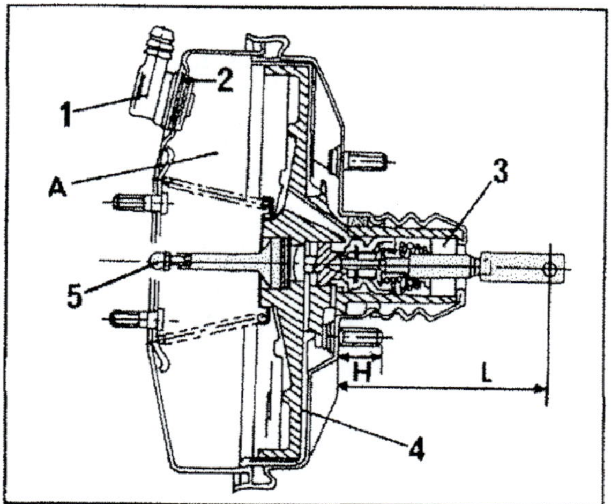

Fig. 8.18. — Sectional view of the brake servo unit with one working chamber (A). Units with 8 and 9 in. in diameter look similar.

1 Non-return valve
2 Rubber grommet
3 Filter
4 Diaphragm
5 Push rod
A = Working chamber
H = Height of securing studs
L = Lenght of push rod

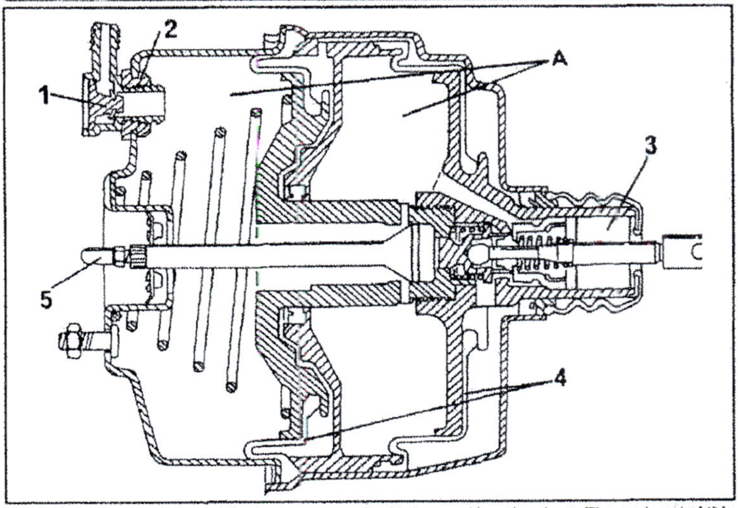

Fig. 8.19. — Sectional view of the brake servo unit with two working chambers. The push rod of this type of servo unit must not be adjusted.

1 Non-return valve
2 Rubber grommet
3 Filter
4 Double diaphragm
5 Push rod
A = Working chamber

Figs. 8.18 and 8.19 show sectional views of the two servo units, where you can see the difference. The push rod (5) has been factory-adjusted on the double-chamber unit and must not be disturbed. The push rod must, however, be adjusted in the case of a single-chamber unit, but differences must be noted. Dimension "L" must be set to 105 - 106 mm if the vehicle is built up to September 1990. After this date the dimension is 113 - 115 mm. We must mention that the new dimension has not been introduced at the same time on all vehicles.

There are times when a brake servo unit can be obtained from a breakers yard. To fit the correct one, follow the guide lines below:

- If the height "H" of the studs is 22.5 mm and the servo unit has a diameter of 8 in. it can be used in a vehicle built before September 1990 (servo unit with one chamber, Fig. 8.18).
- If the height "H" of the studs is 32.0 mm and the servo unit shown in Fig. 8.18 has a diameter of 8 in., you can use it in vehicles build from October 1990.
- If the height "H" of the studs is 35.0 mm and the servo unit shown in Fig. 8.18 has a diameter of 9 in., the unit will be suitable in vehicles build after January 1992.
- If the brake servo unit has the shape shown in Fig. 8.19 (two chambers) the height "H" will be 20.5 mm to June 1990 and then 29.5 mm.

The master cylinder must be removed to gain access to the brake servo unit. The servo unit can be unscrewed from the inside of the vehicle, but the spare wheel carrier may have to be removed to lift out the unit.

A clevis pin is used to connect the push rod to the brake pedal. The vacuum hose (1) in Fig. 8.16 must be disconnected.

Repairs are restricted to replacing the servo unit filters at the push rod end. To do this, pull back the rubber boot, remove the retainer and remove the old filters with a pointed tool. The new filters must be cut with a pair of scissors from the outside towards the inside and then pushed over the push rod. Refit the remaining parts in reverse order.

If the servo unit shown in Fig. 8.18 is fitted, adjust the length of the push rod if the servo unit has been replaced. The push rod can be adjusted after slackening of the locknut. To make sure which of the two dimensions applies, measure the length of the old push rod which will be approximately within the two ranges already given.

The push rod (5) must also be adjusted on a servo unit with one chamber. To find the dimension, place a straight edge over the end face of the unit and measure the distance to the tip of the push rod (5). The push rod must be 0.3 to 0.5 mm below the end face. If this is not the case, slacken the locknut and turn the push rod with a pair of pliers.

The installation of the servo unit is a reversal of the removal procedure.

8.6. Bleeding the Brake System

Bleeding of the brake system is required when the brake circuit has been opened or air has entered the system, for example if the fluid level in the reservoir has dropped too far.

The vehicle must be placed on secure chassis stands. Before commencing the bleeding operation clean the areas around the bleeder screws and the filler cap of the reservoir.

If only one wheel brake cylinder or one caliper has been disconnected it may be sufficient to bleed just the circuit connected to this brake unit. To find out which one it is study Fig. 8.1 and follow the brake lines.

Otherwise start the bleeding at the rear brakes, then the upper bleed screws of the front brakes, followed by the lower bleed screws. You will need a helper, as the fluid level in the reservoir must be continuously observed, as it must not drop below the min. level and of course, to operate the brake pedal. Proceed as follows:

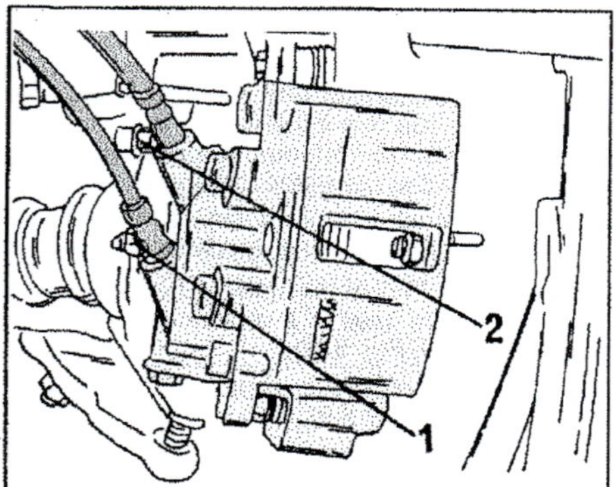

Fig. 8.19a. — The location of the bleeder screws on a front caliper. (1) for the upper circuit, (2) for the lower circuit.

- Remove the rubber dust cap from the bleed screw and push a transparent bleeder hose over the bleeder screw. Bleeder hoses are available from accessory shops. Hold the other end of the hose into a glass jar, filled with some brake fluid. Make sure that the bleeder hose remains at all times below the level of the brake fluid.

- Ask the helper to operate the brake pedal with slow strokes and to signal you when the pedal is contacting the floor. Open the bleeder screw by half a turn. Fluid will run through the hose into the jar. Close the bleed screw.
- Repeat the "pumping" operation and opening and closing of the bleeder screw until brake fluid, free of air bubbles, is entering the glass jar. Remember to replenish the reservoir in between.
- Repeat the bleeding operation in the given order on the other brake units. Fig. 8.20 shows where the bleeder screws of the front calipers are located. Finally top-up the reservoir to the required level. ***Brake fluid drained out the system into the glass jar must, however, nor be used to fill the reservoir.***

Final Note: The brake fluid should be changed every two years. Experience has shown that this necessity is normally overlooked. For your own safety we strongly recommend it. Brake fluid subject to heat and will deteriorate in service.

8.7. Adjusting the Handbrake

The rear wheels must be locked when the handbrake lever has been pulled by 4 to 5 notches. Place the rear of the vehicle on chassis stands to adjust. First rotate the rear wheels to check whether the wheels can move freely. If an adjustment is necessary proceed as follows:

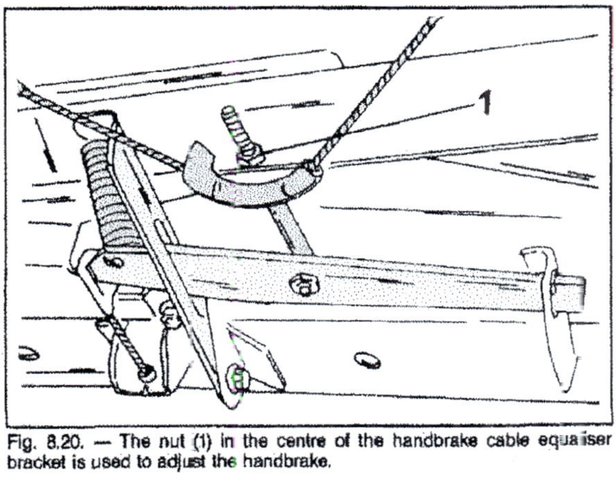

Fig. 8.20. — The nut (1) in the centre of the handbrake cable equaliser bracket is used to adjust the handbrake.

- Pull the handbrake to the third notch.
- Jack up the rear end of the vehicle.
- Tighten the nut in the centre of the handbrake cable equaliser (Fig. 8.20) until the rear wheels can just be rotated under a fair effort. Re-tighten the locknut.
- Pull the handbrake lever one or two notches more and check that the rear wheels can no longer be rotated.

8.8. Brake Pressure Regulator

The brake pressure regulator can only be adjusted with the help of two pressure gauges. Practically every model in the covered range has a different pressure setting, depending on the fitted engine, the wheelbase, the carrying capacity and the type of body. Only your workshop will be able to check and/or adjust the regulator. An adjusting linkage on the mounting of the regulator is used for the adjustment.

8.9. Tightening Torques

Brake caliper housing to steering knuckle:	14.5 kgm (105 ft.lb.)
Brake caliper to mounting bracket:	3.4 kgm (25 ft.lb.)
Brake discs to wheel hubs:	1.5 kgm (11 ft.lb.)
Brake master cylinder to brake servo unit:	2.0 kgm (14.5 ft.lb.)
Brake servo unit to bulkhead:	2.0 kgm (14.5 ft.lb.)
Bleeder screws:	0.8 kgm (6 ft.lb.)
Brake hose connections:	1.3 kgm (9.5 ft.lb.)
Union nuts of brake pipes:	1.4 kgm (10 ft.lb.)
Front drive shaft nuts:	50.0 kgm (360 ft.lb.)
Brake drum screws:	1.5 kgm (11 ft.lb.)
Nuts of rear axle stumps:	
M20 thread:	10.5 kgm (75.5 ft.lb.)
M22 thread:	17.0 kgm (122.5 ft.lb.)
Brake back plates to rear axle:	
M12 bolts:	10.0 kgm (72 ft.lb.)
M14 bolts:	17.0 kgm (122.5 ft.lb.)
With four-wheel drive:	17.0 kgm (122.5 ft.lb.)
Wheel bolts:	18.0 kgm (130 ft.lb.)

9. ELECTRICAL EQUIPMENT

9.0. Battery

Voltage:	12 volts, negative earth
Capacity:	Up to 83 Ah, depending on model and equipment

9.0.0 Battery Care

The 12 volts battery consists of six cells, made-up of positive and negative plates, surrounded by a sulfuric acid solution. The battery provides the current to start the engine, for the glow plug system, the lighting of the vehicle and other current consumers.

The following maintenance operations should be carried out at regular intervals to extend the life of the battery and to always keep it at its peak performance.

- Check the battery level once a week. If the battery case is translucent, the level can be seen through the case. Otherwise the filler plugs will have to be removed for inspection. If the electrolyte is below the separator plates, add distilled water. Do not over-fill the battery and wipe away any spilled water before replacing the filler plugs. Tap water must not be used to top-up the battery.
- Delco batteries incorporate a battery checker, which enables an easy check of

the battery condition. If a green spot can be seen there is no further need for attention, i.e. the battery is sufficiently charged. If the battery checker turns dark, the battery must be re-charged. If the checker turns a light colour, electrolyte is missing in the battery.

- If frequent topping-up is necessary, it may be that the battery is over-charged by the alternator and the latter should be checked accordingly. A cracked battery case can also be the cause.
- The battery cables should always be firmly clamped and the battery terminals must be free of corrosion to ensure good electrical conduct. Corroded areas can be cleaned with a soda solution and a wire brush. A thin coating of petroleum jelly should be smeared on battery posts before cables are re-connected.
- Check the gravity of the electrolyte in each cell using a hydrometer. This is an indication of the charge condition of the battery. All cells should give the same reading and if there is a great variation in one cell, then either the electrolyte in the cell is weak due to being topped-up with distilled water or that cell is defective. In this case, a new battery must be fitted.
- The battery can be charged with a home-charger, but follow the instructions of the manufacturer to avoid damage to the battery.

Note that the following will happen when the battery is disconnected:

- The radio security code will have to be known and set in order to return the radio to service (if a radio of this type is fitted).

9.2. Alternator

9.2.0. TECHNICAL DATA

Types fitted: . . . . Paris-Rhone A14 N91, Motorola 9 AR 5097 or Valeo 29 402 are typical examples fitted (with built-in electronic regulator)

Voltage - All: . . . . 14 volts

Minimum current: . . . . Up to 80 amps

10.2.1. PRECAUTIONS WITH ALTERNATORS

(a) Do not rotate the alternator unless connected to the battery.

(b) Before connecting the alternator, ensure that the battery is correctly connected (negative terminal to earth).

(c) Do not check the operation of the alternator by short- circuiting either the positive terminals and earth.

(d) Take care not to reverse the leads connected to the regulator.

(e) Do not connect a suppressor capacitor to the terminals of the alternator or the regulator, without seeking professional advice.

(f) Do not connect a battery charger to the battery and never carry out any arc welding (or spot welding) on the car chassis unless both the positive and negative leads are disconnected from the battery.

Ir is obvious that many different alternators are fitted over the years into the individual models covered. Always fit one as originally found in the vehicle.

9.2.2. SERVICING

Overhaul and checking of the alternator is best entrusted to a specialist or dealer who will have available the special equipment necessary. It is recommended that the owner should not use test instruments on the unit unless he is familiar with the procedures and precautions necessary. Incorrect application of meters and test equipment can quite easily cause damage to the diodes.

The alternator bearings are pre-lubricated and require no routine maintenance. The brushes should be inspected after a high mileage has been covered and can be replaced if necessary. It should, however, be noted that the brush life can be expected to be quite long under normal conditions.

9.2.3 ALTERNATOR MAINTENANCE

Periodically wipe away any dirt or grease which has accumulated on the outside of the alternator. If a water hose is used to clean the outside of the engine, cover the alternator to prevent water from entering. Check the security of the electrical cable connections on the alternator. The tension of the alternator drive belt should be checked at regular intervals. Refer to Section 9.2.5.

Take extreme care when connecting the battery leads to the battery — positive to positive and negative to negative.

9.2.4. REMOVAL AND INSTALLATION

- Disconnect the battery negative cable, followed by the positive cable.
- Note the location of the alternator supply wires and diconnect them from the rear cover.
- Loosen the adjustment and pivot bolts, swivel the alternator towards the engine and remove the drive belt from the pulley.
- Support the alternator and unscrew the adjustment and pivot bolts. Lift the alternator carefully from the vehicle.

The installation of the alternator is a reversal of the removal procedure. Tension the alternator drive belt as described in Section 9.2.5.

9.2.5. DRIVE BELT TENSION

The alternator drive belt should always be kept at the proper tension. Alternators rotate at high speed and the belt tension is important for proper operation. The first sign of a slipping fan belt is a squealing noise during sudden acceleration

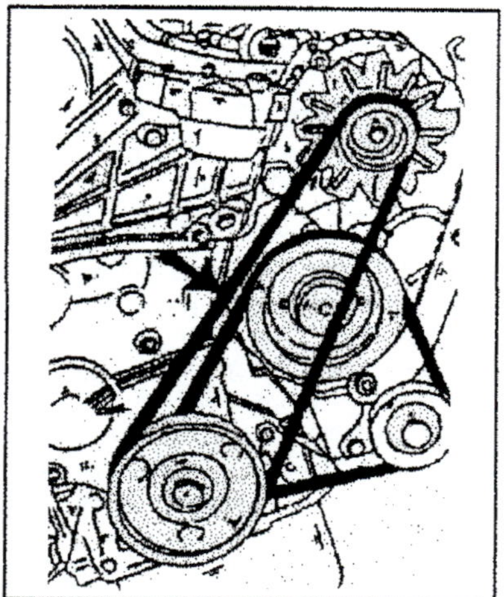

Fig. 9.1. — Details of the alternator belt adjustment, shown on a typical installation. Check the tension at the point shown by the arrow.

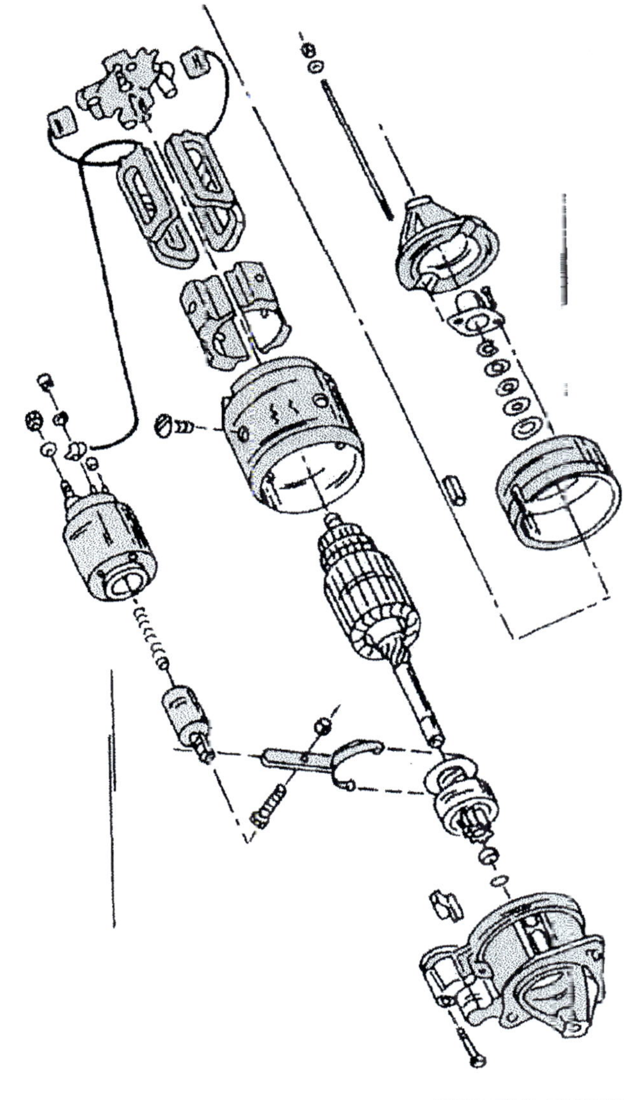

Fig. 9.2. — Exploded view of a Bosch starter motor.

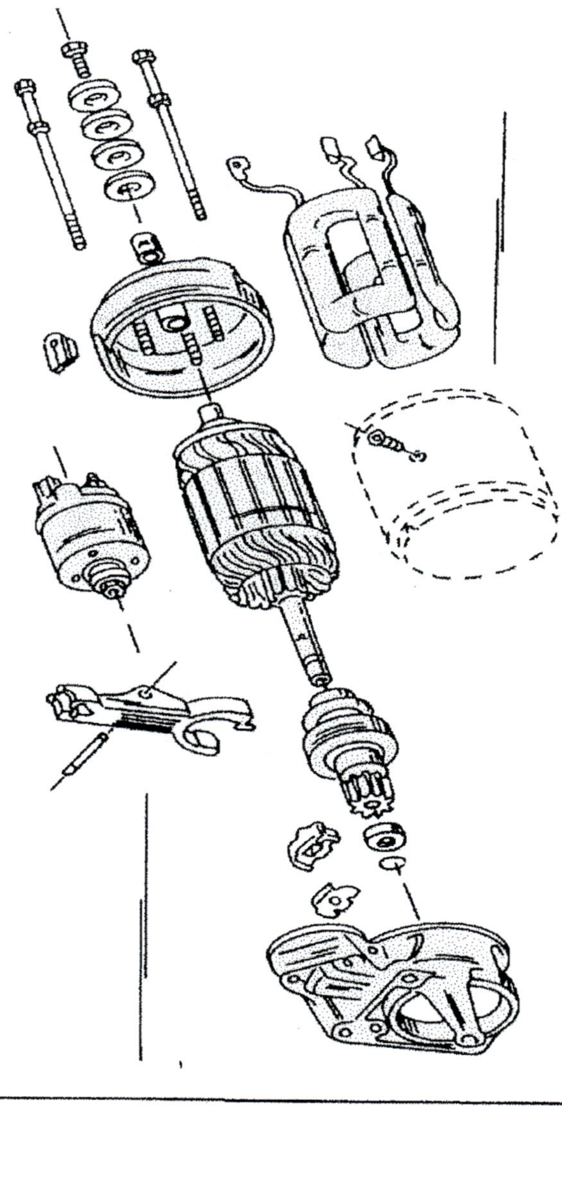

Fig. 9.3. — Exploded view of a Ducellier starter motor.

either during driving off or from low speeds to higher speeds.

In the event of the alternator not charging properly it is certainly a first step to check that the drive belt is not stretched, cracked or defective.

The belt is adjusted by loosening the alternator adjusting link bolt and then moving the alternator towards the outside until the correct tension is obtained. Adjust as follows:

- Slacken the alternator mounting bolts and move the alternator towards the outside with normal hand pressure. Tighten the alternator bolts and check the deflection at the point shown by the arrow in Fig. 9.1. Approx. 1/2 of an inch is a fairly good adjustment, perhaps a little less. Tighten the adjusting strut bolt in this position.

9.3. Starter Motor

A 12 volt solenoid-operated starter motor with positive control, pre- engaged pinion type is fitted.

9.3.0. REMOVAL AND INSTALLATION

The starter motor can be removed from the clutch housing after the battery and the cables at the solenoid switch have been disconnected. The front of the vehicle should be placed on chassis stand to facilitate the access to the starter motor. The installation is a reversal of the removal procedure.

8.3.1. SERVICING

Starter motors are either manufactured by Valeo (Ducellier) or Bosch. Starter motors from Paris-Rhone are also fitted, again depending on the engine and equipment.

We recommend to fit an exchange starter motor if the original unit is no longer functioning. Various specialised companies are around and will always have s starter motor for your specific model. There are, however, two exploded views of two of the starter motors used.

10.4. Fuses

The fuse box contains up to 14 fuses, but it should be noted that different models have a different circuit layout. Your Owner's Manual will give you the protected circuits for you particular model.

Before replacing a fuse, it is necessary to trace the cause of the fuse failure and to rectify it. To check whether a fuse is burnt out, inspect the metal strip across the top of the fuse. There should be no break in the centre. If the metal strip is interrupted, fit a fuse of the same value. Fuses have values from 5 amps to as high as 30 amps. Never fit a fuse with a smaller value to a position where a fuse with a higher value should be situated, or visa versa. Fuses are colour-identified, but again there is no particular guide line. We recommend: If a fuse is required, take the old fuse to the parts department of your dealer. This way you will be assured to obtain the correct fuse for the circuit in question.

Fuses are connected with various sections of the electrical system, i.e. accessories, battery, ignition/starter switch, lighting switch.

9.5. Bulb Table

Headlamp bulbs:	45/40 watts, H4 halogen
Direction indicators:	21 watts
Brake lights/stop lights:	21/5 watts
Reversing lights:	21 watts
Rear fog lamp:	21 watts
Front side lamps:	5 watts
Other bulbs:	See Owner's Handbook

10. GENERAL MAINTENANCE

Most of the maintenance operations can be carried out in modest surroundings. Sometimes it is, however, more advantageous to have certain operations seen to at a dealer, mainly items affecting the fuel injection, as special equipment and experience are required to deal with certain sections of the vehicle. More important are the checks and operations described below which will contribute to the trouble-free operation of your vehicle. Operations to be carried out after 20,000 miles are very important.

Engine Oil Check

The engine oil level should be checked at least once a week, or more often when continuous loss of engine oil can be noticed after a high mileage. The oil level check is described in the Operater's Manuals, but our experience has shown that vehicles purchased second hand are sometimes obtained without it.

To check the engine oil level, park the vehicle on a level surface and withdraw the oil dipstick. Use some tissue paper, wipe off the oil on the dipstick and re-insert it. Withdraw the oil dipstick once more and check the oil level. If the oil is already old, it will be clearly seen. More difficult it will be to see the oil, if it has recently been replaced. Check once more if not 100 % satisfied. The oil must be between the upper and lower mark on the dipstick. Fill in additional oil as necessary. Under no circumstances overfill the engine, thinking that it is better to be on the safe side. Do not forget to replace the filler cap after topping-up — it has happened. **Use only engine oil for diesel engines.**

Checking the Brake Fluid Level

The brake fluid level in the reservoir of the master brake cylinder is a good indicator of the wear rate of brake shoe or brake pad linings. Driving results in a slight drop in the fluid level due to the wear and automatic wear take-up of the brake shoe and brake pad linings. If the brake fluid is near the "Min" mark or slightly above it and there is no leak in the system, have the brake shoes and/or brake pads seen to. Under normal conditions the brake fluid must be between the "Min" and "Max" marks on the fluid reservoir. The reservoir is transparent and the brake fluid can easily be seen. If the brake fluid has dropped below the "Min" mark, check the brake system or have it checked professionally.

Brake fluid should be changed every two years. We recommend to use the brake fluid prescibed by the various manufacturers.

Checking Brake Lights

The operation of the brake lights should be checked at regular intervals. Drive backwards in front of the garage door or similar and depress the brake pedal. The glow of the lamps will be seen in the outside mirror. Replace the bulb if one light is not working; check the brake light switch if both are not working.

Checking Lighting

Check all lights, including the horn, once a week. Tail lights and reversing light are best checked in the dark against a garage door. Otherwise have a second person checking the rear end of the vehicle whilst the brake lights are checked.

Tyes Pressures

Check the tyre pressures at regular intervals, specially before going on a longer trip. The tyre pressures will be given in the Owner's manual and are also given on a sticker on the vehicle. The selection of tyres fitted to the vehicles covered is to extensive to list them all. You will know your tyre pressure. The above note only has the purpose to remind you that you should check the pressures.
the vehicle is fully laden.

Here and then take the opportunity to check the depth of the tyre tread. Remember that the latest regulation require a minimum depth of 1.6 mm. Tread wear indicator bars spaced around the tyre show when the minimum legal limit is reached.

Coolant Level

The cold coolant must be in line with the mark on the expansion tank. If necessary, top-up with anti-freeze solution when the engine is cold. If the engine is hot, allow the engine to cool down before opening the expansion tank cap.

Engine Oil and Oil Filter Change

The engine oil and the oil filter should be changed in accordance with the instructions in the Owner's Handbook.

Air Cleaner

The air cleaner element should be replaced at least every 20,000 miles; earlier if necessary. Clean out the air cleaner casing before fitting a new element.

Steering System Level (Power Steering)

Ever so often check the fluid level in the reservoir for the power-assisted steering. Use fluid as used in automatic transmissions to top-up the reservoir. A reading between the "Mini" and "Maxi" mark should always be seen.

Inspection every 20,000 Miles

The following should be checked every 20,000 miles: Lighting system, hazard warning lights, indicator lamps, horn, windscreen and windscreen washer operation, battery (check electrolyte level and if necessary add destilled water), coolant (check anti-freeze strength and correct if necessary), drive belts (check condition and re-tension if necessary), change engine oil and oil filter, check brake system in general for leaks or damage, check exhaust system for leaks or damage, check track rod ends for excessive play, check transmission, final drive and drive shafts and, if fitted, the rear axle drive, for leaks, check front and rear brake pads/linings, check brake fluid level, check headlamp adjustment or have it checked.

FAULT FINDING SECTION

The following section lists some of the more common faults that can develop in a motor car. The section is divided into various categories and it should be possible to locate faults or damage by referring to the assembly group of the vehicle in question.

The faults are listed in no particular order and their causes are given a number. By referring to this number it is possible to read off the possible cause and to carry out the necessary remedies, if this is within the scope of your facilities.

Engine Faults

Engine will not crank:	1, 2, 3, 4
Engine cranks, but will not start:	5, 6, 7, 8
Engine cranks very slowly:	1, 2, 3
Engine starts, but cuts out:	5, 6, 9, 10
Engine misfires in the lower speed ranges:	5, 6, 9, 11
Engine misfires in the higher speed ranges:	5, 6, 11, 12
Continuous misfiring:	5, 6, 7, 10 to 15, 21, 22
Max. revs not obtained:	5, 6, 12, 22
Faulty idling:	5, 6, 8 to 11, 13, 15, 16, 21 and 22
Lack of power:	3, 5 to 11, 13 to 15, 22
Lack of acceleration:	5 to 8, 12, 14 to 16
Lack of max. speed:	5 to 8, 10, 12, 13 to 15, 22
Excessive fuel consumption:	3, 5, 6, 15, 16
Excessive oil consumption:	16 to 19
Pinking and running-on (dieseling)	5, 6
Low compression:	7, 11 to 13, 16, 20 to 22

Causes and Remedies

NOTE: The faults refer only to carburettor models.

1. Fault in the starter motor or its connection. Refer to "Electrical Faults".
2. Engine oil too thick. This can be caused by using the wrong oil, low temperatures or using oil not suitable for the prevailing climates. Depress the clutch whilst starting. Otherwise refill the engine with the correct oil grade.
3. Moveable parts of the engine not run-in. This fault may be noticed when the engine has been overhauled. It may be possible to free the engine by adding oil to the fuel for a while.
4. Mechanical fault. This may be due to seizure of the piston(s), broken crankshaft, connecting rods, clutch or other moveable parts of the engine. The engine must be stripped for inspection.
5. Faults in the ignition system. Refer to "Ignition Faults".
6. Faults in the fuel system. Refer to "Fuel Faults".
7. Incorrect valve timing. This will only be noticed after the engine has been re- assembled after overhaul. Re-dismantle the engine and check the

timing marks on the timing gear wheels or the timing chain as may be the case.

8. Compression leak due to faulty closing of valves. Check valve clearances. See also under (7) or leakage past worn piston rings or pistons. Cylinder head gasket blown.
9. Entry of air at inlet manifold, due to split manifold or damaged gasket. Correct as necessary.
10. Restriction in exhaust system, due to damaged exhaust pipes, dirt in end of exhaust pipe(s), kinked pipe(s), or collapsed silencer. Repair as necessary.
11. Worn valves or valve seats, no longer closing the valves properly. Top overhaul of engine is asked for.
12. Sticking valves due to excessive carbon deposits or weak valve springs. Top overhaul is asked for.
13. Cylinder head gasket blown. Replace gasket and check block and head surfaces for distortion.
14. Camshaft worn, not opening or closing one of the valves properly, preventing proper combustion. Check and if necessary fit new camshaft.
15. Incorrect valve (tappet) clearance. Re-adjust.
16. Cylinder bores, pistons or piston rings worn. Overhaul is the only cure. Fault may be corrected for a while by adding "Piston Seal Liquid" into the cylinders, but will re- develop.
17. Worn valve guides and/or valve stems. Top overhaul is asked for.
18. Damaged valve stem seals (if fitted). Top overhaul is asked for.
19. Leaking crankshaft oil seal, worn piston rings or pistons, worn cylinders. Correct as necessary.
20. Loose spark plugs, gases escaping past threads, or plug sealing washer damaged. Correct.
21. Cracked cylinder or cylinder block. Dismantle, investigate and replace block or cylinder barrel as necessary and applicable.
22. Broken, weak or collapsed valve spring(s). Top overhaul is asked for.

IGNITION FAULTS

Engine does not start:	1 to 3, 5, 6, 8 to 14, 19
Engine misfires:	2 to 7, 9 to 12, 14, 19
One cylinder not working:	2 to 7, 9 to 14
Engine fails to rev, misfires on acceleration:	2 to 7, 9 to 12, 14, 19
Incorrect idling speed:	1 to 3, 5 to 15, 17, 19
Lack of power:	2 to 12, 14, 15, 17, 19
Poor acceleration:	As for "Lack of Power"
Lack of max. speed:	As for "Lack of Power"
Excessive fuel consumption:	As for "Lack of Power"

Pinking and running-on (dieseling) 2, 3, 5, 6, 8, 11, 12, 15, 16,18

Causes and Remedies

1. Battery discharged or defective. Try charging the battery or replace. Use slave battery to start the engine.
2. Contact breakers (if fitted) not working properly or fault in electronic ignition distributors. Clean old contact breakers or replace and check electronic ignition distributors.
3. Contact breakers connected to earth (conventional ignition). This could happen after replacement of the points.
4. Contact breaker arm spring too weak (conventional ignition). Check with spring scale.
5. Spark plugs need attention. Check condition of plug faces, clean plugs and adjust electrode gaps to specifications. Check when plugs have been replaced last time.
6. Incorrect spark plug gaps. See also under 5.
7. Wrong type of spark plugs fitted. Check with the specifications and install correct plugs.
8. Ignition timing not correctly adjusted. Check and re-time ignition if necessary, using a stroboscopic timing lamp if possible.
9. Coil and condensor defective. No repairs possible, replace,making sure that condensor with correct mfd value is fitted.
10. Loose connection in LT circuit (small lead at side of distributor for example). Check and correct.
11. Open circuit, short circuit to ground (earth) or centre lead of coil not fitted properly. Check all cables and make sure centre lead makes contact.
12. The same as 11, but fault is in the spark plug leads. Check for broken cables and proper connections.
13. Plug leads incorrectly connected. Fault only evident after distributor or spark plugs have been removed and leads incorrectly connected. Follow the wiring order and connect properly.
14. "Tracking" present. This means that HT voltage is creeping to ground (earth) due to dirt or dampness. Various products (damp start) are available to overcome the problem, mainly if caused by dampness (water spray, heavy rain, etc.).
15. Centrifugal advance not working properly. Check by removing distributor cap, turn rotor against tension of flyweight springs and release. Rotor should return to original position (not sticking).
16. Vacuum advance not operating. Pull off hose at distributor with engine running and then re-connect. Engine noise must change if engine speed is increased.

17. Distributor cam or shaft worn. Overhaul distributor or fit replacement (correct one).

18. Fuel with incorrect octane rating used. Check with manufacturers recommendation. Pinking can also be caused by overheating of the engine or too much advanced ignition timing.

19. Carbon brush in distributor cap worn or spring too weak. Check and replace if necessary.

LUBRICATION SYSTEM FAULTS

The only problem the lubrication system should give is excessive oil consumption or low oil pressure, or the oil warning light not going off.

Excessive oil consumption can be caused by worn cylinder bores, pistons and/or piston rings, worn valve guides, worn valve stem seals or a damaged crankshaft oil seal or leaking gasket on any of the engine parts. In most cases the engine must be dismantled to locate the fault.

Low oil pressure can be caused by a faulty oil pressure gauge, sender unit or wiring, a defective relief valve, low oil level, blocked oil pick-up pipe for the oil pump, worn oil pump or damaged main or big end bearings. In most cases it is logical to check the oil level first and then the operation of the oil pressure gauge (if fitted). All other causes require the dismantling and repair of the engine.

If the oil warning light stays on, switch off the engine **immediately**, as delay could cause complete seizure within minutes.

COOLING SYSTEM FAULTS

Common faults are: Overheating, loss of coolant and slow warming-up of the engine:

Overheating:

1. **Lack of coolant:** Open the radiator cap with care to avoid injuries. Never pour cold water into an overheated engine. Wait until engine cools down and pour in coolant whilst engine is running.

2. **Radiator core obstructed by leaves, insects, etc.:** Blow with air line from the back of the radiator or with a water hose to clean.

3. **Fan belt loose or slipping:** Re-adjust the fan belt tension or replace belt. In emergency use a nylon stocking to make up a make-shift fan belt by tieing the stocking around all pulleys.

4. **Thermostat sticking:** If sticking in the closed position, coolant can only circulate within the cylinder head or block. Remove thermostat and check as described in section "Cooling".

5. **Water hose split:** Identified by rising steam from the engine compartment. Slight splits can be repaired with insulation tape. Drive without radiator cap to keep the pressure in the system down, to the nearest service station.
6. **Ignition or carburettor incorrectly adjusted:** Adjust accordingly.
7. **Water pump inoperative:** Overhaul or replace water pump.
8. **Cylinder head gasket blown:** Replace the cylinder head gasket.

Loss of Coolant:

1. **Radiator leaks:** Slight leaks may be stopped by using radiator sealing compound (follow the instructions of the manufacturer). In emergency a raw egg can be cracked open and poured into the radiator filler neck.
2. **Hose leaks:** See under 5, "Overheating".
3. **Water pump leaks:** Check the gasket for proper sealing or overhaul (replace) the pump.

Long Warming-up Periods:

1. **Thermostat sticking in the open position:** Remove thermostat, check and if necessary replace.

FUEL SYSTEM FAULTS

Engine does not start:	1 to 8
Engine starts, but stops soon afterwards:	1, 3 to 6, 8 to 13, 18, 19
Engine misfires at low revs:	3, 4, 8, 9
Engine misfires at high revs:	1, 3, 4, 8, 9
Engine misfires continuously:	1 to 6, 8, 9, 12 to 14
Engine fails to rev:	1, 3, 4, 8, 9, 11 to 17, 21
Bad idling:	4, 8 to 14, 18, 19, 21
Lack of power:	4, 8, 11 to 14, 19, 21
Lack of max. speed:	4, 8, 11 to 15, 17, 19, 21
Excessive fuel consumption:	3, 4, 11, 12, 16, 17, 19, 21
Pinking:	15, 20, 21,
Backfiring:	4, 9, 11, 13, 14

Causes and Remedies

1. Fuel tank empty. Refuel.
2. Fuel line of pipe blocked. Remove pipes and blow through them with compressed air to remove obstructions.
3. Fuel pump not operating. Remove pump and check operation. Repair or replace.

4. Carburettor jets blocked (if applicable). Remove all jets and blow through them with compressed air or in emergency with the mouth.
5. Air lock in fuel pipe. Unscrew pipe and blow through it with compressed air.
6. Fuel filter blocked. Remove filter from its location and clean or replace.
7. Float chamber needle valve sticking. Unscrew float chamber cover, remove needle valve and free off or replace valve. Fit cover with new gasket.
8. Water in carburettor. Clean out float chamber and all jets.
9. Restricted fuel flow due to foreign body in fuel supply line. Clean out lines.
10. Slow-running speed too low. Adjust to proper value.
11. Choke control improperly adjusted. Adjust in the case of manual choke and check setting in the case of automatic choke.
12. Float level out of adjustment. Adjust in accordance with the instructions in section "Fuel System".
13. Carburettor icing up. Very rare fault on modern carburettors. Engine will start after the ice has been thawed up.
14. Inlet manifold sucks in additional air. Check all gaskets on manifold and replace if necessary.
15. Fuel with incorrect octane rating used. Use proper fuel grade. Check with manufacturer.
16. Accelerator pump not operating. Dismantle carburettor and check linkage, lever and diaphragm.
17. Throttle operating linkage wrongly adjusted. Check and adjust as necessary.
18. Slow-running mixture not adjusted properly. Re-adjust slow-running speed in accordance with instructions in Section "Fuel System".
19. Air filter element obstructed. If necessary replace.
20. Ignition timing incorrectly adjusted.
21. Incorrect carburettor jets fitted. Applies not to fixed carburettor jets.

CLUTCH FAULTS

Clutch slipping:	1, 2, 3, 4, 5
Clutch will not disengage fully:	4, 6 to 12, 14
Whining from clutch when pedal is depressed:	13
Clutch judder:	1, 2, 7, 10 to 13
Clutch noise when idling:	2, 3
Clutch noise during engagement:	2

Causes and Remedies

1. Insufficient clutch free play at pedal. Adjust in accordance with instructions in section "Clutch" (if applicable).
2. Clutch disc linings worn, hardened, oiled-up, loose or broken. Disc distorted or hub loose. Clutch disc must be replaced.
3. Pressure plate faulty. Replace clutch.
4. Air in hydraulic system (only applicable to models with hydraulic clutch control). Low fluid level in clutch cylinder reservoir.
5. Insufficient play at clutch pedal and clutch release linkage (the latter in the case of mechanical operation). Adjust as described.
6. Excessive free play in release linkage (only for cable and linkage operated clutch). Adjust or replace worn parts.
7. Misalignment of clutch housing. Very rare fault, but possible on transmissions with separate clutch housings. Re-align to correct.
8. Clutch disc hub binding on splines of main drive shaft (clutch shaft) due to dirt or burrs on splines. Remove clutch and clean and check splines.
9. Clutch disc linings loose or broken. Replace disc.
10. Pressure plate distorted. Replace clutch.
11. Clutch cover distorted. Replace clutch.
12. Fault in transmission or loose engine mountings.
13. Release bearing defective. Remove clutch and replace bearing.
14. Bend clutch release lever. Check lever and replace or straighten, if possible.

- The above faults and remedies are for hydraulic and mechanical clutch operation and should be read as applicable to the vehicle in question

STEERING FAULTS

Steering very heavy:	1 to 6
Steering very loose:	5, 7 to 9, 11 to 13
Steering wheel wobbles:	4, 5, 7 to 9, 11 to 16
Vehicle pulls to one side:	1, 4, 8, 10,14 to 18
Steering wheel does not return to centre position:	1 to 6, 18
Abnormal tyre wear:	1, 4, 7 to 9, 14 to 19
Knocking noise in column:	6, 7, 11, 12

Causes and Remedies

1. Tyre pressures not correct or uneven. Correct.
2. Low oil level in steering gear (if steering is filled with oil). Otherwise lack

of lubricant on rack and pinion steering.

3. Stiff steering linkage ball joints. Re-grease if provisions are made for it, otherwise replace ball joints in question.
4. Incorrect steering wheel alignment. Correct as necessary.
5. Steering needs adjustment. Adjust.
6. Steering column bearings too tight or seized or steering column bent. Correct as necessary.
7. Steering linkage joints loose or worn. Check and replace joints as necessary.
8. Front wheel bearings worn, damaged or loose. Readjust bearing play or replace the bearings if no results can be obtained.
9. Front suspension parts loose. Check and correct.
10. Wheel nuts loose. Re-tighten.
11. Steering wheel loose. Re-tighten nut.
12. Steering gear mounting loose. Check and tighten.
13. Steering gear worn. Although it may be possible to overhaul the steering, the fitting of a replacement steering could be the solution.
14. Steering damper (if fitted) defective or loose.
15. Wheels not properly balanced or tyre pressures uneven. Correct pressures or balance wheels.
16. Suspension springs weak or broken. Replace spring in question or both.
17. Brakes are pulling to one side. See under "Brake Faults".
18. Suspension out of alignment. Have the complete suspension checked by a dealer.
19. Improper driving. We don't intend to tell you how to drive and are quite sure that this is not the cause of the fault.

BRAKE FAULTS

Brake Failure: Brake shoe linings or pads excessively worn, incorrect brake fluid (after overhaul), insufficient brake fluid, fluid leak, master cylinder defective, wheel cylinder or caliper failure. Remedies are obvious in each instance.

Brakes Ineffective: Shoe linings or pads worn, incorrect lining material or brake fluid, linings contaminated, fluid level low, air in brake system (bleed brakes), leak in pipes or cylinders, master cylinder defective. Remedies are obvious in each instance.

Brakes pull to one side: Shoes or linings worn, incorrect linings or pads, contaminated linings, drums or discs scored, fluid pipe blocked, unequal tyre pressures, brake back plate or caliper mounting loose, wheel bearings not properly adjusted, brakes need adjustment (if applicable), wheel cylinder seized.

Brake pedal spongy: Air in hydraulic system. System must be bled of air.

Pedal travel too far: Linings or pads worn, brakes need adjustment (if applicable), drums or discs scored, master cylinder or wheel cylinders defective, system needs bleeding. Rectify as necessary.

Loss of brake pressure: Fluid leak, air in system, leak in master or wheel cylinders, brake servo not operating (vacuum hose disconnected from inlet manifold). Place vehicle on dry ground and depress brake pedal. Check where fluid runs out and rectify as necessary.

Brakes binding: Incorrect brake fluid (boiling), weak shoe return springs, brakes adjusted improperly (if applicable), piston in caliper of wheel cylinder seized, push rod play on master cylinder insufficient (compensation port obstructed), handbrake adjusted too tightly. Rectify as necessary. Swelling of cylinder cups through use of incorrect brake fluid could be another reason.

Handbrake ineffective: Brake shoe linings worn (or pads), linings contaminated, operating lever on brake shoe seized, brake shoes or handbrake need adjustment. Rectify as necessary.

Excessive pedal pressure required: Brake shoe linings or pads worn, linings or pads contaminated brake servo vacuum hose disconnected from manifold, master or wheel cylinders seized. Rectify as necessary.

Brakes squealing: Brake shoe linings or pads worn so far that metal is grinding against drum or disc. Inside of drum is full of lining dust. Remove and replace, or clean out the drum(s).

ELECTRICAL FAULTS

Starter motor failure:	2 to 5, 8, 9
No starter motor drive:	1 to 3, 5 to 7
Slow cranking speed:	1 to 3
Charge warning light remains on:	3, 10, 12
Charge warning light does not come on:	2, 3, 9, 11, 13
Headlamp failure:	2, 3, 11, 13, 14
Battery needs frequent topping-up:	11
Direction indicators not working properly:	2, 3, 9, 13, 14
Battery frequently discharged:	3, 10, 11, 12

Causes and Remedies

1. Tight engine. Check and rectify.
2. Battery discharged or defective. Re-charge battery or replace if older than

2 years.

3. Interrupted connection in circuit. Trace and rectify.
4. Starter motor pinion jammed in flywheel. Release.
5. Also 6, 7 and 8. Starter motor defective, no engagement in flywheel, pinion or flywheel worn or solenoid switch defective. Correct as necessary.
9. Ignition/starter switch inoperative. Replace.
10. drive belt loose or broken. Adjust or replace.
11. Regulator defective. Adjust or replace.
12. Generator inoperative. Overhaul or replace.
13. Bulb burnt out. Replace bulb.
14. Flasher unit defective. Replace unit.

Wiring Diagram Legend for Vehicles with Petrol Engine From Model Year 1991

5 Front cigar lighter
10 Ignition distributor
15 Alternator
21 R.H. horn
35 Battery
40 Instrument cluster
45 Ignition coil
50 Feed junction
100 Spark plugs
152 Engine speed sensor
170 Flasher unit
183 Fan switch
210 Lighting switch
211 L.H. switch
212 R.H. switch
213 Parking light switch
299 Horn switch
300 Ignition switch
301 Glovebox light switch
310 L.H. front door switch
311 R.H. front door switch
314 Reversing lamp switch
315 Handbrake switch
317 Hydraulic fluid level contact
319 Stop lamp switch
350 Starter motor
384 Glovebox lamp
391 L.H. number plate lamp
394 Heater control lighting
436 Idle cut-off solenoid
484 L.H. rear fog lamp
488 L.H. front direction indicator lamp
489 R.H. front direction indicator lamp
490 L.H. rear direction indicator lamp
491 R.H. rear direction indicator lamp
492 L.H. front side light
493 R.H. front side light
494 L.H. stop/tail lamp
495 R.H. stop/tail lamp
496 L.H. tail lamp
497 R.H. tail lamp
499 R.H. reversing lamp
500 L.H. direction indicator side repeater lamp
501 R.H. direction indicator side repeater lamp
504 L.H. stop lamp
505 R.H. stop lamp
540 Fuses
568 Rear fog lamp switch
589 Hazard warning lamp switch
650 Fuel gauge
671 Oil pressure switch
680 Ignition module
694 Front wiper motor and timer unit
720 L.H. cooling fan
L.H. rear interior lamp
R.H. rear interior lamp
742 Centre interior lamp
750 L.H. brake pad wear indicator
751 R.H. brake pad indicator
757 Windscreen washer pump
765 Radio connection
780 Supplementary heater supply
783 Diagnostic socket (TDC sensor)
786 L.H. dipped/main beam
787 R.H. dipped/main beam
790 Heater fan
825 Dipped beam relay
834 Main beam relay
859 Heater fan resistor
910 Coolant temperature sensor
970 Coolant temperature warning switch
971 Radiator water temperature switch

Cable Colour Code

A = Light blue
B = White
BL = Blue
G = Green
J = Yellow
M = Brown
N = Black
O = Orange
R = Red
RO = Pink
V = Green
Vi = Purple

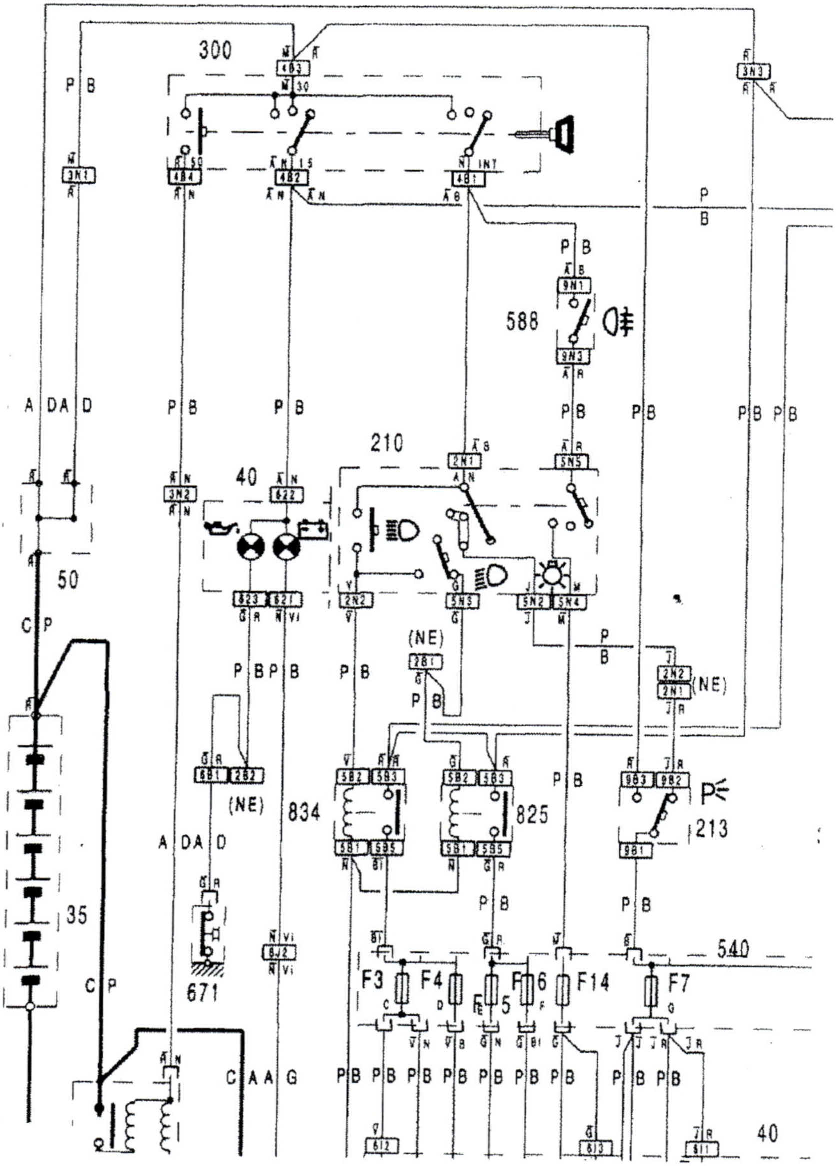
300
588
210
40
50
35
(NE)
834
825
213
671
540
F3
F4
F5
F6
F14
F7
P B
A DA D
C P
C A A G

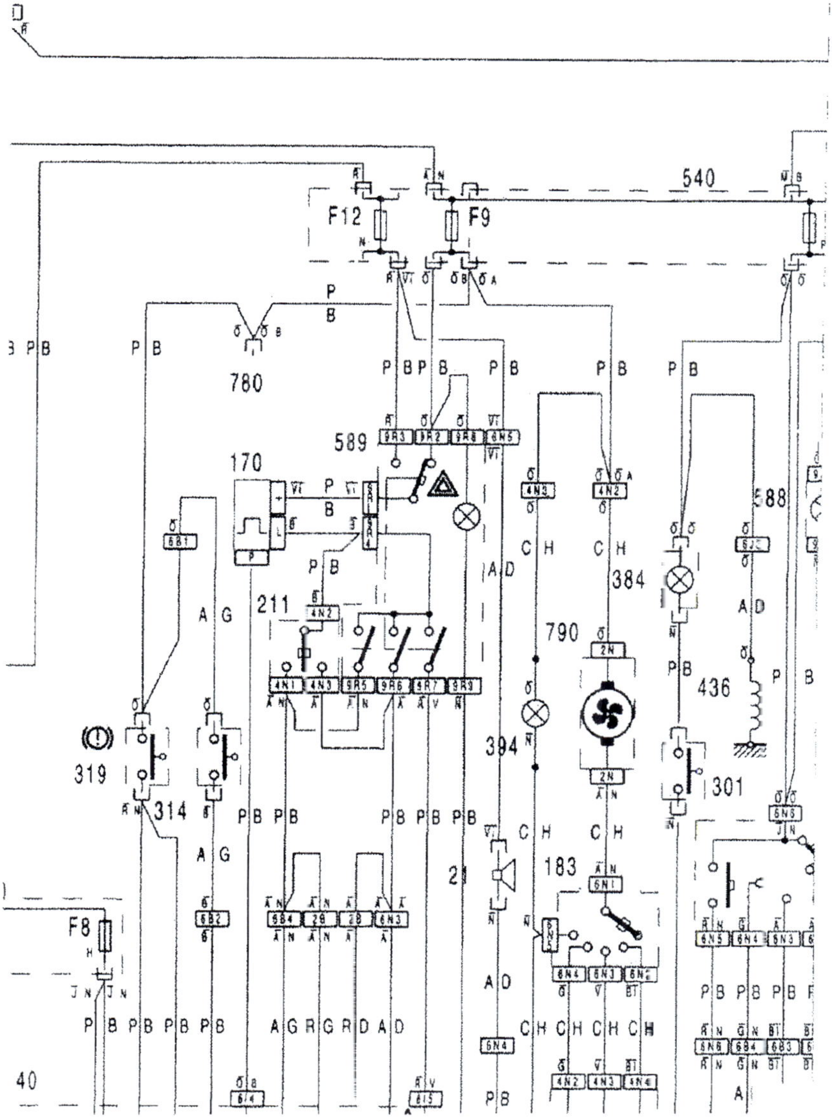
540
F12
F9
780
589
170
211
319
314
F8
384
790
394
183
588
436
301
40

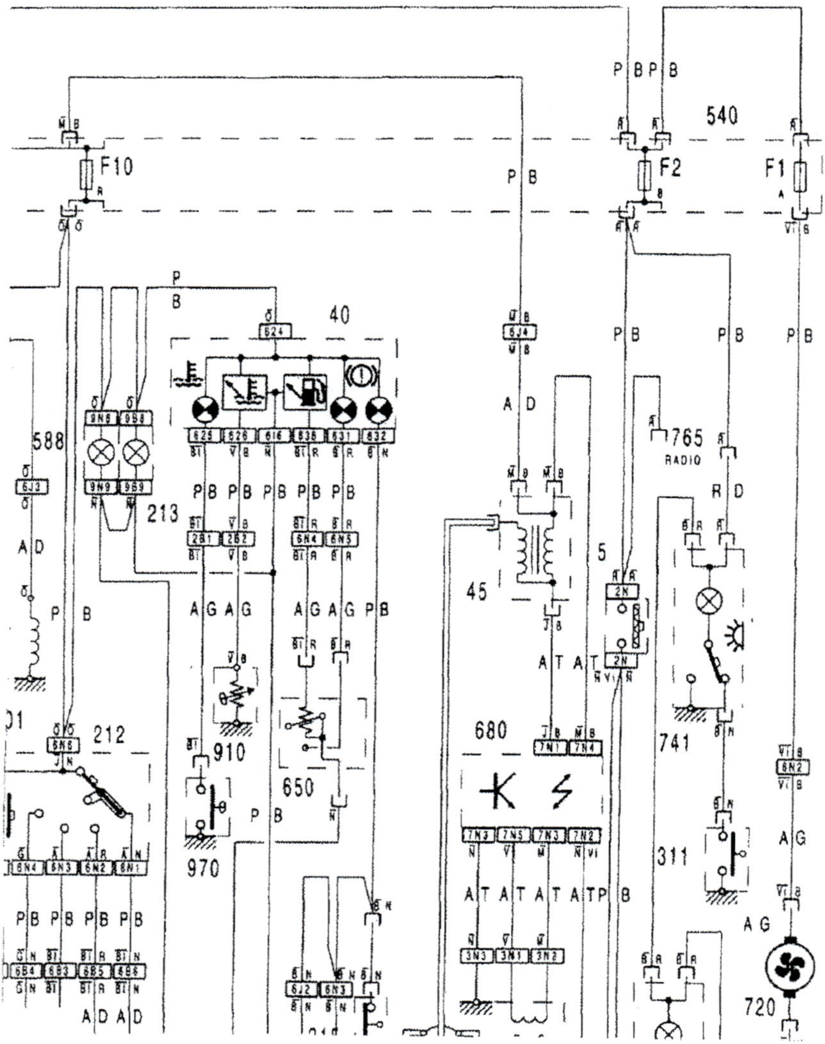

540
F10
F2
F1
RADIO
765
40
588
213
212
910
970
650
45
680
5
741
311
720
P B
A D
A G
A T
R D
624
625
626
616
636
631
632
9N8
9B8
9N9
9B9
2B1
2B2
6N4
6N5
6J3
6J4
6N8
6N3
6N2
6N1
6B4
6B3
6B5
6B6
6J2
7N1
7N4
7N3
7N5
7N2
3N3
3N1
3N2
2N
8N2

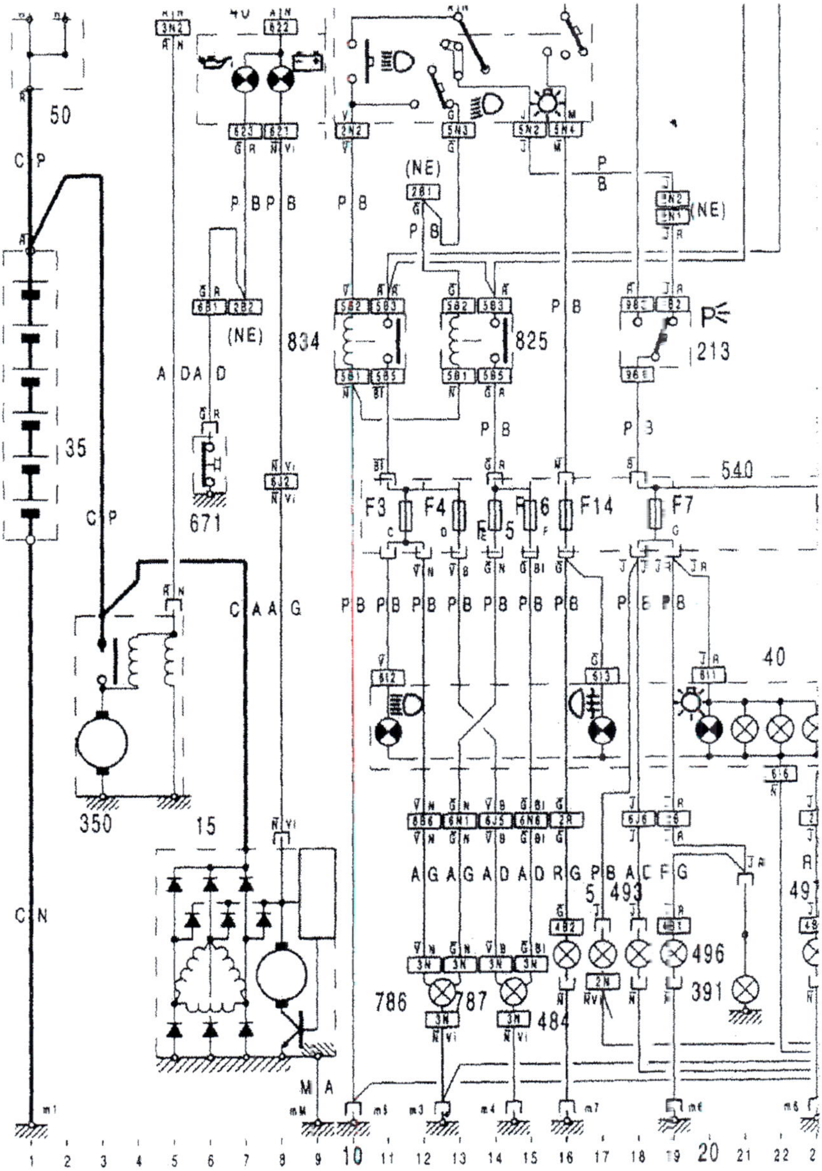
50
35
350
15
671
834
825
213
540
40
F3
F4
F5
F6
F14
F7
786
787
484
493
496
391
497
1 2 3 4 5 6 7 8 9 10 11 12 13 14 15 16 17 18 19 20 21 22

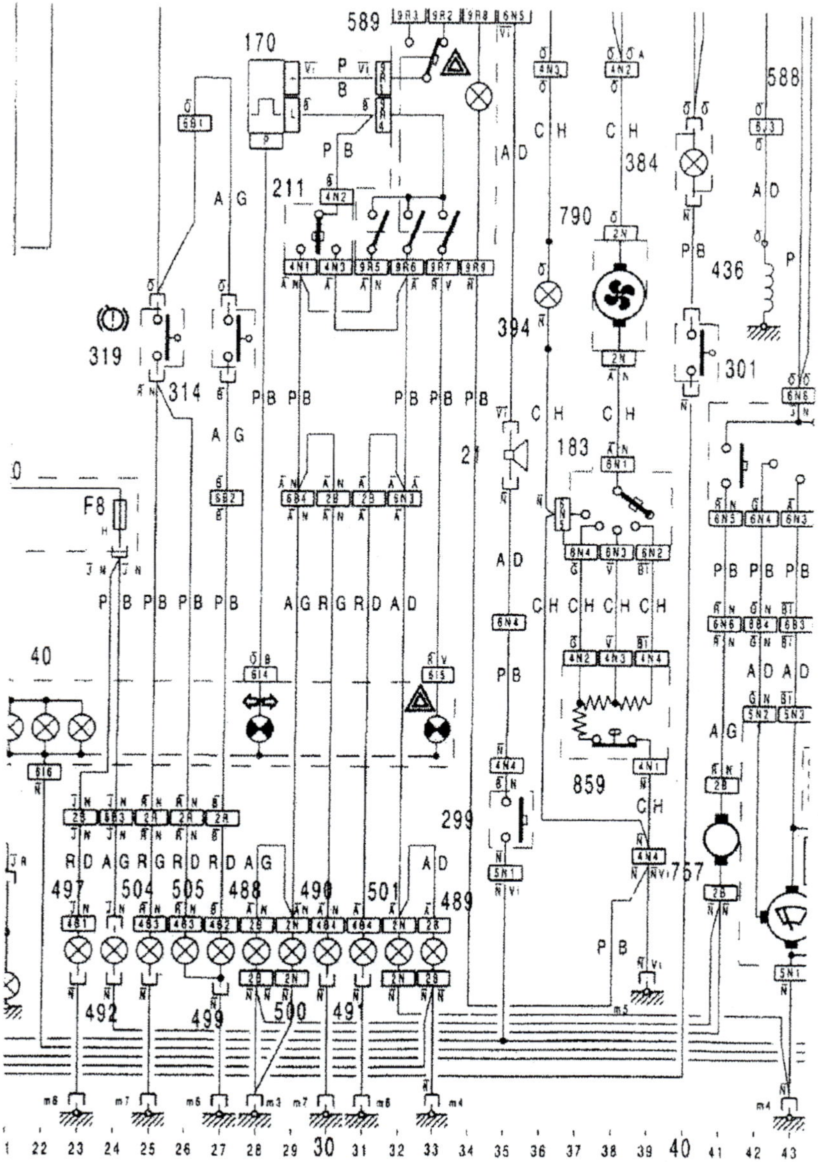

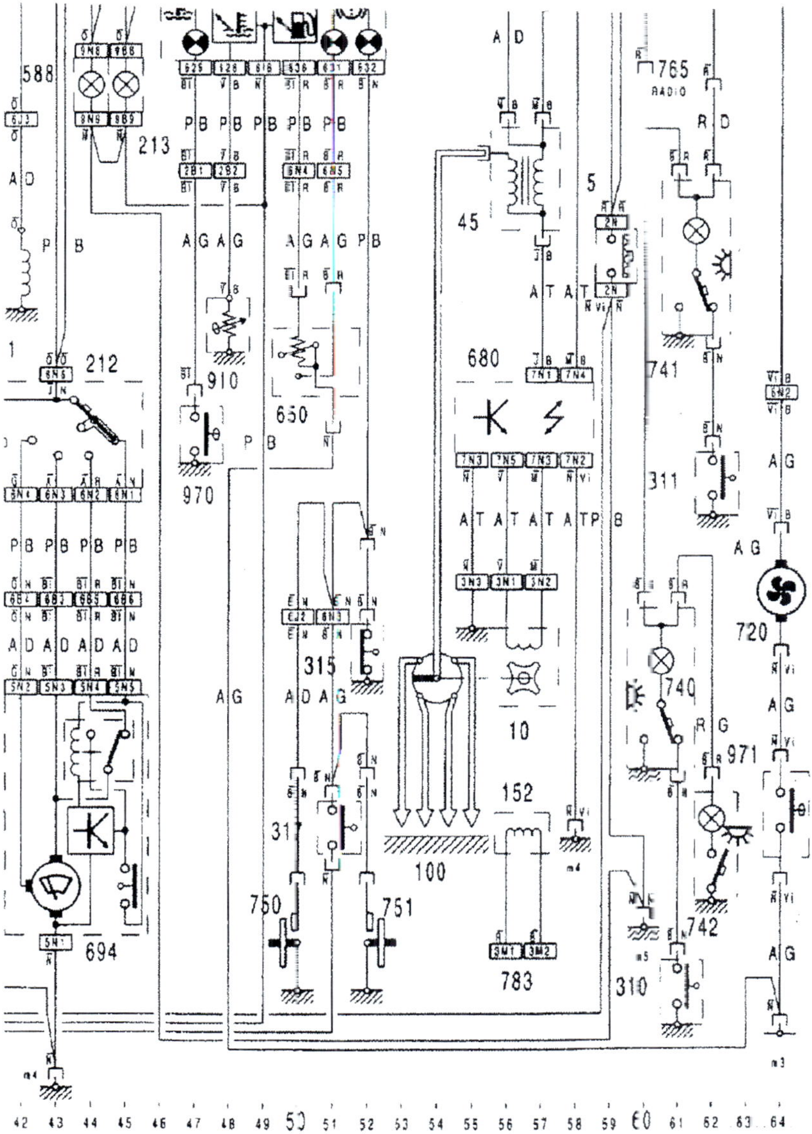
588
213
212
694
910
970
650
315
317
750
751
100
45
680
10
152
783
5
765
RADIO
741
311
740
971
742
310
720
42 43 44 45 46 47 48 49 50 51 52 53 54 55 56 57 58 59 60 61 62 63 64

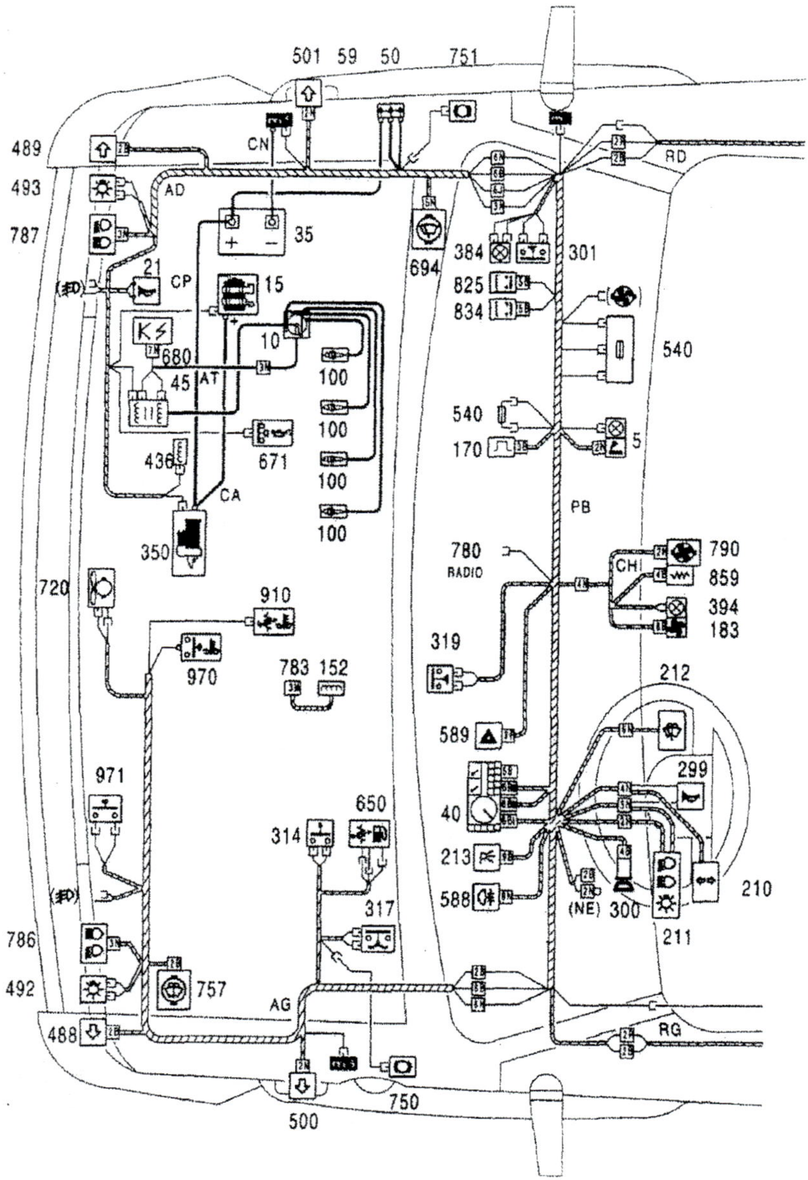
501 59 50 751
489
493
787
CN
AD
35
694
384
301
RD
825
834
21
CP
15
10
680
45
AT
100
540
436
671
CA
350
170
5
PB
780
RADIO
CHI
790
859
394
183
720
910
970
319
783 152
212
589
299
971
40
650
314
213
588
(NE) 300
317
210
211
786
492
757
AG
488
RG
500
750

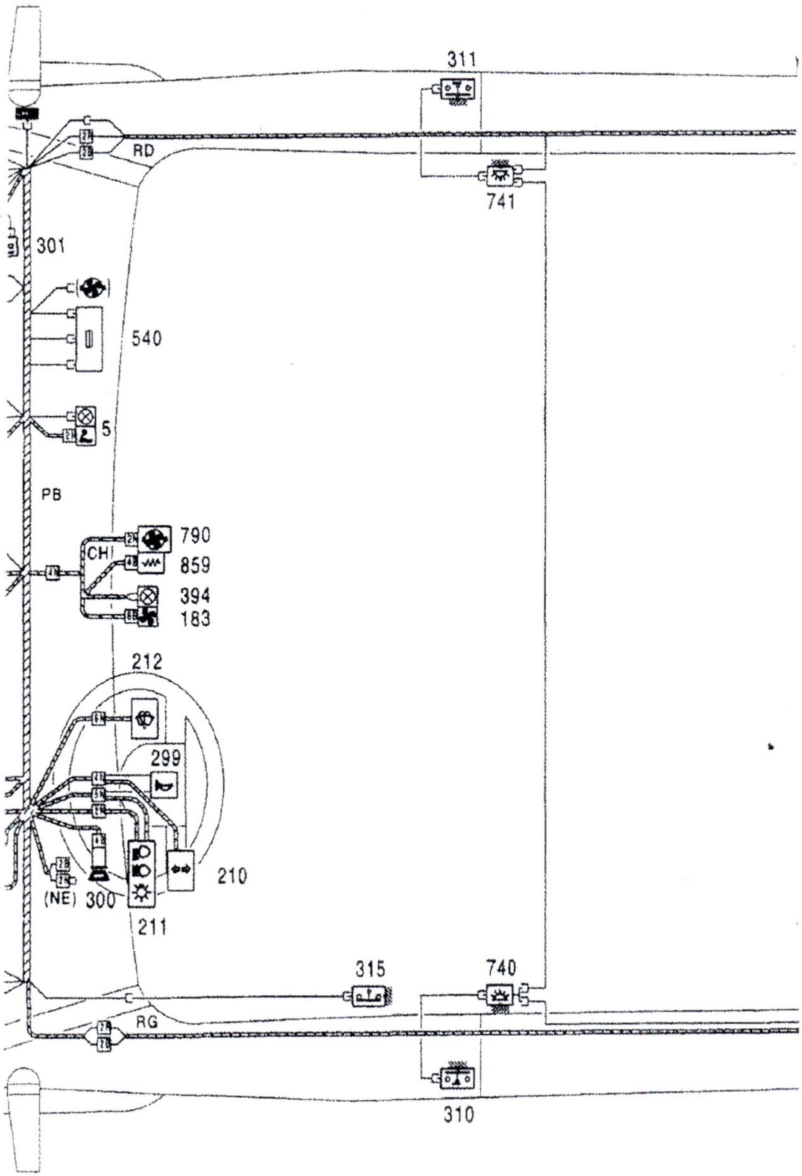
311
RD
741
301
540
5
PB
790
CH
859
394
183
212
299
210
(NE)
300
211
315
740
RG
310

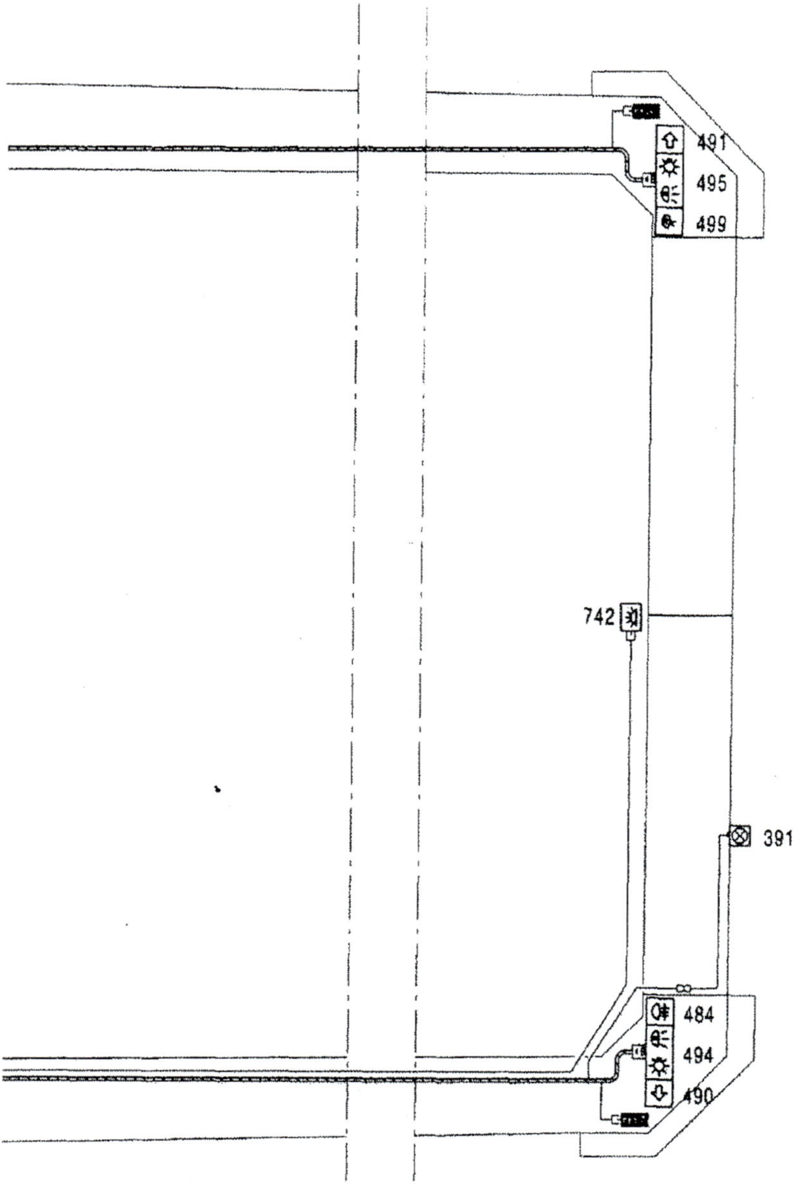
491
495
499
742
391
484
494
490

Wiring Diagram Legend for Vehicles with Petrol Engine From Model Year 1993

5 Front cigar lighter
10 Ignition distributor
15 Alternator
21 R.H. horn
35 Battery
40 Instrument cluster
45 Ignition coil
50 Feed junction
100 Spark plugs
152 Engine speed sensor
170 Flasher unit
183 Fan switch
210 Lighting switch
211 L.H. switch
212 R.H. switch
213 Parking light switch
299 Horn switch
300 Ignition switch
301 Glovebox light switch
310 L.H. front door switch
311 R.H. front door switch
314 Reversing lamp switch
315 Handbrake switch
317 Hydraulic fluid level contact
319 Stop lamp switch
350 Starter motor
384 Glovebox lamp
391 L.H. number plate lamp
394 Heater control lighting
436 Idle cut-off solenoid
484 L.H. rear fog lamp
488 L.H. front direction indicator lamp
489 R.H. front direction indicator lamp
490 L.H. rear direction indicator lamp
491 R.H. rear direction indicator lamp
492 L.H. front side light
493 R.H. front side light
494 L.H. stop/tail lamp
495 R.H. stop/tail lamp
496 L.H. tail lamp
497 R.H. tail lamp
499 R.H. reversing lamp
500 L.H. direction indicator side repeater lamp
501 R.H. direction indicator side repeater lamp
504 L.H. stop lamp
505 R.H. stop lamp
540 Fuses
568 Rear fog lamp switch
589 Hazard warning lamp switch
650 Fuel gauge
671 Oil pressure switch
680 Ignition module
694 Front wiper motor and timer unit
720 L.H. cooling fan
L.H. rear interior lamp
R.H. rear interior lamp
742 Centre interior lamp
750 L.H. brake pad wear indicator
751 R.H. brake pad indicator
757 Windscreen washer pump
765 Radio connection
780 Supplementary heater supply
783 Diagnostic socket (TDC sensor)
786 L.H. dipped/main beam
787 R.H. dipped/main beam
790 Heater fan
825 Dipped beam relay
834 Main beam relay
859 Heater fan resistor
910 Coolant temperature sensor
970 Coolant temperature warning switch
971 Radiator water temperature switch

Cable Colour Code

A = Light blue
B = White
BL = Blue
G = Green
J = Yellow
M = Brown
N = Black
O = Orange
R = Red
RO = Pink
V = Green
Vi = Purple

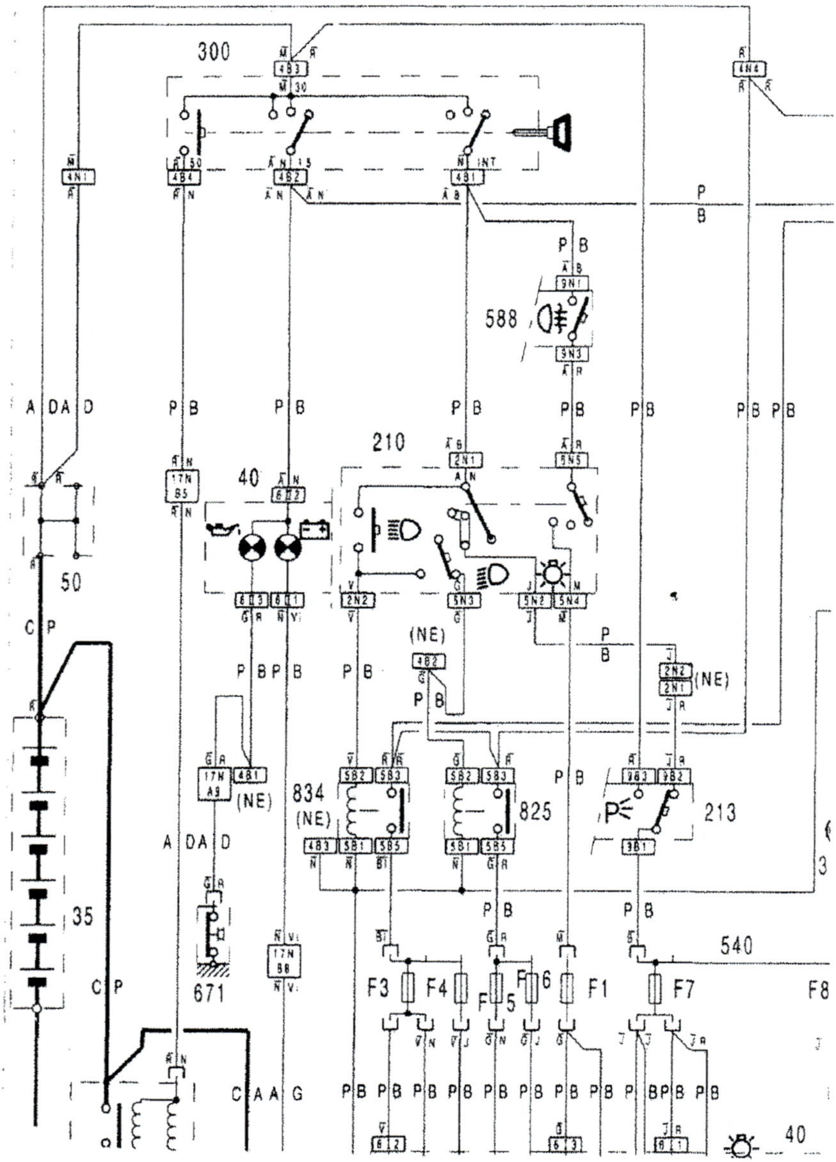
300
588
210
40
50
35
834
(NE)
825
213
671
540
F3
F4
F5
F6
F1
F7
F8

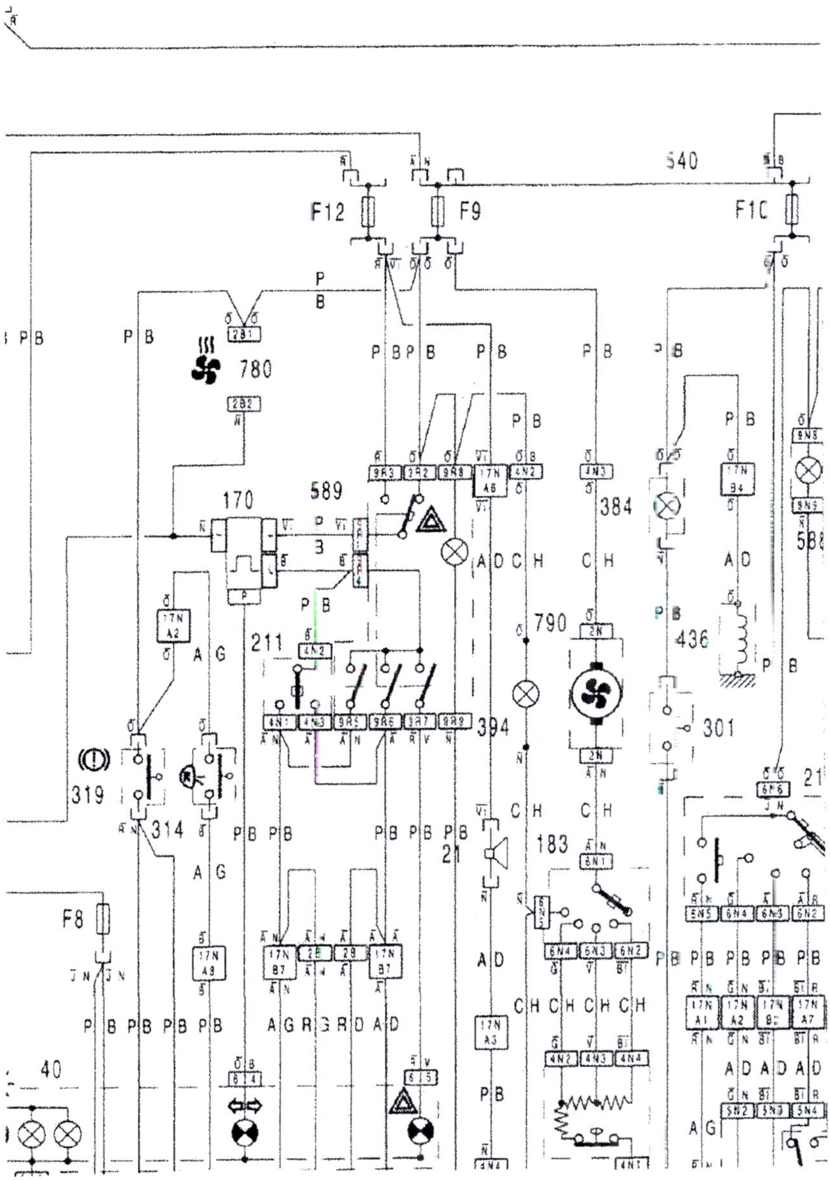
F12
F9
F1C
540
780
170
589
384
436
588
790
211
394
301
319
314
183
21
F8
40

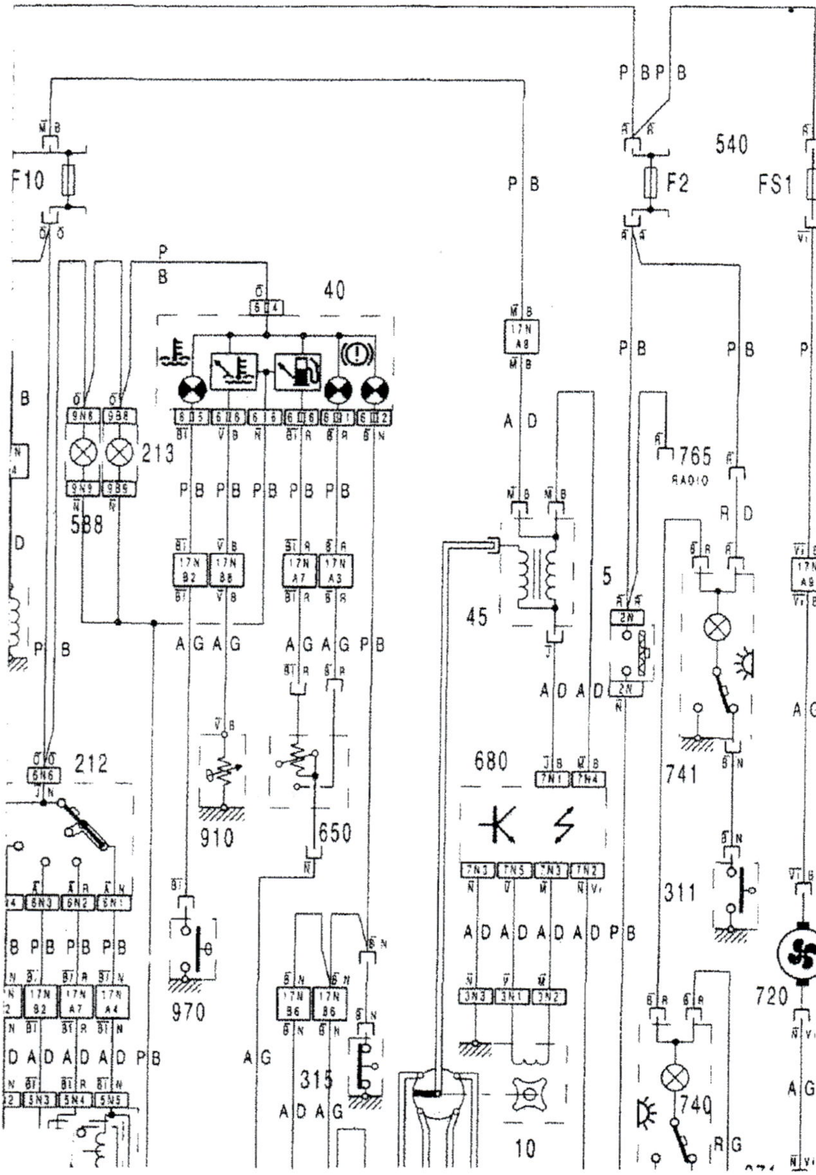

F10
F2
FS1
540
40
213
588
212
910
650
970
315
45
5
765
RADIO
680
741
311
720
740
10

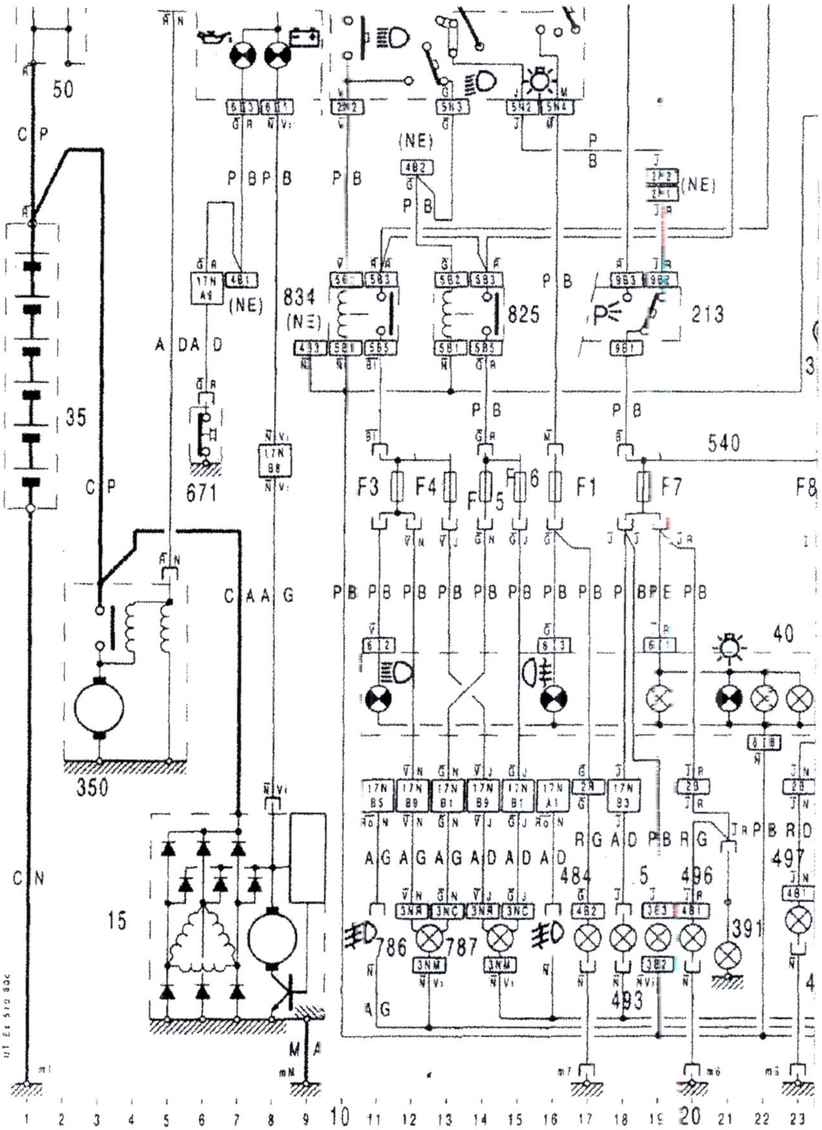

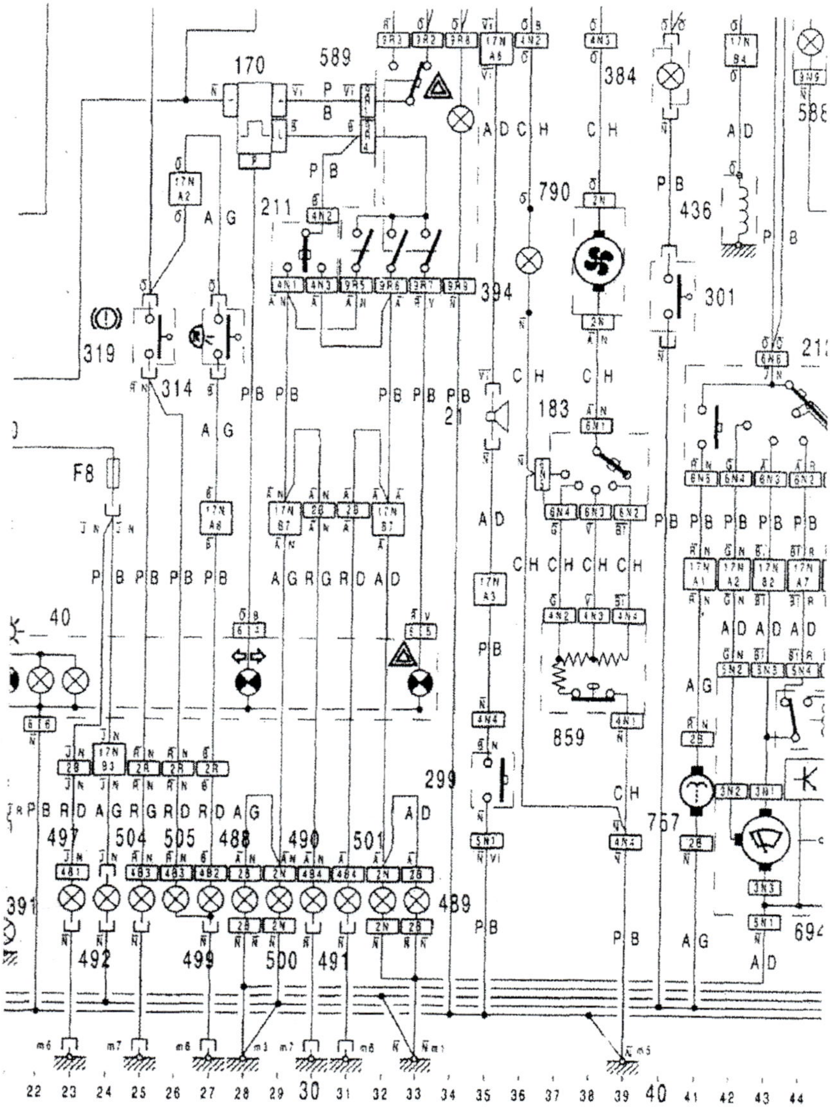
170
589
384
790
436
301
319
314
211
394
21
183
859
F8
40
299
767
694
497
504
505
488
490
501
489
391
492
499
500
491
22 23 24 25 26 27 28 29 30 31 32 33 34 35 36 37 38 39 40 41 42 43 44

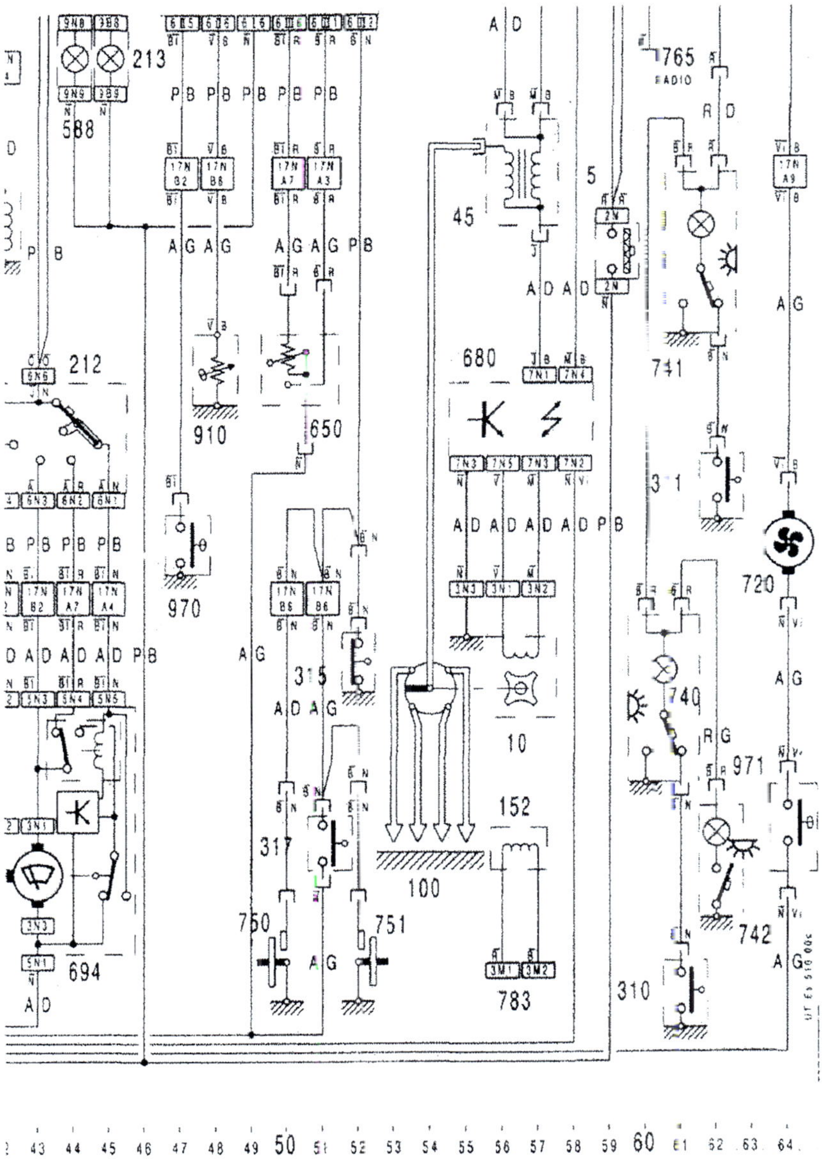
213
588
765
RADIO
5
45
212
910
650
680
741
970
720
315
10
740
971
317
152
100
750
751
742
694
783
310
43 44 45 46 47 48 49 50 51 52 53 54 55 56 57 58 59 60 61 62 63 64

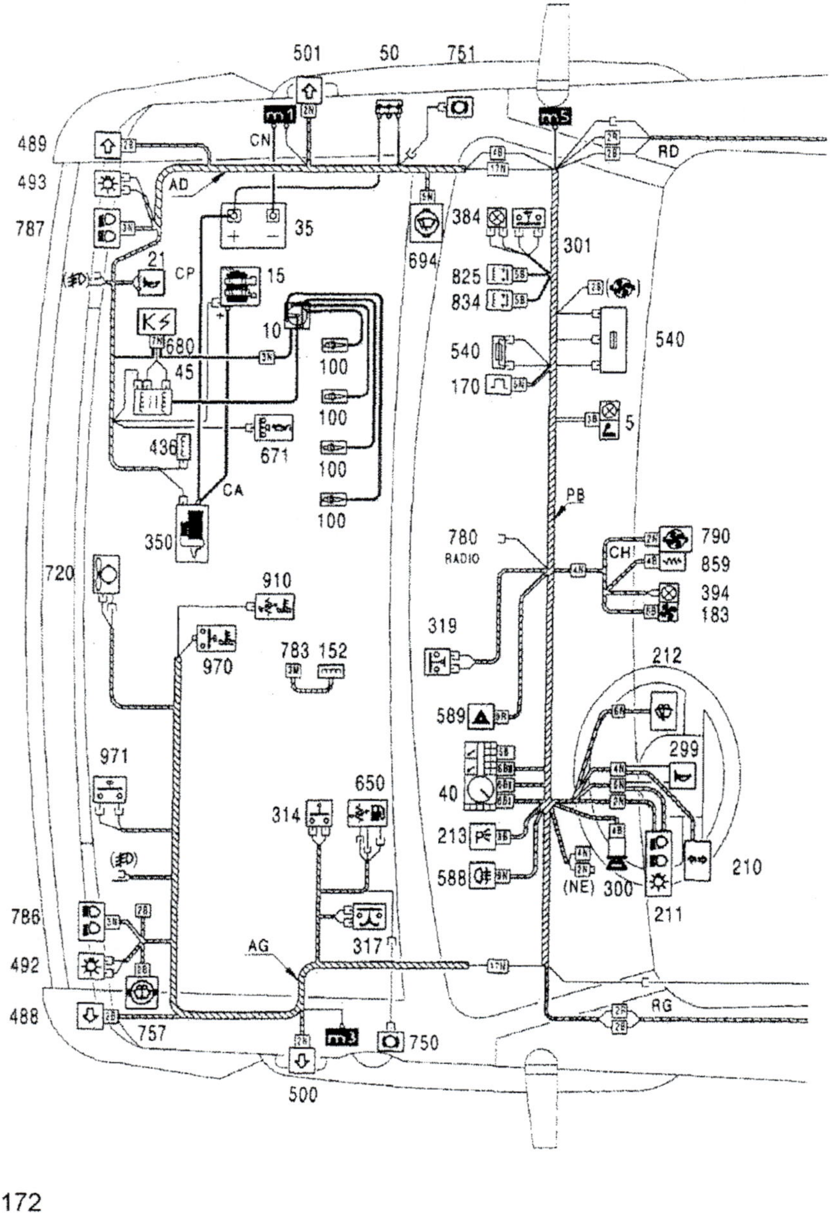
501
50
751
489
493
787
CN
AD
35
694
384
301
825
834
21
CP
15
10
680
45
100
540
170
5
436
671
CA
350
PB
780
RADIO
790
CH!
859
394
183
720
910
970
319
783
152
212
589
299
971
40
650
314
213
588
210
(NE)
300
211
786
317
492
AG
488
757
750
500
RD
RG

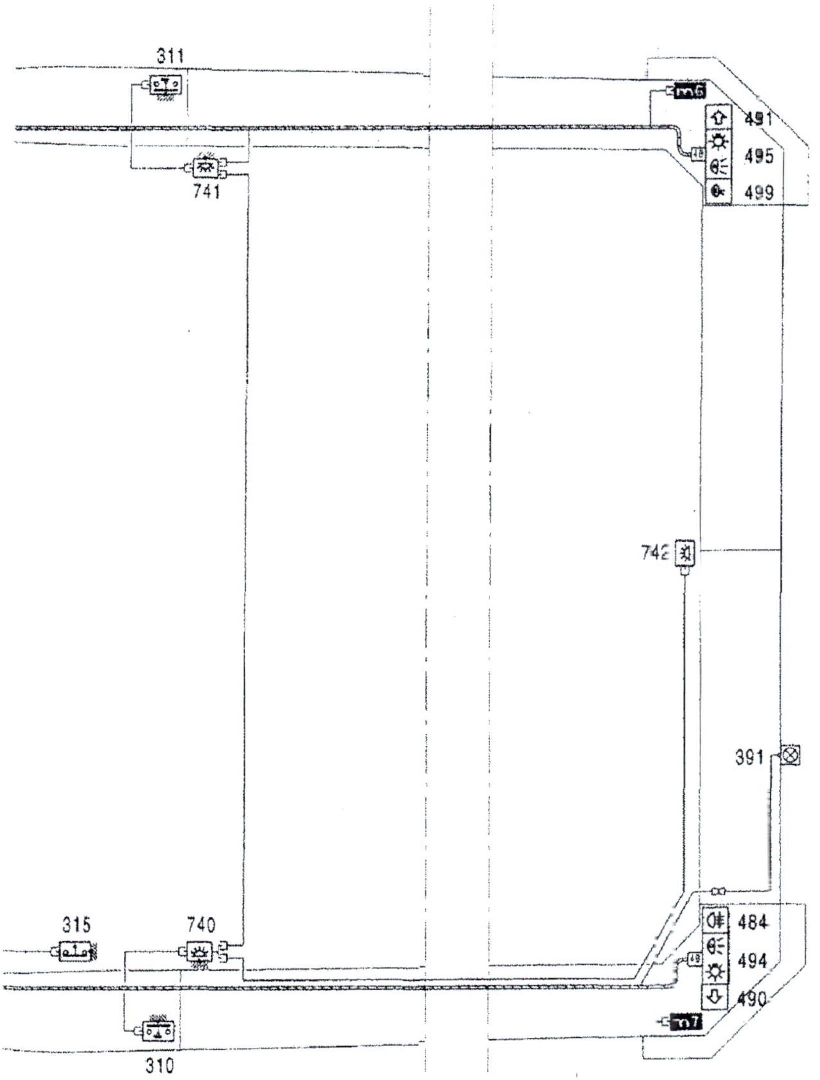
311
m6
491
495
499
741
742
391
315
740
484
494
490
m7
310

Explanation of symbols in Wiring Diagrams (see Page 175)

1 Socket connection
2 Pin conenction
3 Connector connection
4 Screened wire(s)
5 Fuse
6 Diode (rectifier)
7 Accumulator (unit)
8 Condensor
9 Manual switch
10 Switch (fixed position)
11 Manual switch
12 Pressure switch
13 Temperature switch
14 Light
15 Warning lamp
16 Sound equipment
17 Motor
18 Dial
19 Resistance
20 Rheostat
21 Coil winding (relay, etc.)
22 Earth point
23 Electronic control unit
24 Delay unit

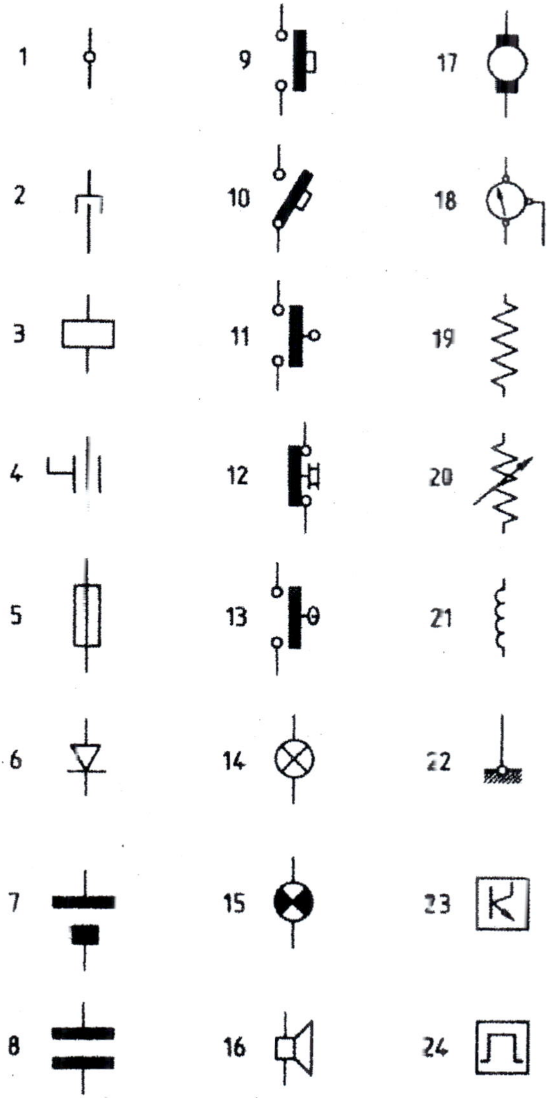

Symbols in wiring diagrams — Explaination see Page 174